FEEDING THE MARKET:
SOUTH AMERICAN FARMERS, TRADE AND GLOBALIZATION

Dedication

For Maya, who entered our lives as we finished writing this book.

FEEDING THE MARKET

South American Farmers, Trade and Globalization

JON HELLIN AND SOPHIE HIGMAN

Kumarian
Press, Inc.

Feeding the Market
South American Farmers, Trade and Globalization

Published 2003 in the United States of America by Kumarian Press, Inc., 1294 Blue Hills Avenue, Bloomfield, CT 06002 USA

Typeset by J&L Composition, Filey, North Yorkshire
Printed and bound in Great Britain by Antony Rowe Limited, Wiltshire

---

Library of Congress Cataloging-in-Publication Data

Hellin, Jon, 1965-
  Feeding the market : South American farmers, trade, and globalization
/ Jon Hellin and Sophie Higman.
      p. cm.
  ISBN 1-56549-172-6
  1. Farms, Small—South America. 2. Agriculture—Economic
aspects—South America. 3. International economic integration. 4.
Agricultural industries—South America—Case studies. I. Higman,
Sophie. II. Title.
  HD1476.S63H45 2003
  382'.41'098—dc21

                              2003003745

---

11 10 09 08 07 06 05 04 03   10 9 8 7 6 5 4 3 2 1   First Printing 2003

Contents

Contents

Contents

Foreword by Jon Snow

We have already travelled a long way on the trail of the effects of globalization. But the road is short on detailed landmarks of evidence and information that support key aspects of the debate. None more so than on the practical obstacles smallholder farmers face in accessing markets. This is a book that makes a major contribution to establishing some fixed points of excellent research from which to take the debate further.

It is a profound departure from the loose generalizations with which much of that debate is beset. Where better to explore the consequences and implications of globalization at the grass roots than in Latin America? This is, after all, a mixed and varied continent that extends from the sweeping grasslands of Patagonia to the snow-capped Andes and on to the dense array of smallholder coffee farms in Ecuador and Colombia.

Jon Hellin and Sophie Higman spent a year working from the very tip of Tierra del Fuego in the south to Ecuador in the north west. Their research encompassed numerous field visits and meetings with farmers, government officials, non-governmental organizations, private companies and international development organizations.

The authors demonstrate that the vast majority of smallholder farmers wish to participate in markets. They focus on no fewer than eight different land uses, including coffee, potatoes, sheep farming, and the lesser known Andean grain, quinoa. The impact of global markets upon smallholder farmers is richly described, especially with respect to the difficulties farmers face in meeting demands for quality of produce along with quantity and continuity of supply.

This is an accessible book which distils the ultimate question – how to reconcile the contradictory demands of the globalized market? The authors identify changes at the policy, research and extension levels that are needed to ensure markets work better for the rural poor and ultimately contribute to sustainable livelihoods.

I'm delighted as Chancellor of Oxford Brookes University, where one of the authors was based while writing this book, and in my capacity as a broadcast journalist, to promote this important work.

Preface

We had both worked in Central and South America on various agriculture and forestry projects during the 1990s. Over the years, the idea of exploring this magical region by bicycle had taken hold. Throwing caution to the wind, we resigned from our respective jobs and flew to Santiago, Chile, at the end of 1999. Our objectives were two-fold: to carry out research on the problems and opportunities facing smallholder farmers in the Andean region of South America; and to travel most of the way by bicycle. We had no idea of the route that we were going to take, we had few clues as to which issues farmers were likely to talk about, and we had only basic bike maintenance skills. As a research methodology it was, perhaps, unconventional.

Over a 12-month period we travelled from the Argentine city of Ushuaia, at the southern tip of Tierra del Fuego to the northern border of Ecuador. We covered almost 7000 km by bicycle, took a few buses and one plane trip. Along the way we visited farmers, non-governmental organizations, academic institutions, private companies, international aid organizations and government bodies. People from these organizations generously took time to explain their work to us, showed us their field work, and introduced us to the farmers with whom they work.

The farmers we met mentioned a number of problems, including technical constraints, land and labour shortages, lack of seed and insecure land tenure. Overwhelmingly, however, smallholder farmers and those working with them talked about the obstacles they face in accessing markets, both national and global. The growth of these markets has accompanied the process of globalization, the economic integration of countries and national economies into a single world system. Time and time again farmers described the difficulty of meeting the demands for quality, quantity and continuity of production. Donors and development practitioners agreed that meeting these market requirements represents an enormous challenge for smallholder farmers, who seldom have the technical and financial resources to understand and adapt quickly to market demands.

Faced with extensive public campaigns against globalization, world economic leaders have now acknowledged that globalization has not led to the benefits that it was claimed to offer, especially for the rural poor. Changes in policies and markets are necessary if the poor are to participate in the potential benefits, but detail is often lacking on the changes that are needed and how they should be implemented.

As we cycled slowly through the Andes, we pondered how seldom farmers themselves are heard in an increasingly shrill and polarized debate on the pros and cons of globalization, a debate largely dominated by ritualistic exchanges between the 'globaphiles' and 'globaphobes'. This book aims to give these farmers a voice. By focusing on eight different products of the Andes, we discuss the reality facing smallholder farmers in South America as they seek access to market opportunities. The chapters on coffee, bananas, potatoes, quinoa, coca, wine, sheep and forestry bring to light a complex web of issues related to production and markets. We identify some of the lessons that can be learnt from the success stories and we suggest changes that are needed to ensure that globalization provides greater benefits to farmers in the developing world.

All the farmers we met participate in markets and wish to continue doing so. A return to subsistence farming is not on their agenda. Our research and travels confirmed to us that globalization is neither inherently bad nor good. It is the way globalization is managed which determines the extent to which smallholder farmers benefit or are disadvantaged. In this respect, the Nobel Laureate Amartya Sen's words ring true: 'to be generically against markets would be almost as odd as being generically against conversations between people'.

By telling the farmers' stories, we hope that this book will contribute to the on-going discussion about how markets can be made to work better for the poor.

Jon Hellin and Sophie Higman
Oxford

Acknowledgements

We could not have written this book without the generous help of innumerable people throughout South America and we are deeply indebted to all of them. However, the views presented in this book are those of the authors, and any mistakes are ours alone. We should like to thank the following people for their time and kindness in helping us with this book.

Chile and Argentina

Adrian Goodall; Boris Simunovic; Dolly and Oscar Gibbons; Franscisco Morón; Gilda Morón; Hector Orlando Baez Torres; Hubert Weber; Jens and Soledad Elers; Katia Gibaja; Luis López; Marcelo Ortega Messina; Maria de Weerdt; Nilo Covacevich; Pablo Bonicholi; Raquel Saravia; Rodrigo Alvarez; Sergio Reyes and colleagues in Aguaray; Tommy Goodall.

Bolivia

Alejandro Bonifacio; Antonio Arce; Antonio Mamani Choquimita; Carlos Yujra; Carmen Doñoso de Aramayo; Circe Aranibar Chávez; Clemente Rodriguez, Dominga and Enrique Padilla; Dani Salvatierra; Don Germán; Doña Alicia Churque; Doña Erminia and Doña Amelia from 16 de Julio; Doña Marina, Tres Rios; Edgar Apaza Torres; Edwin Magariños; Eric Berel Rojas; Felix Valizza Soria; Fortunato Carballo; Francisco Zannier; Franz Terrazas; Freddy Cruz; Freddy Peña Flores; Frederico Magariño and farmers from Arapata; Gerardo Rasens; Gino Aguirre; Guntar Martínez; Hugo Navia; Jaime Caballero and Don Maximo from Ingavi B; James Johnson; Javier Covarrubias E.; Javier Sanchez; Jeff Bentley; Jorge Antezana; Juan Carlos Andrade Salinas; Juan López G.; Juan Ticona Calle; Katrín Linzer; Kathryn Ledbur; Luis Zegada; Mario Suyo; Milton Pereira; Novaldo Mamani; Omar Quiroga; Oscar Barea Montellano; Pierre-Henri Dimanche; Roberto Cayo; Rolando Vargas; Samuel Rodriguez; Severo Alvarez and colleagues at FECAFEB; Simon Macheco; Strico Haciendo; Tomas Wende; Victor Iriarte; Victor Pérez; Yuri Maldonado.

Peru

Adolfo Marocho and family; Alberto B Alanoca Villar; Alfredo Riesco; Angel Mujika Sanchez; Arnaldo de Marzi and colleagues; Carlos César

Acknowledgements

Bendezú López; Jose Rivera; Juan del Mar; Jurenal Mar Farfón; Justo Marín Ludeña; Marlene Gomero Guerra; Minky Reusens; Oscar Ortiz; Oswaldo Hernández; Ramiro Ortega; Rebecca Nelson; Ricardo Orbegoso Carrasco; Roberto Acuña Acuña; Roberto Valdivia; Rómulo Bascope; Ruth Escalante; Sr Calderón.

Ecuador

Alberto Habilo; Alex Noriego; Alvaro Cabrera; Angel Samaniego; Carlos Anibal Dadí Alvarado; Carlos Bonilla; Carlos Nieto; Carlos Otero Alvarado; Charles Chrisman; Cinthya Peñaherrera; Clever Andi; Daniel Selener; David Armas; Don Flavio and Don Maxim (San Antonio); Emelio Grefa; Fanny Rosa Muñoz; Fernando Montenegro; Francisco Gangotena; Ing. Arata; Jamil Ramón, Jeanneth Ordóñez; Joseph Brown; Juan Pérez; Juan Quintuña; Lautaro Andrade; Luis Fernando Rivadeneira; Manuel Yunda; Marcelo Vásquez and family; Mariano and Mercedes Volcar; Maruja Morocho; Mauricio Terán; Mercedes Barrera; Miguel Andrade; Miguel Rea y Cogelena; Miriam Lapo; Patricio Espinoza; Roberto Jimenez Lozano; Rodrigo Aroyo; Rosa Condora; Sergio Larrea; Victor Salinas.

United Kingdom

James Ferguson; John Hedger; Mark Henstridge; Rob Moss; Rob Tripp.

Special thanks to:

Alan Legge; Alistair Smith; Angel and Teresa Salazar; Anne-Claire Chambron; Arthur Morris; Charles Foster; Duncan Green; Eloy, Silvia and Cecilia Larrea; Graham Thiele; Helen Marsden; Javier Luciano Aguerre; John Palmer; Mario Añazco; Martin Haigh; Ramiro Sanhueza; Rob Simons; Scott Wilson; Simón and Paul Cañarte; Steve Sherwood; Sven-Erik Jacobsen; Toby Milner.

Acronyms

ACP Countries	African, Caribbean and Pacific Countries
ACPC	Association of Coffee Producing Countries
ANAPQUI	Asociación Nacional de Productores de Quinua (Bolivia)
ANDEC	Asociación Nacional de Exportadores de Café (Bolivia) (National Coffee Exporters Association)
APPG	Asociación de Pequeños Productores de Guabo (Ecuador) (Guabo Small Producers' Association)
ARPROCA	Asociación Regional de Productores de Café (Bolivia) (Regional Coffee Producers' Association)
ASOPAFT	Asociación de Productores Agroforestales del Tundo (Ecuador)
CAP	Common Agricultural Policy
CENCOOP	Central de Cooperativas Cafetaleras de los Nor Yungas (Bolivia) (Association of the North Yungas Coffee Co-operatives)
CESA	Centro Ecuatoriano de Servicio Agrícola (Ecuador) (Ecuadorian Centre for Agricultural Service)
CIAL	Comité de Investigación Agrícola Local (Local Agricultural Research Committee)
CIAPROT	Proyecto de Asistencia Técnica para la Producción y Comercialización Organizada (Bolivia)
CIP	Centro Internacional de la Papa (Peru and Ecuador) (International Potato Centre)
CIPCA	Centro de Investigación y Promoción del Campesino (Bolivia) (Centre for Farmer Research and Promotion)
CIRNMA	Centro de Investigación de Recursos Naturales y Medio Ambiente (Peru) (Centre for Natural Resource and Environmental Research)
CIT	Centro de Inovación Tecnológica (Peru)
COBOLCA	Comité Boliviano de Café (Bolivia) (Bolivian Coffee Committee)
COCLA	Central de Co-operativas Agrarias Cafetaleras
CODELCA	Consultores del Campo (Bolivia)
COFENAC	Consejo Cafetalero Nacional (Ecuador) (National Council of Coffee Producers)

CONABAN	Corporación Nacional de Bananeros (Ecuador) (National Banana Corporation)
CONCADE	Consolidation of Alternative Development Efforts in the Chapare (Bolivia)
CSU	Colorado State University (USA)
DFC	Programa de Desarrollo Forestal Comunitario (Ecuador) (Community Forestry Development Programme)
DIRECO	Dirección General de Reconversión Agrícola (Bolivia)
Ecuaquinua	El Proyecto Nacional de Quinua en Ecuador
ENACO	Empresa Nacional de la Coca (Peru) (National Coca Company)
EU	European Union
FAO	Food and Agriculture Organization of the United Nations
FECAFEB	Federación de Caficultores Exportadores de Bolivia (Bolivian Federation of Exporting Coffee-growers)
FFS	Farmer field schools
FLO	Fairtrade Labelling Organization
FSC	Forest Stewardship Council
Fundatierra	Fundación Agro-ecologíca Amigos de la Tierra (Ecuador) (Agro-ecological Foundation Friends of the Earth)
GATT	General Agreement on Tariffs and Trade
GDP	Gross Domestic Product
ICA	International Coffee Agreement
ICO	International Coffee Organization
IFOAM	International Federation of Organic Agriculture Movements
IIRR	International Institute for Rural Reconstruction
IMF	International Monetary Fund
INIAP	Instituto Nacional Autónomo de Investigaciones Agropecuarias (Ecuador) (National Autonomous Institute for Agricultural Research)
INV	Instituto Nacional de Vitivinicultura (Argentina)
IPM	Integrated Pest Management
LDCs	Least Developed Countries
ISO	International Organization for Standardization
NGO	Non-governmental organization
NTFP	Non-timber forest products
OCIA	Organic Crop Improvement Association
ODA	Overseas Development Assistance
PROCAFEQ	Productores de Café de Altura de Espíndola y Quilanga (Ecuador) (Espíndola and Quilanga Producers of High Altitude Coffee)

PROFAFOR	Programa Face de Forestación
PROINPA	Fundación para la Promoción e Investigación de Productos Andinos (Bolivia) (Foundation of the Promotion and Research of Andean Products)
PRONAA	Programa Nacional de Apoyo Alimentario (Peru)
RAFI	Rural Advancement Foundation International (USA)
RICANCIE	Red Indígena de Comunidades del Alto Napo para la Convivencia Intercultural y Ecoturismo (Ecuador) (The Indigenous Community Network of the Upper Napo for Intercultural Exchange and Ecotourism)
SETF	La Sociedad Explotadora de Tierra del Fuego (Chile and Argentina)
UK	United Kingdom
UN	United Nations
UNABANA	Unión de Asociaciones de Bananeros (Bolivia)
UNDCP	United Nations Drug Control Program
UNODCCP	United Nations Office for Drug Control and Crime Prevention
UNOPAC	Federación de Organizaciones Populares de Ayora-Cayambe (Ecuador)
USA	United States of America
USAID	United States Agency for International Development
WTO	World Trade Organization
WWF	World Wide Fund for Nature or World Wildlife Fund (US)

Map of South America

VENEZUELA

GUYANA

FRENCH
GUIANA

SURINAM

COLOMBIA

Carchi

Quito

Tena

EQUADOR

Riobamba

Guayaquil

Loja

PERU

Cajamarca

Quillabamba

Caranavi

Yungas

Lima

Cusco

Ica

Puno

La Paz

BOLIVIA

Lake Titicaca

Oruro

Cochabamba

Santa Cruz

Chapare

Potosi

Sucre

Toralapa

Uyuni

CHILE

Aguaray

PARAGUAY

BRAZIL

ARGENTINA

Elqui Valley

Mendoza

URUGUAY

Santiago

Puerto Montt

El Calafate

Puerto Natales

Ushuaia

Punta Arenas

Country boundaries ·················

Towns / Cities •

Areas / Regions ▨

Scale

| 0 | 200 | 400 | 600 | 800 1000 kms |
| 0 | 200 | 400 | 600 miles |

CHAPTER 1

Introduction

Ubiquitous markets

THE MARKET IN the small village square in Escoma, Bolivia, next to the shores of Lake Titicaca appeared overnight, transforming the quiet square into a blaze of colour and noise. Aymara women dressed in bright skirts, set out their goods on the ground, trading every kind of agricultural produce: fruit, vegetables, potatoes, coca leaf. Here the traders arrive with their trucks to buy the farmers' small quantities of potatoes, for resale through the markets of the Bolivian capital, La Paz. At one end of the square, men clustered around machinery, knives, boxes of agrochemicals and agricultural implements, keen to see the new tools on offer. Meanwhile at the other end, bartering was the prevalent means of trade: small quantities of fruit and vegetables changing hands and disappearing into the ladies' voluminous skirts and shawls.

Escoma is at the end of the road; here the farmers from the altiplano and the valleys, from Peru and Bolivia, gather weekly to barter and sell their goods, exchanging or purchasing in return the foods they cannot grow and the consumer goods they need or want. The scene at Escoma is not new and the barter system means that money does not always change hands, but there is no doubt that farmers are involved as buyers and sellers in national and international markets.

It was a recurring theme throughout our trip from Tierra del Fuego to Ecuador: decreasing numbers of farms function in isolation from national and international markets. While many farmers still produce food for themselves and their families, they also sell increasing amounts in local, national and international markets. The farmers we met need and want to sell their produce in the market place. They need money to buy agricultural inputs such as fertilizers and pesticides, to pay for their children's education, to cover medical costs and to purchase consumer goods. Opting out of the market place is not an option for the majority of farmers and they have no wish to return to subsistence farming.

The problem is that, while well-functioning markets are important in generating growth and expanding opportunities for poor people, developing these markets and the institutions to support them is difficult and takes time. Managed well, trade can lift millions of poor people out of poverty; managed badly it will leave whole economies even more marginalized.[1] Even when international and national markets do work properly, poor people

1

need help to overcome obstacles that prevent them from participating on a fair footing.

For many smallholder farmers, markets are not functioning as well as they should. Change is needed to make markets work better for the rural poor. The types of changes that are needed are hotly debated, but the discussion is happening largely in the cities of the rich, developed world. From here, the concerns of poor farmers are all to easily hidden among national statistics, global generalizations and economic theories.

A global picture

Winners and losers

The scenes from various cities around the world are all too familiar: expensively-suited politicians, bankers and business leaders meeting behind closed doors to discuss world trade; a mosaic of protestors waving banners in the surrounding streets, blowing whistles and blaming globalization for society's ills; and the police seeking to keep order, tear gas and water cannon at the ready. Periodically violence breaks out. But what exactly are people protesting about?

Globalization can be defined as a process of rapid economic integration of countries and national economies into a single world system.[2] In the past, governments often protected their populations against world price instability by devices such as fixed exchange rates, high import taxes, or fixed purchase prices. By contrast, globalization – at least that version adopted by countries in the developing world – is driven by the liberalization of trade, investment and capital flows, as well as by rapid technological change. Barriers to internal markets for foreign products are lowered; national producers must increasingly compete with goods imported from elsewhere. In the 1980s and 1990s much of the developing world moved towards implementing 'market-friendly' reforms. The catalyst for these reforms, their scope and their pace varied widely.

Globalization's impacts are diverse and complex. The expansion of world markets through increased flows of trade and finance has created unprecedented opportunities for wealth creation, yet the human development gains have been disappointing.[3] Globalization provides new opportunities created by larger global markets but it also increases economic risk and hence the vulnerability of those with few assets.[2] Farmers are being drawn into a globalized market, where their produce is no longer consumed only by the local community, but also by national, urban and international consumers. At the same time they have to compete with other national and international producers. Competition in international markets is not new, but the extent to which it now occurs is.

Global integration is a selective phenomenon: some countries benefit and others do not.[4] If the world's income distribution had become more equal in the past few decades, it would support the argument that globalization works to the benefit of all. In fact, the 1990s ended with 70 million more people in poverty in the developing world (excluding China) than at the start of the decade.[3] It is becoming clear that global inequality is worsening rapidly and globalization is reinforcing already wide income inequalities at both the international and national levels.[5] The rich are able to grasp the opportunities of globalization, while the poor often pay the costs.

In the 1990s, many of the world's 49 least developed countries (LDCs) liberalized their economies. Among 48 of these countries (excluding Bangladesh, the largest LDC), annual growth of real gross domestic product (GDP) per head was only 0.4 per cent between 1990 and 1998.[6] Most of the LDCs' economies have fared badly, and some even worse than before liberalization. Many also depend on a single export, coffee, and prices have plummeted in recent years. For anti-globalization protestors, there are plenty of examples of those who have suffered from globalization.

In this context, globalization is highly contentious and the debate about its pros and cons has become increasingly polarized. The debate rumbles on as national governments find themselves unable to agree on the rules governing world trade. While developing countries are liberalizing their economies to foreign competition, and reducing protection for their farmers, developed countries maintain high levels of tariff and non-tariff barriers against products from the developing world. Domestic support and export subsidies continue to support farmers in rich countries and to put farmers in the developing world at a disadvantage.[7]

Attempts to launch a new trade round in Seattle, in December 1999, ended in disaster. Gridlock between rich and poor countries about the agenda was set against massive and, at times, violent street protest. At ministerial talks in Doha in November 2001, where a new round of multilateral trade negotiations was launched, developed countries made encouraging commitments to tackle problems of market access and export subsidies, particularly in the agricultural and textiles sectors. These promises of freeing trade were reconfirmed at the United Nations' World Summit on Sustainable Development in Johannesburg in September 2002.

The commitment from the developed world to genuinely tackle these trade issues, however, is doubtful. A few months after the Doha meeting, George Bush signed the United States Farm Bill. This actually increases the subsidies paid to the largest USA farmers by over 80 per cent[8] and runs totally counter to the commitments made at Doha. Meanwhile the European Union (EU) continues to obfuscate about reducing subsidies to European farmers and dismantling its own tariff barriers.

Latin America: a murky picture

Latin America has integrated into the global economy more rapidly than any other developing region[3] and throughout the region there has been a wave of economic liberalization. This has been manifested in the progressive removal of subsidies, tariffs, quotas and trade barriers. Average tariffs were reduced from 50 per cent in 1985 to 10 per cent in 1996, while non-tariff barriers fell from 38 per cent to only 6 per cent of imports over the same period.[9] The aim has been to create a more favourable environment for investment and private sector activity. Despite this, over the past decade another five million people have joined those living on less than US$1 per day.[3]

Largely because of the debt crisis, the 1980s were a lost decade for Latin America.[10] The region fared a little better in the 1990s, but growth averaged only 3.3 per cent per year and income per person rose by only 1.5 per cent per year.[11] The region as a whole slipped into recession in 2001, the second such downturn since 1998. Meanwhile inequality has increased. It is a sobering statistic that only one Guatemalan child in five goes to secondary school but in the capital, Guatemala City, there are more helicopters per person than in any other city in the world.[12]

Although economic growth has been patchy over the past 25 years, agriculture has been of great importance in the economic development of Latin America. Agricultural production still accounts for more than 25 per cent of gross regional product. During the 1980s, the agriculture sector maintained an annual growth rate of over 2 per cent,[13] which underlines its capacity to contribute to the economy as a whole even during a recession. In the 1990s, the sector experienced growth of 3 per cent per year. In many countries, agriculture still employs a high percentage of the workforce. For example, in Bolivia agriculture contributes 15 per cent of gross domestic product and employs over a third of the population. In Ecuador meanwhile, despite the development of the petroleum industry, one third of jobs are in farming, and agro-exports generate around 45 per cent of the country's foreign earning.

Smallholders, agriculture and development

Within the agricultural sector, smallholder farmers have an important role to play in efforts to reduce poverty and inequality and contribute to economic growth, although consensus on exactly what that role should be is lacking. Until recently conventional wisdom was that smallholder agriculture is strategically indispensable to development as a whole. Smallholder agriculture is seen as being a 'win-win strategy', because smallholders are efficient users of resources as well as smallholdings being a relatively equitable means of providing income and food directly to poor people.[14]

More recently, in the late 1990s, the development of 'livelihoods approaches' suggests that smallholder agriculture, while potentially important for the livelihoods of the rural poor, is not the only means of development. Other opportunities for diversification may be available for rural poor people's livelihoods, and agriculture may not be the most appropriate route to take.[14] It is generally expected that as development occurs, a smaller proportion of the population will be involved in farming, and larger numbers of people will be employed in other parts of the rural and urban economy.[15]

However, there are three reasons why it may be right to treat smallholder farmers differently from other sectors of the economy. First, agriculture is not only an economic activity and source of production and income; it is also an important part of rural people's culture and social organization. It is partly for this reason that farming enjoys such protection in the developed countries, where the predominant image of farming is the family farm, despite the reality which is one of dominance by agribusiness.[15]

Second, smallholder farming is linked to reductions in rural poverty and inequality. According to the World Bank growth in agricultural incomes is particularly effective at reducing rural poverty, because it has knock-on or multiplier effects on local markets for other goods and services provided by non-farm rural poor, such as construction, manufacturing and repairs.[9] Strong agricultural growth has been a feature of countries, such as Bangladesh, Indonesia and China, that have successfully reduced poverty.[16]

Third, a more sustainable agriculture provides environmental services such as the conservation of soil and water, the maintenance of biodiversity and also contributes to locking up carbon. These services are important to society in both urban and rural areas as well as locally and globally.[16]

Liberalization of markets, however, poses significant new threats to smallholder farmers[17] and there is little hope that smallholders will be able to continue to survive as full-time farmers on tiny patches of land. Despite this, and within a sustainable livelihoods context, agriculture is still likely to make an important contribution to development as well as being part of the rural livelihoods of many of the world's poorest people.

The human face of globalization

Globalization has enormous impacts on people, through its implications for production and trade worldwide. Yet all too often the human face of globalization is forgotten. Resource-poor people figure in these debates only as marginal spectators.[1] Their voice needs to be heard. Resource-poor people tend to define their poverty in terms that differ from those used by economists: apart from areas such as income and health, they attach considerable weight to less easily measurable determinants of the quality of life, such as insecurity and vulnerability.

In this book, we have portrayed a part of the human face of globalization. We have focused on smallholder farmers in South America. Contrary to the reputation that South America has acquired as a major exporter of manufactured goods, the share of commodities in its export earnings rose during the 1990s. Agriculture still plays a major role in the economies of the region and, in general, smallholder farmers wish to participate in and benefit from national and global markets.

This book is based on discussions with farmers, as well as many individuals working in numerous non-governmental organizations, government offices, academic institutions and private companies. These primary data are supplemented by some secondary sources. It is not, however, an academic tome on globalization; nor it is intended to cover all aspects of smallholder agriculture in South America. This book is written to be accessible and describes a selection of South American farmers' realities as they seek access to markets. Throughout we have given centre stage to the farmers we met, so their problems, opinions, needs and wishes can be heard.

By highlighting the many practical obstacles that farmers have to overcome in order to benefit from market opportunities, this book complements the abundant existing material about the macro-level aspects of globalization. While reform of world trade rules is undeniably essential for improving the livelihoods of smallholder farmers in the developing world, it is not in itself sufficient. As we demonstrate, even if the developed world opened up its markets immediately, most smallholder farmers in the developing world would not be able to benefit in the short term from the new opportunities. This is because of the difficulties in meeting market demands for quality, quantity of produce and continuity of production.

This book points to interventions where development practitioners can have an impact, now. It offers some pointers to the type of practical assistance that smallholder farmers need to help them derive sustainable livelihoods from markets, and to bring some of the benefits of globalization to rural South America and other parts of the developing world. An understanding of global trade issues is useful but not essential to the reading of this book, although we do discuss some of these issues in Chapter 10.

The book is made up of eight thematic chapters, each based around one product of Andean farmers, followed by a concluding chapter. Chapter 2 looks at the banana industry in Ecuador and the power that the banana export companies have over the livelihoods of smallholder farmers. Ecuador is the largest banana producer in Latin America, and the biggest exporter of bananas in the world. Although the fruit are grown by independent farmers, the producers are limited in their choice of market by the small number of exporting companies. Five companies control almost 90 per cent of the country's banana exports. Organic and fair trade markets offer some opportunities to smallholder farmers, but international trade rules and the dominance of the big five companies make it difficult for small banana producers to develop their own, more equitable markets. This chapter looks at the options available to those who have tried to break the power of the banana companies, and the barriers that stand in the way of their access to fairer markets.

In Chapter 3, we look at the options available to coffee producers in Peru, Bolivia and Ecuador. The international coffee market is in crisis, with over-supply worldwide causing a 30-year low in prices. Organic, gourmet and fair trade niche markets offer partial relief from low prices. To meet the require-ments of these niche markets, farmers need to produce coffee of good quality, and to develop marketing chains that ensure consistency in both quality and quantity of supply. In order to do so they require credit, techni-cal and business skills that are often not available to them. This chapter discusses the extent to which these niche markets can offer smallholder farmers a solution to the coffee crisis.

The Andes are home to a vast diversity of potatoes and tubers, which have been used and conserved by generations of farmers. Chapter 4 exam-ines the impact that increasing market integration has had on this store of biodiversity and the other influences at play in farmers' choices about which varieties to plant. Different markets favour different types of potato and tuber, and farmers need new skills and capacities to decide which markets to enter, and how to meet their requirements. Ultimately it is the farmers who will decide whether we conserve or lose potato diversity.

In Chapter 5 we examine the potential of the indigenous Andean grain, quinoa, to contribute to farmers' livelihoods through a direct support to food security, through national markets or through exports to the developed world. Quinoa is one of the most nutritious grains in the world, and grows in some of the most inhospitable areas of the Andes. Increasing demand in the developed world for organic quinoa offers an unparalleled market opportunity to farmers in remote and extreme agricultural lands. National market chains which diminish the quality of quinoa sold locally, combined with cheap alternatives made from imported wheat, have reduced demand nationally. Chapter 5 questions how quinoa can best contribute to farmers' livelihoods and food security in Andean countries, and whether the export or national market routes offer the best future to small farmers.

Chapter 6 focuses on the coca fields of Bolivia and looks at the measures being taken to provide alternative licit agricultural crops to the farmers in those areas where coca is being eradicated. Long before the Spanish arrived in South America, coca was being grown and used by the indigenous people.

In recent decades its potential for producing cocaine has been exploited to the full. Programmes of coca eradication in Bolivia and Peru have been accompanied by the promotion of alternative crops which can offer farmers a decent livelihood. In Bolivia, the search for these alternatives throws light on the difficulties of developing markets for new crops produced by smallholder farmers. Issues of scale of production, price fluctuations and farmers' risk are illustrated. The introduction of alternatives is made doubly difficult by the atmosphere of mistrust engendered by forced eradication of coca and early mistakes in the introduction of alternatives.

The wine industry of Argentina, examined in Chapter 7, is one of the apparent successes of globalization. Unknown internationally less than a decade ago, Argentine wine has improved vastly in quality and become a serious competitor on the international wine stage. Nationally, demand for cheap wine has fallen, while sales of good quality wines are on the increase. Not everyone, however, has been able to move quickly enough to take part in this success story: the smallest farmers who grow grapes were previously protected by layers of state support and protectionist policies, and now find themselves struggling to survive in the harsh new world. Meanwhile, in Peru and Chile, smallholder grape producers demonstrate two contrasting attitudes to production and marketing of the local grape brandy, pisco. It is a competition where working together to produce quality and quantity makes the difference between success and sour grapes.

Chapter 8 takes a look at sheep farming in Patagonia, where a small farm may be several thousand hectares and even the large farms are struggling to survive. With a history of overstocking and environmental degradation, combined with falling demand and prices for wool, Patagonian farmers are faced with a choice: specialize on one market and focus on meeting quality requirements in a tough export market; or diversify away from sheep farming into tourism, forestry or other crops. Farmers' choices are limited by the resources available to them, the packing and freezing facilities available locally, and the desirability of their property for tourism. In the windswept grasslands of Patagonia, farmers may be left with few or no options in the face of change.

In Chapter 9, we examine the opportunities offered by forests and trees, and their potential to contribute to farmers' livelihoods. Forestry offers a multitude of products and services, from timber or non-timber products from forests, through fruit, fodder and shade from trees on farmers' land, to services like watershed protection and opportunities for eco-tourism. Given this abundance of products, it would seem that forests and trees could offer a viable basis for rural people's livelihoods. The use and management of forests is complicated by the range of different and sometimes conflicting alternatives that are possible. New mechanisms are needed to manage and market forest products and services, to the benefit of rural people.

Chapter 10 draws together the main themes of the preceding chapters. This chapter looks at a number of the common issues that have arisen throughout the other chapters, and highlights some of the biggest barriers to smallholders in the Andes as they try to integrate and survive in the market place. Themes arising from the eight chapters are placed in the context of world markets and globalization, and the on-going aid versus trade debate. Finally, some lessons are drawn for the ways in which practical assistance and research can be made more effective in helping smallholders to participate in, and benefit from, markets.

During the research for this book we travelled from the southern coast of Tierra del Fuego in southern Argentina, to the northern border of Ecuador. On the map on page xviii we show some of the main locations mentioned in Chapters 2 to 9 in order to give the reader an idea of the geographical scope of the book.

CHAPTER 2

Green gold: Ecuador's banana producers*

Introduction

THE ECUADORIAN COASTAL plain is separated from the mountains and deeply incised valleys of the Andes by a series of green hills. At 500 metres above sea level, the zone still has a tropical feel about it and we are surrounded by patches of forest and small banana plantations. All around us the dense plants droop under the weight of bunches of ripening bananas. The fruit is clustered at the end of a stem which resembles a toilet brush, each one carrying about 120 bananas. We are helping Marcelo and his family pack bananas for export. Unlike the situation in Central America, the multinational banana companies never secured a foothold in Ecuador and banana production is in the hands of about 5200 independent farmers. Approximately 60 per cent of these producers are smallholders with less than 30 hectares of banana plantations. Marcelo, with 15 hectares of bananas, falls into this category.

We help haul recently cut bunches of bananas to the packing shed. Marcelo's wife, Maria, expertly slices the bananas into clusters of five to seven fruits. These are washed in soapy water, treated to prevent latex appearing at the cut surface and then packed in cardboard boxes that are piled up ready to be transported to the nearest port. Being a banana producer in Ecuador does not seem such a bad life. However, glancing up between packing bunches of bananas, Marcelo explains that 'independent farmer' is a relative term: the large banana companies control the export trade and almost without exception pay farmers less for a box of bananas than the price established under Ecuadorian law[†]. Marcelo, like many of his neighbours, sells his bananas to the American fruit company Dole, but the price they get hardly covers production costs. Consequently Marcelo and some of these same neighbours have formed a farmer association and are trying to circumvent the power of the banana companies by producing organic bananas for the fair trade market in Europe. Fair trade offers farmers a more just price for their produce.

* The authors are grateful to Oxfam and the Overseas Development Institute for allowing us to include material from: Hellin, J. and Higman, S. (2001) 'The impact of the multinational companies on the banana sector in Ecuador'. Oxford, Oxfam; and Hellin, J. and Higman, S. (2002) 'Smallholders and niche markets: lessons from the Andes'. *Agriculture Research & Extension Network Paper*, No. 118. London, Overseas Development Institute.
† Unless otherwise stated, prices in this chapter are from the latter half of 2000 and a box of bananas weighs approximately 43 lb or 19.5 kg.

This chapter examines the structure of the banana sector in Ecuador and the power of the banana companies *vis-à-vis* independent producers. It explores the degree to which producers such as Marcelo are likely to be able to secure a more equitable future for themselves and their families and the role that Western consumers can play in helping to decide the outcome. There is much at stake: Ecuador is the largest banana producer in Latin America and supplies about 35 per cent of the 12 million tonnes of bananas traded annually worldwide. This trade generates large profits for the export companies: it is their 'Green Gold', a reference to the colour of the fruit when harvested. Following the end of the so-called 'Banana War' between the European Union (EU) and the United States of America (USA), Ecuador is well placed to exploit the enormous European market, but if smallholder farmers are to benefit from these market opportunities, policy changes and well-targeted development assistance are needed.

Green gold

Bananas are the fruit of *Musa sapientum* which is the world's largest herb. Wild bananas originated in Asia and have been grown and cultivated for over 4000 years. Cultivation of the fruit spread westward through the Middle East and sub-Saharan Africa. Missionaries brought the banana to the island of Hispaniola in 1516, and it later spread to the rest of the Caribbean and Latin America. Bananas are produced all year round, they are a rich source of carbohydrates, phosphorus, calcium, potassium and Vitamin C, and make a significant contribution to food security in dozens of countries in the developing world. They are also traded widely and, in terms of gross value of production, bananas are the world's fourth most important crop after rice, wheat and maize;[1] banana production has been increasing by around 3 per cent per year over the past decade.[2]

Of the 86 million tonnes of bananas and plantains (a relative of the banana, used in cooking) produced annually, only 14 per cent are traded on the world market.[3] The two biggest banana-producing countries, India and Brazil, are hardly involved in the international banana trade at all. World exports of bananas almost doubled to 12 million tonnes between 1988 and 1998 and have an export value of over US$4 billion.[2] The EU is the biggest banana importer, consuming almost 4 million tonnes of bananas each year.

Ecuador is currently the largest exporter (4 million tonnes per year), followed by Costa Rica (2 million tonnes per year) and Colombia (1.5 million tonnes per year). Latin America accounts for over 83 per cent of world exports, 11 per cent are from the Far East, 3 per cent from Africa and less than 2 per cent from the Caribbean. In the Caribbean, most producers are independent smallholder farmers. In Latin America, with the exception of

Ecuador and Colombia, bananas are grown in large plantations, often directly controlled by multinational companies and vertically integrated operations, incorporating ownership of plantation, packer, shipper and ripener.

World trade is largely controlled by five companies: Chiquita Brands and Dole Food Company each control approximately 25 per cent of the world market while Del Monte Fresh Produce, Noboa and Fyffes each have about 8 per cent of the market. The companies are largely associated with Latin America where they control 60 per cent of production throughout the region. Reflecting the North American origins of the companies with influence in this region, traders still refer to bananas produced in Latin America as 'dollar bananas'. The companies are vertically integrated: they own (or contract) plantations, sea transport facilities and distribution networks in consuming countries.

The world banana trade generates large profits and the big five companies' predominant position allows them unprecedented control of the market and much political influence. The 1990s were characterized by intense competition among the companies for worldwide market share especially within the EU. The banana war with the EU is probably the best-known example of the power of the banana companies (see below).

The banana companies have also exerted immense influence on governments, to such an extent that countries from Colombia to Belize have had to accept impositions with regard to tariff duties, customs preferences, duty-free exports and imports of their products, and preferential financial treatment in the banking systems of the host countries.[3] In the 1940s and in recognition of the influence that the banana companies had over successive governments, Honduras had earned the less than flattering epithet 'The Banana Republic'.

While it is a lucrative business, not all have benefited from bananas. As with the case of coffee, workers on plantations and small independent farmers supplying the world market get only a tiny share of these benefits (generally 1–3 per cent and 7–10 per cent respectively) and only 12 per cent in total of the revenues remain in the producing countries. The remaining 88 per cent is shared between the multinational companies, the ripeners and the retailers.[1]

In Ecuador, independent farmers fare a little better. It has been calculated that 12 per cent of the retail price of a box of bananas goes to the producer, with 20 per cent spent on transport, 30 per cent on ripening costs and the rest are distribution costs and retailing.[4] Growing competition and a fall in prices, however, have led banana companies to seek productivity gains at the cost of an increasingly negative impact on employees and the environment. Many independent producers throughout Latin America receive less than US$2 per 19.5 kg box of bananas. This hardly covers production costs.

Ecuador clearly illustrates both the power of the multinational banana companies and simultaneously the way that independent producers can secure a more equitable future.

The banana sector in Ecuador

Domination, decline and resurgence

If there is one thing that producers and the banana companies agree on it is that lowland Ecuador is ideal for growing bananas. Throughout the nineteenth and early twentieth centuries the principal export crop in Ecuador was cacao. This crop declined irreversibly in the 1920s due to diseases and competition from other suppliers and, in the 1940s, favourable natural and social conditions helped the country convert bananas into its new lead export.[5] Ecuador became the world's largest banana exporter in 1954, an expansion that continued until the mid-1960s.

Several factors facilitated the growth of the Ecuadorian banana sector after World War II. First, global demand rose steadily, mainly centred in the US market. Second, the Central American competitors faced severe banana disease problems as well as periodic devastation of their plantations by cyclones. Ecuador may be further from the USA and Europe than is Central America, but its natural conditions of abundant, disease-free, fertile soils, with sufficient water supplies and few tropical storms, gave it a comparative advantage. This helped to convince companies like United Fruit (now Chiquita) and Standard Fruit (now Dole) to establish their own banana plantations as well as providing credit and technical assistance to independent Ecuadorian banana producers.

Between 1957 and 1965, Ecuador lost ground to the Central American producers. The latter, dominated by the large banana companies, successfully substituted the new and more productive Cavendish banana variety for the Gros Michel variety. The Cavendish variety, being smaller, also happened to be less susceptible to cyclone damage. Within a few years, Central America increased yields and exports two and three-fold respectively.[5] In Ecuador, production was dominated by medium-scale domestic producers and they switched to the Cavendish variety more slowly due to financial constraints and limited know-how. As a result, Ecuador lost its natural comparative advantage. An overvalued exchange rate added to the country's problems. The banana companies stopped producing directly and established contract farming arrangements with local producers. Ecuadorian banana production stagnated from the mid-1960s to the mid-1980s.

The opening of Eastern European markets after the Berlin Wall fell in 1989 helped to fuel higher world demand for bananas. Encouraged by

13

currency devaluations in the 1980s and having switched entirely to the Cavendish variety, Ecuador was again well placed to take advantage of increased world demand. Producers adopted a new technological package that included greater use of fertilizers, insecticides, fungicides, herbicides; regular aerial fumigation, on-farm aerial cable ways (called funiculars) for the transport of harvested bunches of bananas; and irrigation systems.[5]

The adoption of capital-intensive mechanized technologies again made Ecuador very competitive and it is once again dominating the world export market, with exports totalling over 4 million tonnes per year. The banana industry employs over 300 000 people, representing just under 10 per cent of the economically active population. Banana exports from Ecuador generated US$827 million in 2001, some 4.6 per cent of gross domestic product.[6]

Looking good (too good to be true?)

Andrés Arata is the director of the Corporación Nacional de Bananeros (CONABAN), a banana trade union that represents 240 of Ecuador's larger independent banana producers. Although there were strong banana unions until the late 1970s, their influence began to decline as a result of pressure from the banana industry and its allies in government.[7] There is no union that currently represents the interests of the smallholders.

We meet Andrés Arata at CONABAN's tiny office in the hot and sweaty Pacific port city of Guayaquil. Reeling off the industry's statistics, he explains that there are approximately 5200 banana producers in Ecuador farming 150 000 hectares. Of these 5200 producers, 60 per cent are smallholders with less than 30 hectares of bananas, 30 per cent have 30–100 hectares, and 10 per cent have more than 100 hectares. In sharp contrast to the situation in Central America, the better known banana companies such as Dole, Chiquita and Del Monte do not own plantations in Ecuador. Only two Ecuadorian-owned fruit companies have plantations: Favorita and Noboa each own approximately 7000 hectares and they also buy bananas from some of the 5200 independent producers.[8]

The larger plantation owners employ workers and their lot is not always a happy one. Human Rights Watch has reported that on some of the plantations, children as young as 8 are forced to work 12-hour days and are exposed to toxic chemicals and sexual harassment.[6] Furthermore, and contrary to Ecuadorian law, some workers are denied basic rights such as inscription in the social security system and payment for overtime. There are also reports of plantation owners undermining banana workers' attempts to form trade unions.

There are several reasons why Ecuador once again has a comparative advantage over Central America, says Andrés Arata. Ecuador's lowland soils are fertile and banana productivity is high; meanwhile labour costs in Ecuador are low and there are sufficient skilled workers. Ecuador does not suffer from periodic hurricanes and storms such as Hurricane Mitch, which devastated Honduras' banana sector towards the end of 1998. Finally, in the lowlands there is enough water, provided by rivers and rain, but no excess of humidity, and hence there are fewer problems with diseases such as the leaf-browning fungal disease caused by *Micosphaerella fijensis* and known in many parts of Latin America as *sigatoka negra*.

There are more than 200 varieties of bananas in the world, yet worldwide farmers predominantly grow the Cavendish variety. The fruit is genetically identical and, because the plants are established in close proximity and come from the same genetic source, outbreaks of pests and diseases are often a major problem. One of the major diseases facing producers is *sigatoka negra*. This was first identified in the mid-1960s in the Pacific and has subsequently spread to Latin America, the Caribbean and, more recently, Africa. The Cavendish variety is very susceptible to *sigatoka negra*.

It is the reduced incidence of *sigatoka negra* which is perhaps the most important factor behind Ecuador's dominance of world markets. The fungal disease is conventionally controlled by spraying, often by plane. This is an expensive process and is often hazardous and polluting. In Central America, spraying is generally carried out once per week, while in Ecuador is can be reduced to once per month. This, combined with lower labour costs, means that in Ecuador production costs can be half those in Central America.

José Riofrio is a banana expert working at the University of Guayaquil in Ecuador and author of several books on the subject. He puts it another way: Costa Rica needs to produce 2500 boxes/ha per year to break even while in Ecuador the figure is 1600 boxes/ha per year. Ecuador currently exports 1800 boxes/ha per year but if there were sufficient market demand this figure could easily be increased to 3000 boxes/ha per year, suggests Riofrio.

Ecuadorian sales of bananas have fallen in the past few years because of the collapse of the economy in the former Soviet Union, but with an end to the transatlantic banana war (see p. 31), Ecuador is well placed to exploit the growing European market. José Riofrio stresses another advantage: in Central America, banana production peaks between October and December when the demand in Europe is low. In Ecuador production is greatest between December and May when home-grown fruits are not available in Europe, and demand for bananas is high. The only drawback for Ecuador is that its geographical position means that bananas have to be transported through the Panama canal, an additional cost that is not incurred by Central American producers.

The banana sector in Ecuador is vibrant, production is almost entirely in the hands of independent producers and the country is likely to maintain if not increase its dominance of world markets. In this context, you could be forgiven for assuming that banana producers, as opposed to the workers on banana plantations, must be a content group. Not so, explains Arata: 'independent producers' are only nominally so. According to Arata just under 90 per cent of Ecuador's banana exports are controlled by a handful of companies, including Noboa (38 per cent of the export market), Dole (18 per cent), Favorita (16 per cent), Palmar (8 per cent) and Del Monte (8 per cent). Favorita supplies bananas to Chiquita.

The relationship between the companies and the independent producers, as opposed to plantation workers, is often referred to as contract farming. Normally, the grower provides land, labour and tools but is supplied by the exporter with credit inputs and technical advice.[9] Hence, while the farmers cover the production costs and transport to the port, the companies provide the packing material and deal with the paperwork at the ports. In a vertically integrated supply chain the banana companies have enormous influence not only on the prices paid to producers but also on many farm management decisions.

Contract farming is way of allocating risk between producer and exporter. The former takes the risk of production and the latter the risk of marketing. From the companies' perspective, contract farming is often preferable to owning and managing plantations, especially when they can control management decisions at the farm level. Contract farming allows the companies to shift the responsibility for labour and environmental conditions in the plantations on to local shoulders, saying that these conditions are not under their control and that national legislation is in place to ensure that minimum standards are respected. Hence, while most contracts require the producers to follow the company's technical advice, the same company is often absolved of all responsibility for the results.

The main advantage of contract farming from the producer's perspective is that there is an assured market for the produce. Independent smallholder producers either supply the exporting companies direct or sell to a middleman. With a contract, a producer may also be more able to access credit, either from the banana company itself or from the banks, who generally accept a contract as collateral.[10] Some larger producers supply one or more of the exporting companies and employ workers on their plantations. Contract farming in the Ecuadorian banana sector, therefore, encompasses a wide range of situations.

Andrés Arata cites a clear example of the risks to the farmer of contract farming. Excessive rainfall in 1997–98, caused by the weather phenomenon known as *El Niño*, destroyed roads and bridges. The exporters buy ship-side (in the port) and it was the farmers who had to resolve the problem of transporting their produce to the ports. In addition, high rainfall led to an increased problem of *sigatoka negra* which in turn meant that farmers faced higher fumigation costs. Some producers fell into debt.

Contract farming: partnership or exploitation?

Contract farming in practice: the company

With 16 per cent of the banana export market, Favorita is one of Ecuador's biggest exporters. Favorita is actually the holding company: its banana exporting subsidiary is called Reybanpac. Carlos Otero of Reybanpac explains that Favorita also owns companies that make fertilizers, chemicals and cardboard. Another subsidiary owns two large banana plantations. Favorita exports 650 000 boxes of bananas per week. Of these, 200 000 boxes come from Favorita's plantations; the other 450 000 boxes are sourced from 500 independent producers. Approximately 80 per cent of these independent producers are smallholders with less than 30 hectares, although they supply less than a fifth of the 450 000 boxes purchased by Favorita each week.

Carlos Otero is perfectly frank about Favorita's relationship with the producers. The company prefers working with smallholders as it is easier to dictate to them when aerial spraying should be done. Fumigation is carried out by a subsidiary of Favorita's called Aerovic and the farmers pay the costs. Larger producers, on the other hand, are seen as 'too powerful' and less willing to relinquish control over aspects of the production process such as spraying. Irrespective of the size of the independent producers, Favorita pays farmers US$1.90 per box of bananas despite the fact that the legal minimum price is US$2.18. Favorita is not alone, according to Andrés Arata of CONABAN: since 1999 the exporting companies have seldom paid the minimum price. This was confirmed by the various producers and exporters whom we met.

Fernando Rivadeneira, the commercial director of Favorita, is more forthright. The Ecuadorian banana industry has been politicized between producer and exporter, he says, and Favorita cannot pay producers more than the market can sustain. Rivadeneira's argument is that if the market does not pay, Favorita is unable to improve the conditions of local producers. Rivadeneria is particularly critical of the trade barriers imposed by the EU as a means to protect Caribbean banana producers. He sees the EU's protectionism as the main obstacle to growth in Ecuador's banana exports which, he argues, would benefit not only companies like Favorita, but also the myriad independent producers.

Contract farming in practice: the producers and middlemen

Angel Samaniego used to be an employee of Favorita (Reybanpac). When the company sought to streamline its operations, Angel was encouraged to set up his own company to supply Favorita. Angel established his company, called Opervasa S.A. in May 2000 and now oversees 12 producers who manage a total 400 hectares of plantations and produce 9000 boxes of bananas per week. The 12 producers have plantations varying from 10 to 60 hectares in size. They are grouped together and sell to Favorita all year around.

Angel takes us to meet one of his 12 suppliers. Juan Quinteña has 10 hectares of bananas and produces 450 boxes per week. Juan used to sell his bananas to another exporter but he found that they bought his bananas one week and not the next. In the absence of any guaranteed and regular market, at times he had to sell to intermediaries for only US$1 per box. Juan's argument is that it is far better to sell to Reybanpac on a regular basis and for a regular price. José Riofrio from the University of Guayaquil refers to this as the loyalty issue. According to Riofrio, during peak demand at the beginning of the year, producers can secure a higher price per box of bananas by touting their produce around the buyers. However, the same producers will subsequently find that the market disappears during the slacker periods. Hence, for farmers such as Juan stability provided by a guaranteed sale, albeit at a relatively low price, was a strong enough incentive for him to enter into a contract.

One of the difficulties in determining what is a fair price for a box of bananas is that few smallholder producers really know what their production costs are. This problem is not confined to Ecuador and is found worldwide. Juan is no exception, although he does acknowledge that bananas are not very profitable due to the costs of spraying against *sigatoka negra*. Favorita decides when and what to spray. Juan's bananas are sprayed about 15 times per annum at a cost of approximately US$390/ha per year. Juan also adds fertilizer at a cost of US$216/ha per year. While growing bananas may not be very profitable, Juan explains that until 1997 he used to grow cacao. He decided to switch to bananas because, despite low profit margins, it is still a more profitable crop than cacao. In addition, he points out, bananas provide a weekly income all year round; with cacao there are only two harvests a year.

Carlos Sarcis is also a smallholder banana producer. He has 15 hectares of bananas and produces on average 700 boxes per week. Carlos sells his bananas to one of the smaller exporters and is paid US$1.70 per box. Showing us around his rickety packing shed tucked in below the leafy banana plants, he says the company tells him the export price is not high enough to pay him more. As a small producer, he has no way of knowing if that is true.

18

As is the case with many small producers, Carlos is required to sign a form saying that he has received the legal minimum price of US$2.18 per box. Carlos explains that in 1991 the price paid to the producers was good but since then it has fluctuated even though the cost of inputs has risen steadily. *Sigatoka negra* is the biggest problem that he faces and he sprays against the fungus 18 times per year at a cost of US$400/ha per year. Carlos admits that he does not know what his production costs actually are but he calculates that a more equitable price per box of bananas, based on production costs and livelihood security, would be US$2.50. Carlos also points out that, although not very profitable, bananas are better than the alternatives. Like Juan, he used to grow cacao but changed over to bananas at the beginning of the 1990s.

It is surprisingly difficult to reach any consensus on the cost of producing a box of bananas. José Riofrio from the University of Guayaquil, who represents neither producer nor exporter, argues that production costs vary because the calculation methods used are different. He reckons that production costs are approximately US$1.60 to US$1.80 per box (including delivery to the port) and says that those who say that they are higher are probably adding costs of infrastructure development, such as irrigation, into their costs for the first year or two, rather than spreading the cost over seven to ten years. Some exporters refer to production costs of US$1.40 per box, while others mention US$1.80 per box. CONABAN, on the other hand, indicates that production costs are about US$2.20 per box.

Meanwhile, organic banana producers argue that too often the costs of conventional (non-organic) banana production are based on inadequate management practices. If farmers managed their plantations properly, by investing in new plants, fertilizer and irrigation, production costs would be US$2.30–2.40 per box. What is less contentious is that, almost without exception, farmers receive less than the US$2.18 per box stipulated under Ecuadorian law and that as a result their incomes are not healthy. The Ecuadorian government introduced a minimum price of US$2.90 per box on 1 January 2001. Once again, few of the banana exporting companies are paying producers this amount.

Low prices also prevent many farmers from improving their plantations. Many smallholder farmers are reluctant to take out a loan when there is a real danger that they will not be able to pay it back. Banana producers, therefore, need money or credit on favourable terms. Investments are needed to ensure that the produce meets strict quality criteria. Angel Samaniego stresses that funiculars are needed to minimize damage to the harvested bananas. Bruised fruit cannot be sold to the US or EU. There is a possibility that damaged fruit can be sold to Chile but at prices far below those normally paid for a box. Juan Quinteña shows us the stack of assorted second-hand banana boxes he uses to pack the reject bananas: he does not have a funicular system and he sells damaged and rejected bananas for as little as US$0.40 per box.

Pushing the price up

Given the increased concentration in the market and the retail sector, all food companies are obliged to strengthen their market orientation. Dole, for example, is developing an aggressive strategy in this field, leading to partnerships with retailers, wholesalers and distributors, and the establishment of integrated import, ripening and distribution systems. In this context, farmers such as Carlos and Juan seem to be trapped in a system which, in the absence of a strong producer association that defends their interests, offers few opportunities to improve their profit margins.

Furthermore, exporting companies often have more than one method of obtaining supplies. For example, companies such as Favorita have their own company farms and also contract growers. Other exporting companies purchase bananas on the open market. This mix of internal, contract and market purchases, gives the exporting companies a combination of control and flexibility in acquiring bananas.[10] In this context, it is not clear the extent to which producers will benefit from the expanding opportunities for exporting bananas.

On the other hand, Andrés Arata from CONABAN has a vision. He becomes animated as he describes how banana producers could control production and force the price up as long as Ecuadorian bananas remain more competitive than those from Costa Rica or Honduras. According to Arata, CONABAN could 'tax' producers about US$0.10 on each box sold. When the price of bananas drops, CONABAN could subsequently buy up supplies and force the price up. Is this realistic? Would CONABAN have the funds to sustain this over a long enough period to keep prices high? Others caution that the costs of transporting bananas through the Panama Canal are such that a relatively small increase in the price paid to Ecuadorian producers would mean that their bananas were no longer competitive.

Arata further argues that CONABAN also has a role to play in terms of being able to negotiate a better deal for farmers with regards to the costs of inputs. According to CONABAN, Dole sells a chemical called 'Tilt' which banana farmers supplying the company are obliged to use in order to control *sigatoka negra*. In Ecuador the chemical is sold at US$48 per litre while in Central America the price is US$28 per litre. Arata alleges that Ecuadorian banana producers are essentially subsidizing Dole plantations in Central America by paying over the odds for their chemicals. CONABAN is now looking for cheaper alternatives to the chemicals sold by Dole.

While CONABAN is adamant that smallholder producers can benefit from the booming banana sector in Ecuador, it also suggests that the ideal farm size is 70–100 hectares. The reason is economies of scale: a certain size of plantation is needed before it makes economic sense to construct packing sheds and install funiculars and irrigation systems. So where does this leave the smallholder producers? What can they do to gain some degree of autonomy in the export process and improve their livelihoods? The answer may well be to secure a niche in the growing fair trade and organic banana markets. In Ecuador, there are a growing number of examples where banana producers have done just this. They have formed farmer associations, carved out niches in these export markets and have negotiated substantially higher prices for their produce.

Organic and fair trade: a better deal for producers

The power of the consumer

In recent years there has been increased demand in the West, particularly in the EU, for organic produce and also bananas sold through fair trade initiatives. The growth in the fair trade and organic markets is characteristic of the extent to which markets have become consumer driven.[11] Consumers increasingly wish to know where their food comes from and who produces it. The attraction of these markets for farmers is that the product, in this case bananas, is sold at a premium. In the case of fair trade, the premium is always passed on to the farmer, whilst in the organic market it is usually paid to the farmer. Specific environmental and social criteria must be met before the product can be sold in either the fair trade or organic markets. Farmers' compliance with these criteria is checked through a process called certification.

The two markets are distinct, although confusion arises because organic bananas can also be sold in the fair trade market as long they meet the required fair trade criteria and have been certified. Fair trade aims to improve the social, environmental and economic conditions of disadvantaged producers by giving them direct access to a market, guaranteeing better trading and working conditions and thus providing them with the tools that permit them to control their own development, and to invest in environmentally friendly production methods. It seeks to change unfair international trading structures and to offer small-scale farmers (and craftsmen) in developing countries the chance to find outlets for their produce and to make a decent living from the sale.[12] It therefore includes a process of learning and self-help rather than an exclusive focus on the market dimensions of the partnership.[13]

Farmers often have the support of organizations based in the first world who arrange the importing and distribution of the goods and create consumer awareness. The Fairtrade Labelling Organization (FLO) co-ordinates fair trade at the international level and represents national fair trade initiatives in 17 countries; it holds a central register of certified producers for each product type. There are three basic prerequisites for the long-term development of fair trade: high quality produce; access to mainstream food stores; and assurance of compliance with fair trade criteria.[14]

Although the term 'fair trade' is not covered by any legal definition,[12] FLO stipulates that all potential fair trade sources have to meet minimum social and environmental criteria before being accepted for the Fairtrade certifying procedures. The criteria include: a price that covers the cost of production; a social premium for development purposes; contracts that allow long-term production planning; and certain health and safety standards. The assurance that sources comply with the environmental and social criteria is provided by the labels Max Havelaar (in France, Belgium and the Netherlands), Transfair (in Germany, Austria and Italy) and The Fairtrade Foundation (in the United Kingdom and Ireland). Unlike other certification schemes, such as organic certification, FLO does not charge producers for the certification process. Instead importers and retailers are charged a royalty fee for use of the Fairtrade label.

Organic farming aims to produce foods in an environmentally benign way, maintaining natural biological cycles without using chemical inputs. The International Federation of Organic Agriculture Movements (IFOAM) co-ordinates the network of the organic movement around the world. IFOAM has developed Basic Standards which set out international Principles, Recommendations and Standards for organic production. The Basic Standards include provisions for social justice, including recommendations that there be adherence to International Labour Conventions. The IFOAM Basic Standards provide a framework for certification bodies worldwide to develop their own certification standards. In the case of bananas, standards are generally established in importing countries.[14] Farmers who produce food in accordance with these organic standards, and whose compliance is checked by the certification bodies, may be certified as organic.

Benefiting smallholder farmers

Smallholder farmers frequently look to the organic and fair trade markets as niches where they may benefit. These markets offer an escape from the power of the big exporters. Although the two markets may overlap, they may offer different opportunities to farmers.

There is evidence that fair trade initiatives offer independent small-holder banana producers a viable route to more sustainable rural livelihoods. Producers receive a guaranteed fair price, which enables them to survive in the market place and to provide for the basic needs of their families. Worldwide, farmers involved in fair trade initiatives are being offered between US$7.25 and US$11.50 per box of bananas.[7] Producers also benefit from swift payment (net cash against documents), and continuity (buyers and sellers establish a long-term and stable trading relationship).

At the end of November 1996, the first fair trade bananas were imported into Europe. Total sales of all fair trade bananas in Europe were 12 300 tonnes in 1997, rising to over 30 000 tonnes in 2001.[15] The largest fair trade markets are in Switzerland and the Netherlands but growth in the markets is expected in Germany and the United Kingdom. Farmers are already benefiting from these market opportunities; workers in the Dominican Republic who supply fair trade bananas to one of the UK's largest super-markets receive a premium of US$1.75 per box of bananas exported. This money is destined to a social fund for the workers. The fund has been used to build a packing shed and to legalize workers who have come from neighbouring Haiti.

Organic markets operate slightly differently. There is no guaranteed fair price (unless the product is also part of a fair trade initiative). However, organic produce often receives a premium price because demand exceeds supply. Small mixed farms may be less susceptible to pests and diseases than large contiguous blocks of one crop, hence smallholders may have a competitive advantage over large farmers in producing organic crops. In addition, the organic market for bananas is mainly supplied by smallholders and small importers at present because the large companies do not yet see a big enough market to justify their interest. This is not to say they will not do so in future.

In 1997, the EU imported almost 10 000 tonnes of organic bananas, with Germany as the largest market.[14] The main obstacle to the growth of the organic banana market is on the supply side. Bananas are subject to several diseases making them difficult to grow organically, although this is less of a problem in Ecuador. If such constraints can be addressed, it is estimated that organic banana sales would grow in line with the market share of other organic fruit and vegetables, reaching 45 000 tonnes or approximately 1.5 per cent of annual banana consumption in the EU.

While farmers can benefit by selling in the fair trade and organic markets, farmers' initiatives in Ecuador demonstrate the range of obstacles and opportunities facing those seeking to set up marketing channels that are independent of the large banana companies.

Strength through association: orito *producers in Cumandá*

At 300 to 700 metres above sea level, Cumandá is a canton in the low-lying hills that separate the flat coastal plain from the Andes. Smallholder farmers in the region grow bananas, sugar cane, citrus fruits, cacao and coffee. Joseph Brown and Marcelo Vásquez are characteristic of banana farmers in the area, each having approximately 15 hectares of bananas, of which two-thirds are small finger bananas known locally as *oritos*. The remainder are dark red bananas known as *moradas*. These are native varieties of bananas, distant relatives to the improved, cosmopolitan Cavendish banana. Unlike normal-sized bananas, *oritos* are traditionally sold in smaller 7 kg boxes; average productivity is 12–14 boxes/ha per week.

Joseph and Marcelo have embarked on an audacious plan to circumvent the power of the banana companies. They are the driving force behind a group of 15 farmers who currently sell their bananas to Dole, Noboa and Del Monte. Dole and Del Monte do pay the minimum legal price of US$2.50 per box of *oritos*, says Marcelo. However, the farmers do not consider this price to be just and are seeking alternative buyers. The banana companies, they say, pay them the price of conventional *oritos* even though production is organic. They allege that the companies subsequently sell the organic produce at a premium and that this is not passed on to the farmers. The Cumandá farmers have set up a farmer association called the Asociación de Productores Orgánicos de Riochimbo and are currently trying to get the necessary certification so that they can sell their *oritos* direct in the organic and fair trade markets in Europe.[16]

As we work alongside Marcelo packing bananas it becomes clear that he is not exactly a typical farmer. He may end up being the Ecuadorian equivalent of France's José Bové, the one-time 1960s student radical and now, with his much publicized trashing of a McDonalds fast-food outlet, symbol of a growing protest against globalization. Marcelo was also a student radical; he studied in Germany in the 1960s, and befriended a fellow Latin America student, Jorge '*El Loro*' Vázquez-Viaña who died fighting with Che Guevara in the mountains of Bolivia. Marcelo has lost none of his revolutionary zeal. His wife, María, sighs and smiles indulgently as Marcelo describes his family story to us.

Marcelo learnt early on about the problems that smallholder farmers face. His family used to grow sugar cane and, with a concession from the government, produced a locally-distilled alcoholic drink called *aguardiente*. In the early 1980s, the concession system ended and the bigger landowners began to grow sugar cane and produce *aguardiente*. They did so at a more competitive price and undercut producers such as Marcelo. In response, Marcelo switched to growing *oritos* and since then has struggled for a fair price for his produce. He now wishes to use global trade more effectively to benefit the smallholder farmer. He admits that he is more the 'ideas' person and Joseph is the more 'practical, how do we go about it?' person. Politically, they are chalk and cheese but together they make a good team.

Joseph recognizes the importance of quality control, and the need to meet production deadlines and presentational requirements. He has done his homework and is aware that consumers in the developed world can be fickle, and packaging demands are tricky. *Oritos* for the North American market are packed loose, as large hands of 16 relatively large fruits, protected by foam inserts, in 7 kg boxes. However, an alternative method preferred by British importers and retailers, is to pack *oritos* in smaller clusters of six tiny fruits, transported in 12 kg boxes. They want each cluster of six fruit individually packed in a plastic bag, ready to fit the plastic presentation boxes for the supermarket shelves. British consumers are accustomed to tiny finger bananas from Africa, so new sources need to comply with existing preferences. The importers also aim to make a clear distinction between the tiny finger bananas and large, normal bananas.

This poses a challenge for producers. The requirements of the European market are so rigid, says Joseph, that small producers find them difficult to meet. And while small *oritos* can be sent to Europe and larger fruits to North America, the shipping days do not coincide and the fruit harvested for one market do not keep until they can be shipped to the other. The single fruit, cut off to create neat hands or clusters, do not find a market, even locally and are left for the cows. Between 10 and 20 per cent of each plant's production is wasted in loose fingers and damaged clusters or hands.

Packing clusters is a delicate process, which is not helped by the fact that *oritos* have thin skins and are easily bruised. Joseph explains that, because packing clusters entails more handling and potential damage than the larger hands, it is possible to pack seven smaller boxes (i.e. 49 kg) of large hands for every 12 kg box of small clusters. Consumer demands for high quality and presentation in supermarkets are being passed on direct to the producers.

We meet Joseph in his small office. He is well aware of the difficulties and challenges that the association faces. Joseph has already attempted to send *oritos* to Europe. However, the boat was delayed, temperatures in the refrigerated container rose (sabotage was suspected) and the fruits were ruined. In the future, transport will be paid for, and the risk taken, by the independent European importer. It is only by working together that members of the association can achieve the volume of production that is needed to secure a niche in the European market. During the dry season, the association can supply 1300–1400 small boxes of *oritos* per week while during the rains the figure will rise to 3200 boxes per week.

25

These volumes are small fry when one considers the enormous volumes of bananas that are exported weekly from Ecuador. Farmers are well aware that strength and ultimately power can be best achieved through association. Joseph has been busy establishing contacts. He explains that in the lowlands there is a farmer organization called the Asociación de Pequeños Productores de Guabo (APPG) that is already selling 20 000 boxes of bananas to the EU each week. Approximately 12 000 of these are sold in the fair trade market and 8000 in the conventional market. APPG has agreed to help the Riochimbo farmer association transport *oritos* to Europe. APPG is linked to two solidarity groups in Europe: Max Havelaar and a Dutch NGO, Solidaridad. Along with farmer groups in Costa Rica, the Dominican Republic and Ghana, APPG owns 50 per cent of the shares in an organization called Agrofair Europe, while the remainder are held by Solidaridad. The aim is for Agrofair Europe to market the products of its constituent farmer groups.

APPG wants to link up with other organizations, such as the association established by Joseph and Marcelo, to market bananas along with other products such as mango and pineapple. The overall aim is to bring together about 500 farmers from a number of associations to establish a new umbrella organization. The trading arm of this new organization, Agrofair Ecuador, will sell the farmers' produce to Agrofair Europe, who will be responsible for marketing it in Europe. The new organization also aims to enable smallholder farmers to secure credit under favourable terms.

In the absence of any assistance from the Ecuadorian authorities, Joseph and Marcelo need external help. The NGO Solidaridad is helping the Cumandá farmers get organically certified. Joseph has managed to secure the assistance of some Dutch volunteers to work with local farmers on technical and marketing angles. He adds that there are 200 organic *oritos* producers in the Cumandá area. If they all participated, they could produce 20 000 boxes per week. In addition, within the canton there are organic sugar and coffee producers who, Joseph hopes, will eventually join the *oritos* producers.

These are not unrealistic hopes. There are increasing examples throughout Latin America of groups of farmers who have achieved or are struggling for a more equitable future for themselves and their families (see Chapter 3, Niche markets: a solution to the coffee crisis?). But to stand any chance of benefiting from these markets, Marcelo, Joseph and their colleagues will have to meet strict quality criteria and ensure sufficient quantity of produce and continuity of supply.

The Cañartes and organic bananas

The struggle to circumvent the power of the banana exporting companies is also being waged by the larger independent banana producers. One such example is the Cañarte family. Simón Cañarte does not mince his words: 'Now don't get me wrong, I am a capitalist 100 per cent, but capitalism means fair competition and the banana companies are determined to get rid of all competition. They see what we are doing here as a threat'.

The threat that the Cañartes represent is spread out on the ground, about 25m² of organic fertilizer, called *bokashi*, that is drying in the sun. Chickens pick their way cautiously across the fertilizer, pecking periodically at a worm or insect. *Bokashi* is a mixture of residues of mango, pineapple, banana, burnt rice husks, pods of various legume trees, coffee pulp and cattle manure. The Cañartes use special micro-organisms from the US that speed up the decomposition of *bokashi* so that it can be applied to the banana plantations after only 11 days, rather than six months for conventional compost. *Bokashi* is the key to what the Cañartes claim is 100 per cent organic banana production.

While organic production in the cool, low-lying hills of Cumandá is relatively easy, the accepted wisdom is that in the more humid lowlands, *sigatoka negra* can be controlled only by spraying. The Cañartes dispute this and point out that their organic production system has European certification. They believe that they are seen as a threat by the banana companies because these same companies make considerable profits in Ecuador from the sale of chemicals, many of which they produce themselves. 'Did you know,' Simón fumes, 'that Dole makes US$97 million a year in profit in Ecuador and of that about 45 per cent comes from sales of agrochemicals?' If more farmers turn to organic production, the banana companies' profit margin is reduced.

It is easy to understand Simón's concern about the way the banana companies might react to competition. His father had a small banana exporting company in the 1950s which was undercut by the larger banana companies. There is still much anger and resentment against these companies. This partly explains why the Cañartes went into organic production six years ago; by doing so they can carve out a strong market niche for themselves and for others.

With just under 500 hectares of directly managed banana plantations, the Cañartes are not smallholders. They have built a small training centre at their own expense and Simón offers courses on organic banana production free of charge to other producers, small, medium or large. The Cañartes are advising the APPG farmers to turn 20 000 hectares into organic banana production. According to CONABAN this vast area should be totally organic within the next five years. Is banana production in Ecuador about to be revolutionized, the vanguard being producers who will secure market niches in the developed world independently of the large banana companies? Or is this all a sham?

The Cañartes have three plantations of 50, 230 and 200 hectares. The 50 hectare site has recently been replanted; in general the plants are replaced every eight to ten years. The planting stock is of improved varieties that have been identified in their own plantations and then propagated at the University of Guayaquil. Management of the Cañates plantations is based on the theory of trophobiosis. This was put forward by a French scientist called Francis Chaboussou who believed that plant susceptibility to pest or disease attack is directly related to the biochemical state of the plant. The theory is that pests and diseases are a problem only when the plant's biochemical state offers the required nutritional needs. This state can be caused by soil deficiency in trace elements and an excess of nitrogen, caused in part by an imbalance in the fertilizer regime used and the use of pesticides. The argument is that pests starve on healthy plants. Far-fetched? Perhaps, but the Cañartes' plantations have been tested and certified as organic.

We wander through the 200 hectare plantation at the San Humberto farm to see how bananas are produced organically. At San Humberto, the Cañartes produce a staggering 210 tonnes of *bokashi* per month. Approximately 6 kg of the mixture is applied to each banana plant four times a year. In addition, workers spray the plants with an organic and home-made foliar spray called *Biol*. The spray is made from whey yeast of milk, cattle manure, liquid drained from the decomposing *bokashi* and micro-organisms. The spray is applied to 50 hectares of plantation each day.

As we talk to the Cañartes, two workers fill up back packs with the brown liquid. They start the motor and then walk through the plantation aiming large nozzles at the leaves of the plants. Spraying takes place in the late afternoon when stomata on the leaves are open, making uptake of the fertilizer more efficient. Simón is adamant that smallholder farmers can replicate the system: many have cattle and can get hold of the other ingredients to make *bokashi* and the spray. The brothers add that many of their plantation workers are now using *bokashi* to produce organic vegetables at home.

We move on to the subject of costs. How profitable is it to grow organic bananas? Where are the markets? Paul, Simón's brother, explains that organic production is more profitable than conventionally-managed bananas. Labour costs on an organic farm are 30–40 per cent higher than on a conventional plantation. Hence, the Cañartes employ on average 1 person per hectare in comparison with the standard 0.6 person per hectare. Furthermore, productivity in the organic system (even when well managed) is only 80–90 per cent of that in conventionally-managed plantations. Despite this, the 230 hectare plantation block produces 11 000 boxes per week and there are a further 10 000 boxes a week from the 200 hectare plantation.

The key to profitability is the premium that organic bananas command. The farm-gate price for organic bananas is US$ 5–6 per box; delivered to the port, the price is US$6–7 per box, which includes US$1.60–1.70 per box for packing and transport. Unlike those selling on the conventional market, organic producers have to pay for the cardboard boxes. According to Simón, organic production costs are US$2.30–2.40 per box. There are no costs for applications of pesticides; fertilizer is home-made and is low cost to apply.

As far as Simón is concerned organic production makes economic sense. He is highly sceptical that production costs for conventional bananas are under US$1.80 per box. He agrees that farmers who sell conventional bananas for US$1.90 per box or less are hardly covering production costs, and yet they could secure a substantial premium, with marginally higher production costs, were they to produce organic bananas.

Almost the entire production of the Cañarte farms is sold to Italy, with a small fraction going to the rest of the EU and Chile. Organic bananas are not subject to complicated EU rules for licences and quotas. The advantage that Simón has, and one that the producers in Cumandá are striving for, is volume. Each container on a ship bound for Europe or the US contains approximately 950 boxes and there are 350 containers per boat, making a total of approximately 330 000 boxes per ship.

The Cañartes export about 20 000 boxes a week to Europe. This translates as 21 containers, a sufficiently large volume for the European importer to have influence over the shipper. Ironically, the organic bananas are transported on boats belonging to Noboa, an Ecuadorian company and the largest banana exporter in the country. According to the contract, Noboa is responsible for ensuring that the Cañartes' bananas arrive in good condition in Europe. In this way, the Cañartes avoid the problems encountered by the Cumandá *oritos* producers when shipping was delayed and the fruit was ruined.

The Cañartes' one complaint is that although their plantations have been organically certified by an Italian certifier and the bananas are sold in Italy, attempts to break into other national markets, such as the UK, have been hampered by each country's preference for its own certification scheme.

According to the Soil Association, the UK's main organic certifying body, produce certified by a legally recognized EU certifier can be sold legally anywhere within the EU. The main advantage of being certified by a national organization is that the national logo is likely to be better recognized than, in this case, an Italian one. Hence, there may well be marketing advantages to having a national logo. Potentially, the Cañartes' organic bananas could be sold in the UK with a Soil Association logo once the Soil Association has ascertained the credibility of the Italian certifier. The process can be costly because it involves the Soil Association verifying the Italian certifier's degree of quality control and standards of operation.

Jumping on the organic bandwagon?

There are many in the banana sector who are very sceptical of the Cañartes' claims about organic production. Their argument is that if the Cañartes were doing what they claim to be doing, then others would have cottoned on and followed suit. Even those who are supportive of organic production argue that chemical applications will still be needed in a large plantation during the rainy season when *sigatoka negra* is more prevalent. Sceptics are less dismissive of the attempts of the APPG producers in El Oro province to turn 20 000 ha over to organic production: in this case the plantations are found in a drier area where *sigatoka negra* is not such a problem. However, even the most hardened sceptics of the Cañarte's work are not blind to the advantages that the environmentally conscious market offers.

Favorita is proud that its two directly owned plantations have been certified under the ECO-OK scheme. This certification scheme was developed by the Rainforest Alliance, a US-based NGO and certification body, specifically for the banana sector. The scheme certifies that bananas have been produced under good – although not organic – management practices. For example, it requires that chemical applications are reduced (but not eliminated); that aerial spraying does not contaminate neighbouring land, and that corridors of natural vegetation are left between blocks of bananas.

Favorita claims that at the moment there is no premium for ECO-OK bananas (as opposed to organic bananas) but that this will change and the market will eventually pay more for 'ecological' bananas. The company is also suspicious that the EU may at any stage seek to exclude dollar bananas by using strict environmental criteria in place of the old system of quotas and licences.

The company therefore wants to get its medium and large independent producers ECO-OK certified so that it is able to take advantage of more lucrative market niches. However, it is much more difficult for smallholder producers to qualify for the ECO-OK label, as they cannot spray their plantations by air without contaminating surrounding areas: on very small farms, it is not possible to be this accurate.

Chiquita started the ECO-OK programme with the Rainforest Alliance in 1995. On the world stage, the ECO-OK label is being used by Chiquita to establish itself as the environmental leader of the banana companies. It is part of the company's marketing image, a means of strengthening its presence in the wholesale/retail sector and to improving brand awareness. In Europe, ECO-OK certification is not well known as an eco-label, and the programme has been criticized for permitting the use of agrochemicals.[2] The Cañartes, likewise, claim that the ECO-OK label is potentially misleading to consumers, who may believe they are buying an organic product.

Likewise, Dole claims to be developing and implementing an Integrated Pest Management (IPM) programme on its plantations and stresses that it complies with the international environmental management standard ISO 14001 which is set by the International Organization for Standardization (ISO). However, this standard sets out the way in which a company should manage its environmental performance, rather than the results of that performance. The company is required to identify its environmental impacts, and set targets for reducing them. Compliance with ISO 14001 means that a plantation is achieving its own objectives and targets, rather than achieving an externally fixed performance. In the case of chemical usage, the company can set its own targets for reduction in application, which may be minimal.

Banana production is not alone in the sense that there are a number of different labelling schemes available. Proponents of one scheme tend to criticize the quality of others. The banana companies will generally apply whichever scheme has most market acceptance and lower costs.

According to Alistair Smith of the UK-based NGO Banana Link, the large banana companies are watching developments in Ecuador very carefully. At the moment the Cumandá *oritos* producers, APPG and the Cañartes do not really represent a serious threat to the banana companies. But if the organic initiatives take off, the large banana companies will enter the market as ruthlessly as in the conventional banana market, competing with, and ultimately undermining, the farmers' associations.

Organic and fair trade markets may offer a better deal for small producers, but bananas also provide an illuminating example of how farmers' access to these markets has been hampered by restrictive trading practices, the extent to which current trade rules are stacked in favour of the large banana companies, and the degree to which these same companies will fight to maintain and expand their share of world markets. The banana war between the United States of America and the European Union was an acrimonious trade dispute that lasted for several years and was resolved only at the beginning of 2001. Although Ecuadorian producers were not directly involved in the banana war, the terms under which it was resolved have a direct bearing on the Ecuadorian banana sector.

The transatlantic banana dispute

Regulation 404/93

The EU is the biggest importer of bananas in the world, consuming some 35 per cent of total exports. For this reason its policy on banana imports has a strong impact on patterns of production and trade.[7] Prior to 1992, a number of different arrangements for the import of bananas existed in Europe. While Germany had a tariff-free banana market, the UK gave preferential treatment to imports from its former colonies in the Caribbean. Support for smallholder banana farmers in the Caribbean was considered necessary because the lack of economies of scale and unfavourable growing conditions mean that production costs in the Caribbean are twice as high as those in Latin America.

Following the formation of the Single European Market in 1992, a new banana regime was agreed in 1993. The EU had two objectives: to create an integrated market for bananas harmonizing different banana trade agreements, and to guarantee that access to this market for its traditional African, Caribbean and Pacific (ACP) countries, was not hampered by the foreseen influx of cheap 'dollar' bananas.[2] Preferential treatment of the ACP countries dated back to the Lomé Convention that was signed in 1975. The process of harmonizing the European market was further complicated by the fact that preferential treatment of the ACP countries contradicted the need to comply with the General Agreement on Tariffs and Trade (GATT).

The result was EC Regulation 404/93. It used a system of licences, quotas and tariffs to limit the volumes of cheaper imports from Latin America. Regulation 404/93 sparked an acrimonious trade dispute between the United States and the EU. Encouraged by the multinational fruit trading companies, and particularly Chiquita, much of whose banana trade is located in Latin America, the USA challenged the European banana regime first at GATT and then at its successor, the World Trade Organization (WTO). The WTO insisted that the EU cease its preferential access for ACP countries' bananas, even though the annual revenue from banana exports from the ACP countries represented a fraction of the combined annual revenue of Chiquita, Dole and Del Monte. The EU refused and, in 1999, the US imposed 100 per cent tariffs on American imports of a long list of European products, almost all of which had nothing to do with bananas.

Regulation 404/93 also did few favours for the growing fair trade movement. The allocation of licences was based on past performance of the operators, which favoured the large banana companies and considerably hampered the trade in fair trade bananas. Under Regulation 404/93 fair trade operators were classified as 'newcomers' on the market. As such, they could access only the 'newcomer category' which represented 8 per cent of the total licences. Due to constant over-applications, there were never enough licences, and fair trade importers were forced to buy licences from their 'unfair' competitors at a high cost.

Sacrificed on the altar of WTO compatibility?

In the first half of 2001, a new agreement was finally reached between the EU and USA. The system of tariffs, quotas and licences was modified, with 83 per cent of licences going to 'traditional operators' and 17 per cent to 'non-traditional operators'. The allocation of licences to fill quotas is based on trade volumes between 1994 and 1996. The 'traditional operators' during this reference period were principally the large banana companies. The main losers are the 'non-traditional operators', which include many independent producers and traders who have built up their business since the mid-1990s, and particularly the smaller players who have built up trade in organic and fair trade bananas.

According to the NGO Banana link, fair trade bananas have been sacrificed on the altar of WTO compatibility. A further obstacle to the development of fair trade is that a non-traditional importer has the right to apply for a maximum of 12.5 per cent of the licences available. If the total of the applications from 'non-traditional' importers exceeds the available quota, all applications are reduced by the same factor. To date, none of the fair trade operators has actually gone out of business as a result of the new regime but there is little or no room to grow.[17]

Chiquita and the other banana companies are the main beneficiaries of the new EU regime. Under the new EU regime, country quotas (which had existed under Regulation 404/93) will be abolished and there will be a tendency for operators to seek the cheapest bananas available on the world market. Ecuador is likely to benefit from this, but it will be those who are tied into the banana companies' marketing structures who will benefit most. Independent producers like the Cumandá farmers are not favoured by the new rules and smallholder Caribbean producers will suffer under intensified competition.

Circles within circles: Ecuador and the Caribbean

Throughout the protracted banana dispute, and unable to compete with the cheaper dollar bananas, Caribbean banana exports to the EU have declined significantly. Across the EU, Chiquita, Dole and Del Monte control approximately 43 per cent of the market. Some 64 per cent of all imports come from Latin America, with less than 10 per cent from the Caribbean.[1] The UK is virtually the only market for Caribbean bananas. In the period between 1992 and 1998, UK banana imports from the Caribbean fell from 65 per cent to less than 35 per cent, while imports of bananas from Latin America have increased inexorably. Caribbean banana producers have been leaving the industry in large numbers and what has not yet been quantified are the associated economic and social consequences of this change.

Bananas used to provide the major export revenue of this region: banana exports made up almost half of all export earnings in the Windward Islands. This dependence goes back to the early 1950s, when the islands were British colonies. Prior to bananas, sugar cane had been the main export, but when sugar beet grown in Europe began to compete, the price on the world market fell and the islands began to grow bananas. There is now much speculation as to what can possibly replace the employment and income that the banana industry used to provide to the Windward Islanders.

There are signs that Caribbean farmers have 'discovered' an alternative to growing bananas. This alternative grows well in the hot and humid conditions found on many of the islands and can be very profitable. It is also illegal. Reacting to the supply and demand rules of the free market, Caribbean farmers are beginning to grow marijuana in ever greater quantities. This phenomenon is no different to those farmers throughout the Andes who grow coca because it is the most viable crop (see Chapter 6, Coca eradication and alternative development). The Caribbean is also a very convenient transit point for those smuggling cocaine from South America to the USA. The temptation to get involved in the cocaine supply chain may prove irresistible for farmers whose livelihoods used to depend on banana production. The USA may discover that victory in the banana war for companies such as Chiquita is a hollow victory.

Aiming for diversity

It is ironic that while diversity is a feature of other world commodities such as coffee, the world banana trade still focuses almost exclusively on the Cavendish variety. An independent banana importer in the UK stresses that although supermarkets in countries like the UK are interested in marketing other banana varieties, the banana companies have such a stranglehold over world trade that diversification is difficult. The independent importer's argument is that the exporting companies benefit from dealing with one banana variety; from a marketing perspective, the system is almost perfect. For example, a boat off the Central American Atlantic coast line (with bananas originating from Honduras, Costa Rica, Colombia, Panama or Ecuador) is carrying a product that can be sold either in Europe or the USA. At the last moment, the exporting company can divert the boat to the USA coastline or European ports such as Hamburg and Rotterdam.

In addition, the process of harvesting, transporting and subsequently ripening bananas has been developed for the Cavendish variety, creating a further obstacle to diversification. Research and development would be needed to identify the necessary modifications to this process in order to ensure that other varieties of banana arrive on supermarket shelves in an optimum condition. Under the current system, there is little incentive for the exporting companies to invest financial resources in exploring the market potential of other banana varieties. Increasing banana diversity would make marketing considerably more complicated.

Perhaps it is time to encourage consumers to complicate the process and seek sources of 'alternative' banana varieties from the myriad smallholder producers found throughout the developing world. Developing a diverse market would not take that much imagination. However, there are some extraordinary EU rules and regulations that seemingly serve no purpose at all but stymie changes to the market. For example, the *oritos* producers in Cumandá point out that they are blocked from exporting to the EU the single bananas that inevitably accumulate as the clusters are prepared for packing. Independent banana importers in the UK confirm that under EU regulations it is indeed prohibited to import clusters of green *oritos* with fewer than four fruits per cluster, in the same way that it is illegal to import single green bananas.

It is not, however, illegal to sell single bananas within the EU once they have been ripened. Certainly farmers like those in Cumandá would benefit from a change in the rules. Single *oritos* could quite easily be imported into the EU and used in baby food or coated in fair trade chocolate ice-cream and sold in supermarkets. As it happens, some Ecuadorian producers do sell single *oritos* to the USA; the destination is the US army along with some of the US airline companies and hotel chains.

The Cumandá farmers and the Cañarte family clearly illustrate how much can be achieved when farmers have a vision and take the initiative to achieve it. Farmers seeking a niche in fair trade and organic markets face a number of challenges: leadership qualities are needed; contacts need to be forged; negotiations carried out; capital is needed to improve plantation infrastructure; and the farmers have to produce high-quality bananas.

What is clearly lacking are the policies that support these initiatives. An enabling policy environment is needed, one in which carefully targeted assistance can be directed at smallholder farmer associations and which provides them with fair access to the market. Furthermore, there is growing evidence that such assistance can contribute to long-term development by providing smallholder farmers with precisely the type of wide-ranging capacity building that enables them develop their own linkages and eventually secure better deals in conventional markets.[18]

CHAPTER 3

Niche markets: a solution to the coffee crisis?*

Introduction

WE ARRIVE AT Doña Alicia's little wooden house just after the rainstorm has ended. All around us the mud is slippery after the rain, but under the tree canopy the ground is protected by a thick layer of leaves and the coffee plants thrive. Against a backdrop of the coffee plantation climbing the steep hillside behind the house, Doña Alicia shows us the new concrete tank for washing coffee in the yard. At US$400, the tank represents a significant investment. The coffee tank allows her and her husband to produce better quality coffee than before, potentially opening the door to higher prices for the produce from the 8-hectare plot that they own in the hills above Caranavi in Bolivia. The challenge is for Alicia and her husband to capitalize on that improved quality and ensure that they sell their coffee in the more equitable organic coffee market. It is a challenge facing increasing numbers of Latin American coffee producers.

Coffee originated in Ethiopia and is now grown in 80 countries in Latin America, the Caribbean, Africa, Asia and the Pacific. Worldwide, coffee now covers over 100 000 square kilometres. Annual yields are in excess of 5.7 million tonnes and it is one of the most valuable agricultural commodities in world trade.[1] In the United Kingdom alone, over 31 billion cups of coffee are drunk each year.[1] Coffee provides a living for over 10 million producers, of whom over two-thirds are smallholder farmers with less than five hectares of coffee.[2]

In recent years the world market price of coffee has fluctuated dramatically. For example, between 1988 and 2001 coffee prices fell by two-thirds,[3] but within this period the market was very volatile. From 1989 to 1993 there was a 50 per cent reduction in the world price of coffee.[1] Prices then soared in 1994 after a frost severely damaged Brazil's coffee plantations, and then plummeted again. In December 2001, international coffee prices hit a 30-year low. For many smallholder coffee producers worldwide, including those in Ecuador, Peru and Bolivia, the price of coffee has dropped below the costs of production. A big recovery in coffee prices in the short to medium term is unlikely.[4]

---

* Throughout this chapter, and following the convention in the coffee sector, prices for coffee are given in US cents per pound (¢/lb). Unless otherwise stated, prices are from the latter half of 2000.

Low coffee prices have forced many farmers either to abandon coffee production or increasingly to seek temporary off-farm employment. The latter is the cause of a vicious circle whereby farmers' neglect of their coffee plantations leads to a deterioration in the quality of coffee produced and a further reduction in the price that they receive for their crop. The key question is how can smallholder coffee producers in Bolivia, Peru and Ecuador deal with the problems of low and fluctuating world coffee prices, distant markets and the vicious circle of neglect?

The answer might lie with the example set by a growing number of smallholder farmers. Faced with the vagaries of world markets in terms of low and fluctuating prices, increasing numbers of coffee producers are also beginning to work together to pool their resources and improve their negotiating position in the market. These groups of farmers are being encouraged to produce high-quality coffee for the fair trade, organic and gourmet coffee markets. These niche markets offer higher prices than the markets for conventional coffee. But how great are the opportunities offered by these growing niche markets and what are the obstacles to farmers securing a foothold in them? This chapter examines these issues and considers whether niche markets offer a sustainable solution to the coffee crisis.

Low and fluctuating prices

Oversupply and more power in fewer hands

The adverse market conditions faced by smallholder farmers are the result of world oversupply of coffee and high volatility of international coffee prices. Since the price peaked in 1994, there has been increased investment in coffee to the extent that coffee production now exceeds demand by up to 10 per cent.[5] While world demand has risen slowly at about 1 per cent per year over the past two decades, world production of coffee increased by an estimated 18 per cent between 1980 and 1999.[2] This is due to the introduction of higher-yielding trees (such as the 'Catura' variety in Colombia), advanced technology, and the emergence of new producer countries such as Vietnam, which in the 1990s increased coffee production by 400 per cent and now produces 11 per cent of the world's coffee.[3] Almost all of the coffee grown in Vietnam is lower-quality Robusta as opposed to higher-quality Arabica coffee.

In Brazil, the 1994 price rise led to an increase in the area planted to coffee, and in some cases a greater density of planting along with the planting of more Robusta coffee. The large-scale mechanized farms in Bahía can now produce 4.2 tonnes per hectare (t/ha), although production on the majority of smaller farms averages approximately 1 t/ha. This compares to yields of 0.6 t/ha achieved by smallholder farmers in the Andean region. Brazil now accounts for approximately 25 per cent of all coffee exports.

The International Coffee Agreement (ICA) was established in 1962 and between the date of its establishment and 1989 a total of 24 import and 44 export countries worked together to stabilize coffee prices through export quotas and buffer stocks. Coffee prices have been highly volatile since 1989, when the price control clause of the ICA was suspended largely because coffee exporting countries could not agree on quotas.[6] Producer countries flooded the market with stocks that had originally been withheld to sustain prices. The coffee price subsequently plummeted.

Until the late 1980s, most producing countries regulated their coffee sectors. Government organizations offered a price stabilization scheme to coffee producers by fixing the internal price. Since the later 1980s, and partly under pressure from international organizations such as The World Bank and International Monetary Fund, most coffee-producing countries have liberalized their markets as part of structural adjustment. One of the consequences has been that subsidies for coffee production and agricultural services have been reduced[7] and private exporters have become the main players in world trading. Although farmers do now receive a greater share of the export price, they are much more exposed to sudden price fluctuations associated with free market forces. The farm-gate price can be around 60 per cent of the export price, but the reality is that farmers often sell to intermediaries and receive far less for their coffee.

The price of coffee is set in international coffee exchanges in New York and London, where future contracts are traded. Futures are agreements to buy and sell coffee at an agreed price at some time in the future.[1] The international coffee market is dominated by a handful of large roasting companies such as Nestlé, Philip Morris and Sara Lee, along with large trading companies such as the Neumann Group, Volcafé and Ecom. It is these companies that capture most of the value-added associated with coffee processing (which takes place largely outside the producer countries) and retailing. They are able to do so because of the volumes they buy, the strength of their brands and products, and their ability to mix and match blends.

The price that producers receive for their coffee is a small fraction of the retail price on the supermarket shelves in developed countries. By the time that the coffee beans arrive in the USA or Europe, the importer has incurred freight and insurance costs, as well as port and customs charges. The coffee is then sold to a roasting company which roasts and blends it with coffee from other sources, prior to its marketing in retail outlets such as supermarkets.

Coffee buyers are in a very strong position to determine price, especially when supply exceeds demand. It has been calculated that farmers receive approximately 5–10 per cent of the retail price of coffee. Approximately 70 per cent of the wealth generated by world coffee sales is captured outside of the producing countries. The share taken by international intermediaries is increasing and is reflected in the growing difference between consumer and producer prices in the past 20 years. For example, between 1975 and 1993 the international price of coffee declined by 18 per cent but that paid by consumers in the USA increased by 240 per cent.[8]

The differential: issues of quantity, management and quality

Although there is an international price for coffee in New York and London, export prices from individual countries vary widely and depend on crop quality, demand for particular varieties, and the reputation of the exporting country. The degree to which an exporting country's coffee varies from the international price is known as the differential. In Ecuador, Bolivia and Peru the price differential is known as the *castigo* (punishment) because for these countries the export price is well below the international price. For example, the differential for Bolivian conventional coffee is 26¢/lb. Therefore, when Arabica coffee is trading on the international markets at 77¢/lb, Bolivian coffee sells for 51¢/lb.

In Bolivia, coffee producers and exporters agree that there is an urgent need to reduce the differential. What is less clear is how this can be achieved. Bolivia produces between 7100 and 9700 tonnes of coffee per year. This represents less than one quarter of 1 per cent of world sales and is significantly less than Peru and Ecuador. In Bolivia, representatives of the coffee exporters such as the Asociación Nacional de Exportadores de Café (ANDEC) and the Comité Boliviano de Café (COBOLCA) argue that their negotiating position with world buyers could be improved were Bolivia to increase production ten-fold. They cite the fact that there is a lower differential for Peruvian coffee partly because Peru sells larger volumes of coffee on the world market and is better able to negotiate with the international buyers.

ANDEC and COBOLCA suggest that in Bolivia a ten-fold increase in production can be brought about by bringing more areas into production, increasing the density of planting and hiring labour during the harvest (to ensure that coffee is picked at the optimum time). However, are these realistic options? Should Bolivia be trying to increase production when there is a worldwide surplus of coffee and a differential of 26¢/lb? And how realistic is it to increase the density of planting? In Bolivia there are often 900–1000 coffee plants/ha while in Colombia there may be as many as 5000 plants/ha. Coffee producers in Peru point out that on poor soils lower densities are needed so as to ensure that there are sufficient nutrients for the coffee trees. Are the soils in the coffee growing regions in Bolivia rich enough to sustain the planting densities found in Colombia? These issues need to be addressed before embarking on an intensification of coffee production in Bolivia.

The Bolivian coffee exporters also lament the fact that many farmers do not manage their plantations well. Badly managed plantations lead to poor-quality coffee and this, in turn, contributes to the high differential levied on Bolivian coffee. From the farmers' perspective, poor management of their coffee is rational. The production of high-quality coffee is a labour-intensive exercise. Many coffee producers migrated from the Bolivian highlands and still have land there. With coffee sales barely covering production costs, farmers are returning to the highlands more frequently. In their absence, their coffee plantations remain unmanaged. Faced with depressed prices for their coffee there is little incentive to improve quality. Farmers are seemingly caught in a vicious circle whereby without a market that gives them a decent income, they cannot deliver a high-quality product to the market.[1]

Two examples demonstrate the link between low world prices and poor management. When coffee prices were low in the early 1990s, farmers in Colombia neglected their coffee plots. As a result, a coffee pest known as *la broca*, a worm that bores into the coffee fruits, spread widely and led to a reduction in the quality of coffee. Similarly, in the Espíndola coffee area in southern Ecuador, farmers explained that 25–30 years ago coffee prices deteriorated relative to cattle. Subsequently, farmers neglected their coffee plots and focused on raising cattle. As a result, the quality of coffee declined. Efforts are now being made to improve the quality of coffee from the Espíndola area and a major component is improved management of coffee plantations. This is an attempt to break out of the vicious circle of low prices and poor management by producing higher-quality coffee for those niche markets that offer farmers higher prices.

Intermediaries: villain or scapegoat?

Another option to secure higher prices is for farmers to work together and to shorten or bypass the chain of intermediaries that exists between the producers and exporters. Intermediaries have a poor reputation among coffee producers. Farmers accuse the intermediaries of exploiting them. Farmers' dependency on intermediaries is both a result and a cause of their marginalization. Coffee producers are often geographically isolated and lack transport to get their coffee to market. They often have little choice but to sell their coffee to the intermediaries and are, therefore, vulnerable to underpricing.

Caranavi in Bolivia is located to the north of La Paz, just where the peaks of the Andes drop into the western reaches of the Amazon basin. To reach Caranavi, the road climbs from La Paz, over a 4500-metre high pass, and then drops terrifyingly along a dusty, single track road which clings impossibly to the sheer cliff face. Trucks fall off the road so frequently that no-one really knows how many lie at the bottom of the cliffs. Coffee producers in Caranavi are dependent on the intermediaries to transport their coffee along this perilous road to the capital.

Doña Alicia and her husband sell some of their coffee in Caranavi to the intermediaries who transport it to La Paz. The biggest problem, she says, is not the diseases that inevitably afflict their coffee, but the intermediaries they have to sell their coffee to. The intermediaries offer the producers low prices and cheat them on their measures, as well as cheating the coffee exporters to whom they sell. But the producers have no choice but to accept the low prices if they want money for family expenditure.

Farmers in Caranavi and Loja, Ecuador, complain bitterly that, when buying coffee, the intermediaries use adulterated scales that do not reflect the true weight of the coffee. This use of inaccurate scales was confirmed by ANDEC and COBOLCA in La Paz, Bolivia. Bolivian coffee producers add that one of the disincentives to improve the quality of coffee is that the intermediaries do not differentiate between good and poor quality coffee. They mix the purchased coffee and pay the same price irrespective of quality, that is to say, there is no premium for improved quality coffee. This is a phenomenon found in other parts the world such as Tanzania,[9] and with other products such as the Andean grain quinoa (see Chapter 5, Quinoa and food security).

Bolivian coffee exporters also accuse the intermediaries of cheating them by increasing the moisture content and hence weight of the coffee when it is transported from the coffee-producing areas. Coffee sometimes arrives in La Paz with a moisture content of 45–55 per cent, and during processing there is much weight loss when the moisture content is reduced to 12 per cent. In the absence of a transparent system whereby farmers are more aware of the costs associated with processing the coffee, they are convinced that the intermediaries and exporters are exploiting them.

Farmers increasingly have access to the Internet and are becoming aware of the world price of coffee. For example, coffee producers in Caranavi check the world price of coffee on a regular basis. In June 2000, they received 22¢/lb of coffee when they sold it via the intermediaries. They argue that based on the New York price and the differential on Bolivian coffee, they should have been paid at least 25¢/lb. Meanwhile, in La Paz, the

41

exporters argue that processing costs are high, typically 9 –14¢/lb of export coffee, and that the prices paid to farmers for conventional coffee are therefore fair.

ANDEC claims that it wishes to work direct with producers and aims to establish a coffee-buying centre in Caranavi so as to bypass some of the intermediaries. Until this happens farmers and exporters are caught up in a commercial enterprise that breeds suspicions. For example, reconciliation talks in Caranavi in July 2000 between the exporters and producers broke down in a mass of recriminations, with farmers threatening to withhold coffee.

An alternative point of view, however, is that the intermediaries play an essential role because they buy coffee from farmers in isolated and remote areas. Were it not for the intermediaries, the farmers would not be able to sell their coffee, nor secure cash payments long before the harvest.

Desperate for cash

Farmers are often in a weak negotiating position, not only because they seldom have the means to process or transport their crop to market, but also because, with only one harvest per year, they are often desperate for cash before or by the time the coffee is ripe.[1] Hence, they rarely have a choice regarding the timing of the sale or the identity of the buyer. Often they are forced to sell their coffee for whatever price they can secure. More often than not this has meant selling to intermediaries. A major cause of this problem is that it is extremely difficult for farmers to secure loans at a fair interest rate from banks or other lending organizations.

Coffee producers face similar problems to many other smallholder farmers in Latin America in gaining access to credit. Lending institutions are often not prepared to give credit to farmers, and few smallholders are able or willing to offer their land as collateral. The supply of credit, especially from institutional sources, frequently depends on the borrower's ownership security.[10] Provision of collateral is a common prerequisite for commercial bank loans and land is useful as collateral only if ownership by the borrower can be proven. Farmers may not be the legal owners of the land they farm or may not have all the necessary documentation. Even if farmers own their land, they may be very reluctant to offer it as collateral because coffee is such an uncertain asset. For example, international coffee prices tripled in the first six months of 1997 before losing half their value in the next six months.[2]

In the absence of formal sources of credit it can be argued that the intermediaries play an important role as 'unofficial banks' although they tend to charge exorbitant interest rates and demand land and homes as guarantees to be forfeited if they default. However, if farmers could secure credit on favourable terms, there would be less need to sell their coffee to the intermediaries months before it is harvested or as soon as the coffee is picked and when prices may be depressed by oversupply within the region or country. At harvest time, farmers are not only desperate for cash but there are also logistical problems to storing coffee while waiting for more favourable prices.

According to The Fairtrade Foundation,[1] the lack of access to credit has become one of the key factors undermining the position of smallholder farmers. The situation has been exacerbated in recent years by structural adjustments which have led to the demise of agricultural extension services, which in the past would have provided some farmers with access to credit. The problem of securing finance at favourable interest rates is also one faced today by the more successful farming co-operatives.

Quality and niche markets

The niche markets: fair trade, organic and gourmet

Throughout the Andean region, coffee producers are working together to pool their resources and strengthen their negotiating position. Many farmer groups are now able to pay for technical advice, buy equipment to process and grade their coffee, organize transport and market the crop.[1] The main incentive behind the movement to empower farmers is the growth, since the early 1990s, of niche markets that offer farmers a significantly higher price for their coffee than that offered by the conventional markets and which do not suffer from the price fluctuations associated with conventional coffee. From the farmer's point of view, they also often offer a means of bypassing the intermediaries and exporters who are their usual route to the market.

Niche markets are seen as the key to breaking out of the vicious circle of low prices and poor-quality coffee. These markets can be divided into the fair trade, organic and gourmet coffee markets (for a fuller explanation of the organic and fair trade markets see Chapter 2, Green gold: Ecuador's banana producers). Gourmet coffees are usually high-quality Arabica coffees that are sold as a brand rather than a commodity. Often they are single-estate coffees in the same way that some high-quality wine is marketed on the basis of its source. The combination of high quality and limited availability gives the coffee an exclusivity which means that it often commands a very high price. In recent years there has been a growth in the gourmet coffee market. Examples of gourmet coffee include Blue Mountain Coffee from Jamaica and Antigua Coffee from Guatemala.

Organic, fair trade and gourmet coffees are also sometimes referred to as 'speciality coffees' and there is overlap between them. For example, some gourmet coffee is organic and, whether produced conventionally or organically, gourmet coffee may also be sold as fair trade coffee if the smallholder producers have been certified as such.

Fair trade schemes mean that, irrespective of the world price, buyers pay a price for coffee that covers the cost of production, a basic living wage and allows for investment. The price is agreed by producers and the Fairtrade Labelling Organization. Fair trade coffee from Peru, Ecuador and Bolivia receives a price of 124¢/lb. In order to qualify, participating farmers must have less than 10 hectares of coffee, be a member of a growers' association and contribute to the costs of running the association. Organic coffee sold in the fair trade market sells for 139¢/lb. These prices are significantly higher than the New York price of 77¢/lb for conventional coffee.

The scheme depends on consumers, largely in the developed world, being prepared to pay this higher price. Fair trade labelled coffee was launched at the end of the 1980s and over half a million farmers worldwide are now producing coffee for this market. Fair trade coffee sales grew by 12 per cent in 2001 and fair trade coffee now accounts for approximately 1.7 per cent of the European coffee market.[2]

Farmers selling fair trade coffee benefit from being members of farmer co-operatives and associations. Even if they are unable to sell their coffee in the fair trade market, they benefit from working together. First, they are often able to bypass some of the intermediaries. They may also receive more for their coffee, because processing prior to export can add almost 50 per cent to the value: if this is done by a farmers' organization, the proceeds return to the farmers rather than the exporter. Increasingly, they are also able to sell coffee in the organic and gourmet coffee markets.

Many smallholder producers in Peru, Ecuador and Bolivia are also being encouraged to produce organic coffee. For many farmers the transition to organic production is not especially difficult because traditionally they have used few chemicals, the main reason being that external inputs such as insecticides are often prohibitively expensive. Organic production is more labour intensive and production costs can be 20 per cent higher than conventional coffee. However, the improved management associated with organic production has also led to higher yields. In Bolivia, promoters of organic coffee see this as a means of generally improving the quality of Bolivian coffee and ultimately reducing the price differential. Conversion to organic production, however, presents a challenge to some farmers. In Brazil, where production has traditionally relied on the use of pesticides and herbicides, the focus on organic production has not occurred. Here, less use of chemical inputs means lower production. In addition, as Alberto Habilo, a coffee producer in Loja, Ecuador explained as we walked around his small farm where he produces citrus fruit, banana, honey, chickens, cows and sheep, in order to qualify for organic certification under most schemes, the entire farm needs to be organic, not just the coffee. This may have severe implications for the rest of his production.

The Andean countries also have the advantage that they have enormous ranges of altitude and numerous types of coffee that are adapted to local conditions. This enables these countries to exploit the specialized markets for gourmet coffee which comes from specific areas. The best quality coffee is generally produced between altitudes of 1200 and 1800 metres. The Andes provide plenty of such high altitude zones. Producers in Ecuador and Peru proudly point out that better-known coffee-producing countries, such as Costa Rica, have fewer types of coffee because they lack the altitudinal range of the Andes.

In addition, technical advances in the past few decades have led to a homogenization of coffee types in Costa Rica, a process that has not occurred to large degree in Peru, Bolivia or Ecuador. In the Andean region, the locally adapted coffee varieties of the Andes turn out to be ideal for producing gourmet coffee.

Quality and higher prices

Niche markets, and particularly gourmet coffee markets, demand high-quality Arabica coffee. The key to producing higher-quality coffee is careful management of the coffee plots and post-harvest handling. Improved management includes optimum spacing between coffee plants, weeding of the plantation, cutting back the plants, and regular replacement of old planting stock.

Coffee beans are harvested inside cherry-like fruits and the beans have to be extracted, processed and graded before export. In the Andean region, Arabica coffee beans are processed in two different ways. The first process involves farmers drying the recently harvested coffee, still encased in the fruit, on the ground and then selling it to the intermediaries who oversee further processing. A variation of this process is that the farmer transports the dried whole berries to a factory where the fruit is removed at the farmers' expense. The coffee is then sold to the intermediary. This coffee can be of a poor quality if it is dried directly on the ground; it absorbs the smell of the soil and can often go mouldy; this affects the taste and can irritate the stomach. Coffee produced this way is known as 'natural Arabica'.

The second method involves the farmer milling the coffee berries to remove the pulpy fruit, then fermenting the bean in water for 12 hours, separating out the bad grains which rise to the top. However, poor coffee can also arise from over-fermentation. The coffee bean, which is still encased in a thin skin known as the parchment, is sun-dried to lower the moisture content. This parchment coffee, also known as 'washed Arabica' is then sold to a factory or intermediary.

Further processing removes the parchment, prior to grading and export. This 'wet' method produces a better-quality coffee. Coffee can best be washed in large concrete tanks like Doña Alicia's, but at US$400 per tank this represents a significant investment for a small producer. The process also has environmental costs because large quantities of water are needed to ferment and wash the coffee cherries, and polluted water is often subsequently discharged into streams and rivers. About 30 litres of water are needed to produce 1 kg of parchment coffee. Colombian researchers have developed a water-saving coffee processing technology that uses significantly less water than the conventional method,[6] but this is not widely in use.

COCLA: a successful coffee co-operative in Peru

The Central de Co-operativas Agrarias Cafetaleras (COCLA) is an association of 21 co-operatives in the coffee-growing region of Quillabamba in Southern Peru. It was established to assist in the production and marketing of the co-operatives' coffee production. The co-operatives represent some 5000 coffee producers of a total of 25 000 in the Cuzco region. COCLA offers technical advice to its members and buys and sells coffee from the producers. An additional 7000 producers sell their coffee to COCLA although they do not receive technical advice. COCLA has a sound reputation and survived the withdrawal of state support for the co-operative movement when the now disgraced Fujimori became President.

COCLA stresses the importance of quality and the overriding need to improve the quality and reputation of Peruvian coffee. In his small office next to the processing plant in Quillabamba, COCLA's finance manager, Romulo Bascopé, points out that if countries like El Salvador, with altitudes of only 600–800 m, can produce coffee with a premium on the New York price, there are few technical obstacles to Peru doing the same. The issues are quality control and marketing. Quality control extends to COCLA's processing plant in Quillabamba. Each of the 21 co-operatives delivers parchment coffee to the processing plant at 13 per cent humidity. A sample is taken from each sack of delivered coffee. The sample is evaluated for physical defects and is then roasted to judge further the quality of the coffee. The second test is necessary as the coffee could have few physical defects but may have been stored badly. The coffee is then processed to remove the parchment and graded. The export-quality coffee, known as *café oro*, is transported to Lima by truck, a journey that takes about one week.

COCLA is successful because farmers benefit from being members of the co-operative. Farmers are paid relatively quickly for the coffee they deliver and also receive a share of the profit (liquidation) at the end of the year. COCLA offers farmers fair prices and prompt payment, it seeks out international markets and the system is transparent. Coffee producers know that for every 100 lb of coffee delivered to COCLA's processing plant at 12–13 per cent humidity, about 70 lb are exportable (approximately 4.5 lb is relegated to a poorer-quality category and the remaining loss of weight is made up of the parchment). The system is transparent and farmers trust that their local co-operative and those in the higher echelons of COCLA are genuinely working for the benefit of all participating farmers. The contrast to the situation in Caranavi in Bolivia could not be more striking.

There is competition to sell in the fair trade, organic and gourmet coffee markets. COCLA is well placed because it has a solid reputation internationally for delivering good-quality coffee as stipulated in agreements. It also has a commercial section dedicated to seeking out market openings. At COCLA's office in Lima, the capital of Peru, the marketing manager, José Rivera explains that COCLA produces and sells around 5500 tonnes of coffee per annum (1999 figures). Approximately 36 per cent of this total is sold in the niche markets: fair trade coffee makes up 11 per cent of sales (approximately 20 per cent of this is also organic) while a further 25 per cent is sold exclusively in the organic markets. The remaining 64 per cent of the coffee COCLA deals with is sold on the conventional market, even though it might have been produced organically.

The current emphasis is on organic coffee. COCLA's organic programme started in 1995. There are six technical staff in the organic coffee programme, who in turn have trained 400 farmer extension workers. All organic coffee producers are certified to internationally acceptable organic standards. COCLA pays the certification costs and divides these among 1300 organic producers. It has established a competent internal monitoring system so that during the actual certification, external auditors can inspect the system and a few sample farms. This is particularly important because organic coffee sold by COCLA is certified by three different organizations: the Organic Crop Improvement Association (OCIA) for the USA market; BioLatina for sales to Germany; and Naturland for the Dutch market. Scale is important because the more farmers there are, the lower the certification costs per farmer.

In 1999, COCLA launched a new organic gourmet brand called *Machu Picchu*, which is sold in the United Kingdom by Cafedirect. Similarly a specialized organic coffee, *Café Amigo de los Aves* (Friends of the Birds) is being marketed as a joint initiative with the Smithsonian Migratory Bird Centre. In order to qualify, the organic coffee producers must enhance the environment for birds by ensuring that there are at least eight species of tree providing shade for the coffee plantation.

Most of the coffee producers who are members of COCLA have 2–3 hectares of coffee and produce on average 0.6t/ha per year, although well-managed plantations can produce up to 1.2t/ha per year. COCLA offers these farmers the chance to break out of the vicious circle of low prices and poor quality coffee. Members of COCLA benefit directly from producing good-quality coffee even though some of this coffee may be sold on the conventional markets.

One of COCLA's strengths is that it is able to raise capital so that when farmers deliver coffee at the processing plant in Quillabamba, they receive a high percentage of the final sale price of the coffee. Romulo Bascopé explains that the differential on conventional coffee from Peru is 13¢/lb, so when the New York price is 80¢/lb, the price of coffee at export from Peru is 67¢/lb. The costs of processing and marketing are 11¢/lb. Hence farmers eventually receive a total of 56¢/lb of exported coffee. On delivery, farmers are paid 37¢/lb, with the rest of the money being paid at the end of the year. In addition, if COCLA makes a profit, some of this is also passed on to the farmers at the end of the year. These prices compare very favourably with those paid to farmers in Caranavi in Bolivia.

Ruth Escalante is one of those farmers who has benefited from selling organic coffee through COCLA. She lives in a small village approximately 20 km from COCLA's processing plant in Quillabamba and is a member of the Maranura Alta organic coffee co-operative affiliated to COCLA. Ruth and her husband own four hectares of land, half of which is planted with organic coffee. In the front room of the wooden house the family also runs a small shop, where we drink fizzy lemonade before wandering through the small coffee plantation behind the house. Here banana, citrus, mango and yucca mingle with the coffee, providing household basics to supplement the coffee income. Further up the hill away from the river is Ruth's main coffee plantation.

The costs of certification were divided among the 350 members of the local co-operative. Ruth explains that she could sell her organic coffee to the intermediaries for an immediate payment of 43¢/lb, but prefers to sell via her local co-operative to COCLA. In 1999, Ruth was paid 40¢/lb on delivery of the coffee to COCLA, a further 11¢/lb at liquidation and a premium of 14¢/lb for the fact that the coffee was organic. 'Yes, coffee is profitable if you produce good quality', she says. But even with the prices paid by COCLA, she earns only about US$1500 for the year's harvest from their two hectares. Every year Ruth and her husband are increasing the area under coffee. Meanwhile, the shop helps them get by during the year.

Another farmer affiliated to COCLA explains that globalization is a challenge that can be met by improving quality. Romero Gonzalez is a member of a 350–strong co-operative called Alto Urubamba. He admits that in the past very few farmers recognized the importance of quality. Once the buyers started to separate coffee by quality, he says, the growers were forced to improve by better management and processing. The co-operative is now affiliated to COCLA and with their land at 1700 m, farmers can produce good-quality coffee with respectable yields of 0.6t/ha per year.

Although COCLA is a success, there are still many farmers who are unable or unwilling to join the organization and who still choose to sell their coffee to the handful of intermediaries in Quillabamba. Some farmers are so desperate for cash that the price offered by COCLA on delivery of the coffee, compared to that offered by the intermediaries, is not sufficiently attractive even though COCLA pays another instalment later on in the year. Intermediaries offering credit and immediate payment may still be the only option for some. Farmers are also suspicious of the poor management and corruption associated with the co-operative movement in the past. New co-operatives that apply to join COCLA need to pass a five-year probation period in order to prove they are stable and competent.

Caranavi and the Yungas, Bolivia: an uphill struggle

Twenty organizations in Bolivia are affiliated to the Federación de Caficultores Exportadores de Bolivia (FECAFEB). The organization was founded in 1991 and represents approximately 8000 producers. The majority of the producers are in the Caranavi area of the Yungas region. This lowland area was colonized in 1952–53 and coffee production began in the 1960s. Approximately 85 per cent of Bolivia's coffee production comes from the Caranavi area.

FECAFEB, like COCLA in Peru, recognizes the benefits of organic coffee and has been promoting organic coffee production since the early 1990s. The Federation offers technical advice and seeks specialized markets for organic coffee especially in the Netherlands and Germany. According to FECAFEB there is no oversupply of organic coffee and there is still much market potential.

FECAFEB helps to market the coffee produced by people like Doña Alicia and her husband in the village of Illimani, near Caranavi. They have been growing coffee for 20 years and started growing organic coffee with the help of FECAFEB. Doña Alicia is now one of 80 members of an organic coffee growers' association know as La Asociación Regional de Productores de Café (ARPROCA). She sells some of her coffee to the intermediaries in Caranavi but most is sold by ARPROCA as organic coffee via FECAFEB or direct to the coffee brokers in La Paz. According to Samuel Ramirez of FECAFEB, a farmer with three hectares of well-managed organic coffee can live reasonably comfortably, assuming the coffee is sold as organic with the associated premium.

FECAFEB's goals are admirable. It is too easy to blame the intermediaries and exporters for all the problems faced by smallholder producers, says Gustavo Lugones, technical consultant to FECAFEB. Farmers have to accept greater responsibility; they need a change of heart and attitude to coffee production that leads to improved management, careful post-harvest handling and the ability to deliver coffee as stipulated in agreements. FECAFEB's argument is that by focusing on the organic market and the improved management associated with producing organic coffee, the general quality of Bolivian coffee will also improve and it will eventually be possible to reduce the price differential of 26¢/lb. The problem is that in the absence of markets, most organic coffee is sold as conventional coffee. This need not be a problem were the coffee sold to an organization like COCLA, but in the case of farmers in Caranavi the coffee is sold at relatively low prices to the intermediaries.

Some farmer-leaders attached to FECAFEB argue that they have the knowledge and marketing skills to export coffee direct. What they believe they currently lack is the capital to set up a processing plant in Caranavi similar to COCLA's plant in Quillabamba. FECAFEB is therefore unable to take advantage of the substantial gain in value as a result of processing. Faced with limited sales of organic coffee and low prices for conventional coffee, there is less incentive for farmers to invest time and money in producing higher-quality coffee.

The exporters and some members of FECAFEB, however, dispute this. In order to export coffee, one needs to have contacts with international coffee brokers and to know the market intimately, says Gustavo Lugones. This sort of marketing expertise cannot be built up overnight and is not easily done from Caranavi. Hence, in the short term at least, and until they have marketing expertise, coffee producers need the assistance of exporters such as ANDEC and COBOLCA. This argument is partly borne out by the experience of FECAFEB's marketing section. A rapid changeover of staff has lead to poor sales: a marketing specialist taken on in 1999 did not actually sell any coffee on the export market, members grumble. The lack of success in developing a strong sales base reduces the confidence that farmers have in the organization.

On the vertiginous slopes of the Coroico area up the road from Caranavi, coffee has been grown for almost 500 years. The altitude of about 1500 m helps to produce high-quality coffee. However, production has declined as the plants have aged and the soil has become more impoverished. Farmers have not invested in replacing their coffee plants, and soil fertility has not been maintained over the past few decades. Coffee still grows well in some areas but the steeper and more eroded hillsides can now support only coca (see Chapter 6, Coca eradication and alternative development).

There are, however, examples in the Yungas region of farmer groups that have successfully marketed high-quality organic coffee. Five farmer co-operatives representing 245 farmers are affiliated to the Central de Cooperativas Cafetaleras de los Nor Yungas (CENCOOP). This co-operative offers technical advice to farmers, assists them to secure credit and helps them sell high-quality organic coffee direct and via coffee buyers in La Paz. CENCOOP is the sixth largest exporter of coffee in Bolivia, but despite this relative success, it represents only about 10 per cent of the producers in the area. Past problems of corruption and debt have left farmers suspicious of the co-operative and CENCOOP faces an uphill struggle to win back previous levels of support. Furthermore, many farmers are cultivating land that is not suitable for coffee.

The technical advice offered to farmers is similar to that provided by FECAFEB and COCLA. Coffee plants should replaced every six years, organic compost and chicken manure should be used as a natural fertilizer, the amount of shade needs to be carefully controlled and plantations regularly cleaned. Advice is provided on the use of selected seed of local breeds and improved varieties for raising coffee plants in a nursery. CENCOOP also oversees the washing process to ensure quality.

Felix Valizza Soria is the charismatic and articulate ex-president of CENCOOP; he passionately believes the co-operative can be rebuilt into a successful exporter of high-quality organic coffee. The intermediaries are not the only ones to blame for poor prices, he asserts disparagingly: farmers themselves do not control the quality of their washed coffee. They harvest their coffee on Monday to Thursday and wash it on Friday in time for the market. But the coffee harvested early in the week has fermented too much by Friday: the quality is mixed right from the start, so of course exporters will not pay good prices. Farmers need to wash and dry their coffee every day to produce the quality that CENCOOP requires.

The incentive to improve management is that CENCOOP sells organic coffee to the USA at 100¢/lb. This is a good price and the farmers receive over 33¢/lb for their coffee, compared to the 22¢/lb paid by the intermediaries to producers in Caranavi. Don Felix explains that, faced with labour shortages it is better to focus on quality rather than quantity. Farmers are encouraged to manage one hectare of coffee well rather than several hectares badly, to avoid the risk that coffee berries will be left rotting on the ground or will be poorly washed at harvest time because of the shortage of labour.

Loja, Ecuador: a determined start

Jamil Ramón is the head of a coffee project run by the Fundación Agro-ecológica Amigos de la Tierra (Fundatierra). The project is working in the district of Espíndola in the Loja region of southern Ecuador, an isolated area of poor communications and high emigration close to the border with Peru. There are 5000 families in Espíndola of which 3000 are coffee producers. Fundatierra currently works with 400 families and hopes to reach 600 over the three-year project lifespan. The project started in 2000 and is relatively small but Jamil and his colleagues have a vision. Fundatierra recognizes that coffee farming will become profitable only if farmers can sell their coffee in the specialized markets. According to Jamil, the fair trade market is not growing, but there is a future in organic and gourmet coffee, with the price of the former being 15¢/lb above the New York price for conventional coffee.

Coffee in Espíndola has traditionally been grown at different altitudes. Unlike other parts of Ecuador, exotic coffee varieties have not been introduced by the national coffee organization, the Consejo Cafetalero Nacional (COFENAC). Hence, like COCLA, there exists the possibility of producing locally differentiated gourmet coffee. In Espíndola, farmers often have less than one hectare of coffee and production is low at 0.14–0.23t/ha per year. Farmers traditionally sell coffee to intermediaries even though they are well aware that the same intermediaries often fiddle the scales and offer them poor prices.

Frequently a bad harvest in one year leads to poor management in the subsequent year as farmers seek better incomes off-farm. Fundatierra is trying to persuade farmers to manage their plantations well, irrespective of whether the harvest is good or bad. The message is that good management can increase yields to 0.7–0.9t/ha per year, a four- or five-fold increase on current production levels. Moreover, in future, farmers can receive higher prices for organic coffee. However, nothing short of a revolution is needed because many farmers do not appreciate that their soils can be improved and production increased. All too commonly farmers complain that 'my soils do not produce'.

Fundatierra is under no illusions about the challenge. It receives funds from Canada but has only three years to make the project work. Towards the end of 2000 it established a local coffee producers' union, the Productores de Café de Altura de Espíndola y Quilanga (PROCAFEQ). In the coming years, PROCAFEQ is expected gradually to take over the running of the project until eventually it becomes a sustainable enterprise. There are few co-operatives in Espíndola but there are agroforestry farmer groups and PROCAFEQ will work through these groups to ensure that producers meet the market demands of quality, quantity and continuity of supply. Jamil and his colleagues are aware that the success of the project rests on improvements to the quality of the coffee produced – Fundatierra having continued access to capital so that farmers can be paid in advance and on delivery – and an ability to secure markets.

In the village of Sucupa, Alberto Habilo is a deceptively young-looking farmer who evidently thrives on experimenting with new ideas. He explains that he has always grown organic coffee, but over the past 30 years he has favoured cattle over coffee as prices for the latter dropped. His coffee plantations were, therefore, largely abandoned and the quality has been poor. Some coffee plantations are over 80 years old and produce a very poor and variable harvest. People in the area have tended to work the coffee in good years and leave it abandoned in bad years, but to produce good coffee you need to be there all the time, says Alberto.

Nurseries are needed as largely abandoned plantations have to be improved with new planting stock. Fundatierra has helped farmers establish a communal nursery behind Alberto's house where coffee seed from the best fruits of the best branch of the best trees are planted in seed-beds prior to being transplanted to plastic bags and eventually to farmers' coffee plantations. Fundatierra encourages group work in the nurseries even though coffee plots are individually owned. Farmers receive plants in proportion to the amount of time they contribute to the nursery.

Above the nursery, coffee grows on the steep slope beneath a canopy of shade trees and tall bananas. Farmers are encouraged to use organic fertilizers made from the crop residues, chicken manure and the discarded pulp from already-harvested coffee. Three years after planting, the coffee starts producing fruit. In year ten, the bush can be cut back to a stump about 30 cm high. This produces new shoots, three of which are selected and allowed to grow. In year fifteen, the coffee plant should be replaced again. Because most of the plantations are semi-abandoned and the plants often all beyond their productive lifespan, farmers are encouraged initially to replace 20 per cent of the plants every year, with new plants sown between the old ones. The rejuvenation of coffee plantations requires investment of time, money and energy.

In the village of San Antonio, 200 families grow coffee and 25 of them are working with Fundatierra. Victor Salinas is typical of the type of farmer that Fundatierra is targeting. He accompanies us on a visit to his four hectares of coffee, perched on a steep hillside just outside the village. He never used chemicals in the plantation and previously replaced his coffee plants infrequently. The incentive to invest his time in improved management is the higher price that he will get for his coffee when it is sold via Fundatierra. 'We've been told there's too much production of coffee in the world', he says, 'so if we don't improve the quality we won't have a market, or get a decent price.'

Victor Salinas traditionally sold his coffee dried in the berry to intermediaries in the nearby town of Caraymanga. He had to pay for the transport of the coffee to the town. The intermediaries paid him between 44¢/lb and

52¢/lb, but he had to pay for the processing so he was really getting about 38¢/lb, from which he also has to pay for transport to Caraymanga. Now Don Victor and some of his neighbours produce parchment coffee in San Antonio. The problem that they face when soaking and washing the coffee is that water is in short supply and they sometimes have to delay washing it for a day, which reduces the quality of the coffee.

A further problem is that large numbers of people are emigrating from Loja. Fundatierra is increasingly worried that a shortage of labour, especially at harvest time, will jeopardize the coffee project. Some farmers are put off processing coffee to the parchment stage because drying the berries, the traditional way of processing coffee, is normally regarded as women's work, to be done in the back yard while carrying out other daily chores. On the other hand, washing and subsequently drying parchment coffee is more intensive work, requires labour input from the men and, therefore, represents a change in roles within the household.

Farmers like Victor Salinas hope, however, that the parchment coffee (washed Arabica) will be sold in the USA and Europe for a much higher price than the intermediaries pay for natural Arabica. Victor is adamant that more families will participate in Fundatierra's project when they see the benefits that come from producing parchment coffee. This is a view endorsed by another farmer in the scheme, Don Maxim. He has 1.5 hectares of well-managed coffee and produces a total of 1.4t/yr of coffee. Like Don Victor he used to sell his coffee to middlemen but he now produces parchment coffee and receives a much better price for his coffee from Fundatierra.

The trust between Fundatierra and the farmers is enhanced because, in a similar way to COCLA, there is transparency at all stages of the process. Farmers know that approximately 16 buckets of harvested coffee in the berry produces 125 lb of parchment coffee at 14 per cent humidity (this part of the processing is carried out on their farms). Further processing leads to 100 lb of export-quality *café oro*, with the difference in weight made up by the discarded parchment and rejected coffee beans.

The advantage that Fundatierra has over FECAFEB in Bolivia is its access to funds from Canada, which allows it to pay farmers in advance for their coffee. Fundatierra pays farmers three times: an advance of US$2 per bucket at harvest, a delivery payment of US$1.20 per bucket for the parchment coffee and a final payment when the coffee is actually sold on the world market. Farmers can make approximately 51¢/lb from the advance and delivery payments. Organic coffee can sell for 72¢/lb, taking account of the price differential. Farmers are charged 12¢/lb for processing so when the coffee is sold they receive a final payment of 9¢/lb.

Much of the success of Fundatierra's programme will rest on it having sufficient capital to pay farmers before the coffee is actually sold. A group of women working in one of the communal nurseries in the village of Tundurama sums up the dilemma that they face. As they sit in the hot sun, using sticks to break up hardened pieces of chicken manure for planting bags, they explain that each of them has 1–1.5 hectares of coffee and that this is their main source of income. In a good year they produce 0.5–0.6t/ha organic coffee. However, in January, several months before the coffee harvest, they have used up all their savings and are forced to sell some of their coffee in advance to the intermediaries. 'We can't sell all our coffee to the project,' says one, 'because sometimes we have to borrow money before the harvest.' At this stage the best that they can hope for is gradually to sell less to the middlemen as they build up savings from the higher prices paid by Fundatierra until there is no need to sell coffee to the intermediaries. Even with abundant harvests, a good price from Fundatierra and 1.5 hectares of land, each farmer's total annual income from coffee amounts to only US$1080: it is difficult to save on this level of income.

Obstacles to accessing niche markets

Identifying markets

In 1999, Fundatierra sold 45 tonnes of coffee from Espíndola to the USA and Germany. Roberto Jiménez, Fundatierra's marketing analyst, explains that this is a good start, but he recognizes that the project will work only if farmers can secure a longer-term niche in the volatile markets. Fundatierra is not alone: marketing is given much prominence by COCLA in Peru and FECAFEB in Bolivia. It is a skilled job that initially requires outside assistance.

In 1994 COCLA exported 1600 tonnes of coffee; by 1999 this had risen to 5500 tonnes. José Rivera, COCLA's head of sales, explains that there are really two coffee markets: a market based on volume, which is controlled by a handful of multinational companies, and the smaller specialized coffee market which includes fair trade, gourmet and organic coffees. Approximately 35 per cent of COCLA's sales are to the specialized markets while 65 per cent are in the conventional market. Niche markets cannot become the prime business strategy for COCLA, says José Rivera, because they do not know for how long these markets will grow. They need to carry on selling to the bulk market.

COCLA seeks an interdependent relationship with buyers and focuses on the smaller specialized market for this. Two multinational companies control over 60 per cent of coffee exports from Peru, buying over 100 000 tonnes of coffee per year. COCLA's annual exports of 5500 tonnes pale into insignificance in this light, which leaves COCLA with little or no room for negotiation with the big buyers. It is better for COCLA to sell to smaller buyers who deal in perhaps 22 000 tonnes of coffee per year. At this level, COCLA's coffee can form a significant proportion of the buyer's stock, offering COCLA a better negotiating position.

The reality faced by COCLA, Fundatierra and FECAFEB is that even if farmers produce organic coffee there is no guarantee that it can be sold as organic coffee. The situation is more problematic because in order to sell organic coffee the producers have to be certified. This is generally done by external certification organizations with repeated visits. The costs can be substantial and may form a serious barrier to entry into the market. This is less of a burden for farmers if their coffee is sold at a premium as organic coffee, but can be a problem if farmers are then forced to sell organic coffee in the conventional coffee market. This is the case in Bolivia, where 14 per cent of Bolivian coffee is produced organically but only 4 per cent is actually sold as organic. As FECAFEB encourages more farmers to grow organic coffee, a major concern voiced by the organization is whether these farmers will be able to find a niche in the organic market. Is the market big enough to absorb new organic producers?

Securing credit to expand

Roberto Jiménez from Fundatierra explains that raising capital is another major challenge for the organization. Fundatierra has identified markets for 90 tonnes of organic coffee per year, twice the volume of coffee that it sold in 1999. The problem is that Fundatierra does not have sufficient capital to pay more farmers the advance and delivery payments. With approximately US$40 000 made available by the Canadian fund, Fundatierra is able to pay advances for about 45 tonnes of coffee. If Fundatierra were dealing with 90 tonnes of coffee per year it would need US$100 000. The long-term sustainability of the project, following the end of international donor funding after three years, will depend on there being continued access to credit. Money is also needed to buy the pulping machines that are sold at cost to the communities. Credit at reasonable interest rates is available to some coffee farmers, but in the case of Ecuador the national coffee organization, COFENAC, tends to give credit almost exclusively to larger landowners, those with 4–10 hectares of coffee.

COCLA, despite its larger size and longer history, faces the same problem. COCLA's strength, says Romulo Bascopé, is its good record on repayment of credit to the banks. This allows them now to borrow at lower rates of interest than newer organizations without a track record. Even so, as their production has risen 250 per cent over the past five years, so COCLA's requirement for credit has grown too. The 21 co-operatives that make up

COCLA face the same problem of raising credit: being smaller and less stable than COCLA, the private banks are wary of lending them money. Without a specific government lending facility for agriculture, they are reliant on private banks. Shortage of credit essentially undermines attempts by farmers to set up collective schemes such as COCLA in Peru and Fundatierra in Ecuador. Even once they are established, organizations like COCLA find it difficult to compete with the large international exporters because they do not have access to cheap financing, a facility more readily available to the multinational companies.

Standing on their own feet: the need for external support

Following the liberalization of the coffee sector in many countries, producers trying to secure a place in the niche markets face the same three fundamental challenges as smallholder producers throughout Latin America: quality of produce as well as quantity and continuity of supply. The free market environment also offers opportunities, and the examples of COCLA in Peru and CENCOOP in Bolivia show what can be achieved through establishing well-managed producers' associations. Despite these success stories there are producers who are reluctant to join farmer associations. One of the reasons for this is that the co-operative movement was tainted in the 1970s and 1980s by blatant corruption and mismanagement, followed by an abrupt demise when government support was withdrawn. In Peru, for example, government support for the co-operative movement came to an end with the neo-liberal policies introduced by ex-President Alberto Fujimori. Once state support was withdrawn, the number of coffee co-operatives dropped from 300 to about 10.

The examples of COCLA and Fundatierra are encouraging. However, while they demonstrate that there are relatively few insurmountable technical obstacles to the production of high-quality coffee, they also show that farmers are often prevented from exploiting global markets because they lack capital and marketing skills. As the Fairtrade Foundation points out: 'Individual small farmers and . . . the co-operative ventures they embark upon, lack knowledge of the markets and the capacity to deal as equal partners in world trade . . . To regain control of their lives, farmers and their associations must become adept at financial planning and control, forecasting, deal making, logistics and quality control. In other words, they must become more business-like'.[1] This raises a question of the degree to which farmers can take advantage of the opportunities of the global market without the type of external support that empowers them and makes them more 'business-like'.

Both COCLA and Fundatierra have staff who are engaged exclusively in securing international buyers and, while COCLA is largely sustainable,

Fundatierra has yet to reach a stage of development whereby it can survive without donor support. A German government-funded organic coffee project in the eastern lowlands of Bolivia collapsed when donor money was withdrawn, partly because the conditions were not suitable for coffee, but also because farmers had been insufficiently empowered to run the operation on their own.[11]

The Federación Nacional de Cafeteros in Colombia represents almost 500 000 farmers and has been held up as a model for all aspiring coffee growers' organizations.[6] The organization was established in 1927 and runs a research centre and a coffee fund that is designed to stabilize farm-gate prices. As a result, Colombian farmers receive a high proportion of the export price and the Federation pays producers the same price for their coffee when it is delivered to the co-operative's warehouse, irrespective of the distance from roads and ports.

However, experts caution that the situation in Colombia is unique and that aspiring federations in the Andean region are very unlikely to achieve the success enjoyed by Colombian coffee producers.[12] It is also important to note that Colombia's success has not been based on exploiting niche markets; it has come from a long-standing reputation for producing high-quality coffee which attracts a positive differential or premium of 10¢/lb over other Arabica coffees.[13] Furthermore, the Federation is not isolated from the downturn in world coffee prices, and coffee producers are going out of business. In fact the Federation has now run into severe financial difficulty: the coffee fund has actually run out and it is now being supported by central government funds.

State support?

Policy changes are needed that lead to higher and more stable incomes for smallholder farmers.[2] The problem is that the slump in coffee prices and coffee growers' pleas for aid coincide with a general economic downturn in which governments are cutting spending in order to reduce budget deficits.[13] Few producer countries have policies that provide smallholder farmers with a level playing field. Farmer organizations in Peru complain that there is no state interest in the coffee sector and that international companies are favoured to the detriment of the smallholder farmers. They cite the example of the United States Agency for International Development (USAID) which wanted to invest US$12 million in institutional strengthening for specialized coffee sellers. According to farmer organizations, the large international coffee exporters sabotaged efforts by the coffee producers to establish direct links with specialized coffee brokers in the USA and the project was dropped.

Indirect state support focuses on issues such as transport and the difficulties that producers face in getting their coffee to market. Farmers affiliated to COCLA point out that the road from Quillabamba to Lima is so appalling that it costs US$2000 and takes up to a week to transport a container (approximately 32 tonnes of coffee) to Lima. From Lima to Europe by ship costs only US$900 per container. The co-operatives also have to pay for transport to the processing plant in Quillabamba and this can add 4–7¢/lb to the processing costs. The situation would be dramatically improved were a section of railway between Quillabamba and Cusco reopened after the flood damage caused by the weather phenomenon *El Niño* in 1997. As José Rivera of COCLA points out, coffee makes up 50 per cent of Peru's agricultural exports, yet coffee producers receive no government support or assistance to make infrastructure improvements to promote exports.

What does the future hold?

How big is a niche?

Many coffee producers see their salvation in growing high-quality coffee for the fair trade, organic and gourmet coffee markets. These niche markets have grown considerably over the past decade. COCLA estimates that in 1994 about 17 per cent of their coffee was considered high quality. By 1999, this percentage had risen to 80 per cent, marking their move into the specialized markets.

It is, however, unclear how much coffee these markets can absorb. Fair trade initiatives cover only 1 per cent of the world coffee market[2] and are therefore available to a very small percentage of producers. There are currently around 500 000 smallholder coffee producers who have been registered to sell coffee in the fair trade market. Retailers such as the main supermarket chains are willing to stock fair trade products, although very few of them have a fair trade own-brand coffee. As a result, products such as fair trade coffee still account for a fraction of overall coffee sales. Hence, while The Fairtrade Foundation[1] refers to opinion surveys that demonstrate that 75 per cent of people surveyed indicate a willingness to pay more for a fairly traded product, supermarket sales demonstrate that there is a huge gulf between 'willing to pay more' and 'actually paying more'.

The reality is that the fair trade market is expanding too slowly to absorb all the potential supply. In Loja, Ecuador, another coffee project, which receives financial assistance from Canada, received its fair trade Max Havelaar certificate status in 1999, but the organisers could not find a fair trade market on which to sell their coffee. Supply appears to outstrip demand. One of the problems in the United Kingdom to date has been the relatively poor quality of fair trade instant coffee.[14] There is also the problem of having to compete with established brands such as Nescafé. The growth in the organic and gourmet coffee markets is encouraging but these markets are also unlikely to absorb all the supply.[13] Many smallholder coffee producers will still have to sell coffee in the conventional market if they choose to continue growing the crop.

Interdependency

José Rivera, marketing manager of COCLA explains that relatively small producers' organizations may be able to get a better deal from international brokers if they sell their coffee to the small to medium brokers. With these brokers, there is some interdependency as producers and exporters need each other's services. In general, it is also these smaller brokers who are interested in the higher-value, higher-cost, specialized coffees.

In the increasingly competitive international market, however, smaller companies cannot compete with the large transnationals and are being bought up. As the large companies increase their buying networks and the smaller companies are pushed out, producers' organizations like COCLA will find it harder and harder to place their coffee with the small to medium-sized brokers. And as these brokers disappear, so COCLA's opportunities for interdependence and negotiation go with them.

Stabilizing the price of conventional coffee

Following the demise of the International Coffee Agreement in 1989, the Association of Coffee Producing Countries (ACPC) was established in 1993. In 2000, producer countries began trying to raise the price of coffee by once again withholding stock. Signatories agreed, among other things, to retain 20 per cent of their stock when the price fell below 95¢/lb.[2] The approach was plagued by difficulties, not least the non-compliance of some producer countries,[5] the financial costs of physically storing the surpluses in producer countries,[15] and the fact that consumer countries have high stocks of coffee.[16] In addition, higher prices could lead to a reduction in demand for coffee, especially in new markets, along with increased production as farmers seek to take advantage of the increase in international prices.

Even after the scheme was inaugurated in May 2000, coffee prices continued to fall and countries like Brazil threatened to leave the scheme if other producer countries did not pull their weight.[4] Finally at the end of September, 2001 the ACPC retention scheme was abandoned[13] and the ACPC exists in name only. Despite this, attempts to raise the price of coffee have not been abandoned. The International Coffee Organization (ICO) has approved a scheme to set minimum standards for exportable coffee whereby lower-quality coffee would be removed from the export marketing chain.[17] The idea is that by reducing the amount of coffee being sold, prices will rise. The scheme faces the same problems as the ACPC attempt to raise prices, and experts are sceptical about the possibility of success. One of the major problems is that the scheme does not have the backing of the roasting companies or consumer country governments.

There are now attempts to widen the access of smallholder coffee producers to insurance cover that provides some protection against price volatility. However, there are no serious attempts actually to reduce international price volatility directly.[2] The initiative, launched by the World Bank's International Taskforce on Commodity Risk Management is, however, faced with many obstacles including farmers' inability to pay for the crop insurance and the logistics of administering such a scheme.

Perhaps anticipating that the insurance initiative is not going to get off the ground, the development charity Oxfam has launched a 'Coffee Rescue Plan'.[18] The plan calls for all the major players in the coffee sector to work together in order to overcome the current crisis facing smallholder coffee producers and to create a more stable market. One of Oxfam's arguments is that if fair trade is to have a wider impact, it has to be brought out of the 'niche' market. Roasting companies and supermarket chains should follow the example set by the fair trade movement and offer decent prices to coffee producers. Other recommendations include support for producer countries to capture more of the value-added associated with coffee processing. It remains to be seen whether the plan will actually improve the livelihoods of smallholder coffee producers.

Coffee as an alternative to coca: does it make sense?

Coffee producers in Peru, Bolivia and Ecuador would be better off if their respective countries' differential were reduced. This is partly linked to the quality of the coffee produced. A problem facing those seeking to improve quality is that coffee production is being promoted in areas that are not suited to coffee. In Bolivia and Peru, this is often linked to the eradication of coca and alternative development initiatives (see Chapter 6, Coca eradication and alternative development). The fundamental question is whether international organizations such as the United Nations (UN) should be promoting coffee in areas where it is unlikely to be of sufficiently high quality to meet the demands of the specialized markets, and when the price for conventional coffee is so low.

In Bolivia, coffee was promoted in the Chapare coca-growing region at the beginning of the 1980s. In 2000, a UN-funded alternative development programme in the Chapare began promoting coffee again as one of several alternatives to coca, despite the reservations of local farmers who remain unconvinced by coffee. 'We tried growing coffee before. It kept getting attacked by pests and diseases and what is more the prices were all over the place, we're not interested in coffee', said Don Germán, a farmers' leader in the Chapare. In Caranavi there is a mixture of concern and support for the plight of ex-coca producers in the Chapare. At an altitude of only 300 m, the Chapare cannot produce high-quality coffee and organic production there will be hampered by higher rainfall leading to increased pest and disease problems. An increase in coffee production in the Chapare is therefore unlikely to contribute to the urgent task of improving the overall quality of Bolivian coffee and thereby reducing the price differential.

Coffee has also been promoted in the traditional and legal coca-growing area in Bolivia known as the Yungas. Here coffee has been grown for the past 500 years, but the availability and quality of land is an issue for coffee production. In the Coroico area, farmers have about one hectare of land and productivity is 0.5–0.7t/ha per year. In the Caranavi area, by contrast, farmers have 5–6 hectares and productivity is 0.9–1.4t/ha per year. Once again the wisdom of promoting coffee in areas such as the Yungas is questionable.

Farmers in the Quillabamba region of Peru have also experienced alternative development programmes. They explained that at the beginning of the 1990s approximately 50 per cent of farmers grew coffee. The figure now is about 70 per cent. The increase is largely due to the fact that the Peruvian government has sought to reduce the area planted to coca. Coffee producers explain that the option to switch from coca to coffee is available only to those farmers with land suitable for growing coffee. Those with unsuitable land have become marginalized or have migrated to the Amazon region.

On-farm diversification

Faced with a continuation of low prices, Oxfam[2] contends that the balance between supply and demand needs to be re-established through diversification out of the coffee sector. According to the laws of supply and demand this should happen automatically: declining coffee prices should lead to a decline in supply with fewer farmers continuing to produce coffee, and a subsequent increase in prices. This has not happened, partly because the prices of alternative crops such as cocoa are often just as low and the production costs of the alternative crops may be higher. In addition, coffee is often grown in South America on family-owned farms which are so dependent on the crop that they go on producing, however low the price.[5]

Another reason is that coffee is a tree crop and many farmers have invested much time and money in establishing a plantation. Psychologically it is far harder to eliminate a tree crop than it is to substitute one annual crop for another. With severe fluctuations in the price of coffee, producers can always hope that the price will rise again, especially if the large producer countries, such as Brazil, suffer from devastating frosts. The costs of switching to other crops may be so high that farmers have no choice but to continue with coffee: the only real alternative may be to sell the land.

If the international coffee price is unlikely to improve in the immediate future, and if the specialized coffee markets are not able to absorb growing supplies, should projects be encouraging farmers to grow coffee? The cruel irony is that as coffee prices have plummeted there is growing evidence that some coffee producers in the Andean region are indeed diversifying production. They are increasingly switching to the cultivation of coca,[19] which is hardly the type of on-farm diversification that will be readily supported by the international community. In this context, international development projects should consider the long-term implications of encouraging farmers to increase their coffee production, either through more intense management of existing plantations or through new plantings.

There is an argument that smallholder producers, including those growing coffee, just have to get used to the reality of deregulated markets and accept low and fluctuating prices as part of that reality. However, it is a reality from which many farmers in the developed world are shielded. Despite externally-enforced deregulation in many developing countries, both the USA and the EU protect their farmers by stabilizing producer prices. In addition, the USA provides subsidies for insurance cover against price decline and crop loss due to bad weather. More recently in the EU, farmers whose livestock were slaughtered as a result of the outbreak of foot-and-mouth disease in 2001 were compensated for each of the animals killed. None of these safeguards is available to the majority of coffee producers in the developing world.

CHAPTER 4

Potatoes and Andean tubers: losing diversity?

Introduction

IN A BIG concrete warehouse with a sliding metal door, crates of potatoes are stacked on shelves, floor to ceiling. Victor Pérez enthusiastically hauls down crates, pulls out a selection of misshapen, oddly coloured tubers in string bags, and sets them out on the floor: small, knobbly yellow ones, long smooth pink ones, grubby looking black ones, all neatly labelled. The variation is remarkable. This is the potato germplasm bank, run by the Fundación para la Promoción e Investigación de Productos Andinos (PROINPA) at Toralapa in Bolivia. The 20 varieties Don Victor shows us are a fraction of the 1290 samples stored; these include 725 different varieties of seven different potato species found in Bolivia. And this does not even count the varieties of other species of tubers and roots such as *papalisa*, *oca* and *isaño*, which are almost unknown outside the Andes.

At the potato wholesale market in Colomí, some 50 km away from Toralapa, there is less evidence of potato diversity. Local women sell huge sacks of their potatoes to the merchants from the cities of Cochabamba and Santa Cruz. In one region of Colomí called Candalaria, people cultivate some 56 varieties of potatoes, but looking around this market we see only about ten different types and, of those, two or three predominate. The Colomí area is well known as a centre of potato diversity, but where are all the other varieties?

In the McDonald's restaurant in Lima, the capital of Peru, the urban population flocks to buy their beefburgers and French fries. Nearby, the fried chicken restaurants are doing a roaring trade in French fries. However, only one type of potato is being used and it does not originate in the Andes. French fries are made from an improved potato variety, cultivated to ensure homogeneity and quality. In the case of McDonald's, the potatoes are not even cultivated in the Andes. For some of the big multi-national food chains, it is cheaper and easier to import their French fries already chipped from big producers in the USA, Canada or Europe.

What is happening to potato diversity in the Andes? Does the germplasm bank at Toralapa represent the diversity of potatoes still grown by Andean farmers or is the small selection of potatoes at the market in Colomí indicative of reduced diversity? What effect do market demands have on potato diversity and how does this affect farmers' livelihoods? And if potato diversity is declining, what can be done about it?

Why is potato diversity important?

Historical potatoes

Machu Picchu is an extraordinary sight. The lost city sits on the sharp shoulder of a hill, hidden in the folds of the Peruvian Andes. Terraces and staircases cling to the steep hillside leading between palaces, temples and towers. The complexity of the architecture and the density of temples and religious sites in this area and throughout the southern Andes, are demonstrative of the advanced and stratified ancient Andean societies. The agricultural foundation which supported the development of these complex societies was based on potatoes and maize.

It was the extreme climate of the south-central Andean region, with heavy frosts and hot sun, that permitted the production and storage of the freeze-dried potato known as *chuño*, which in turn facilitated the development of complex ancient societies.[1] Although Inca society was initially based on maize growing, the development of *chuño* may be linked to pre-Inca kingdoms that developed around Lake Titicaca and which were subsumed later into the Inca Empire. The ability to store and transport large quantities of food helped to sustain a non-agricultural population of artisans, priests, armies and rulers. In the milder *páramo* Andes of Ecuador and Colombia, production of *chuño* was not possible, and perhaps for this reason the complex societies seen further south did not develop.

The common potato (*Solanum tuberosum* subsp. *tuberosum*) is the fourth most important food crop worldwide.[2] Potatoes originated in the Andes and have been cultivated in the region for more than 8000 years. During this period they have been refined by an ever-changing population of people who constantly adapted and selected the tubers they wanted. Within Latin America, seven species of *Solanum* are recognized, and with thousands of variants throughout the 4000 km long range of the Andes, they form one of the most diverse crops in the world.

The ancestral *Andigena* type of potato (*Solanum tuberosum* subsp. *andigena*), was probably brought to Europe in the late 1500s. Over the following 500 years it was selected and bred to grow in a vast array of countries with resistance to a range of pests and diseases, including late blight, a serious diseases caused by the fungus *Phytophthora infestans*.

In addition to potatoes, the Andes is also home to numerous varieties of other tubers: *oca* (*Oxalis tuberosa*), *papalisa* (*Ullucus tuberosus*) and *isaño* (*Tropaeolum tuberosum*). Most of us have never heard of these crops, but together with a range of Andean roots and grains, they form the traditional basis for Andean livelihoods.

Supporting farmers' livelihoods

The Andean region is one of violent extremes: the vast 4000 m high altiplano of Bolivia, a cold, high, windswept desert; the valley systems that cut 1000 m gashes into the altiplano; the Peruvian sierra where snow-capped mountains rise from warm, almost tropical valleys; and the lower, wetter hills of northern Ecuador, where thick, dark soils and daily rainfall produce some of the best potato growing lands of the Andes. The mountain chain stretches from 55° south – as far south as the United Kingdom is north – to 10° north of the equator.

In the major potato centres of Bolivia, Peru and Ecuador, this array of ecosystems falls into three broad zones: the 'Green' Andes of Ecuador and northern Peru, with good rainfall and little climatic variability; the 'Yellow' Andes of central Peru and eastern Bolivia, with very variable rainfall; and the 'high climatic risk' Andes of southern Peru and the Bolivian Altiplano.[3] Each of these produces its own set of ecological niches. Add to this a seasonal variation in climate, which can bring drought, floods, frost or hail within one growing season, and a variation in altitude from sea level to 4500 m, and you have a very variable environment in which to grow a crop.

Traditionally farmers use the great diversity of potatoes to cope with the range of environmental risks that they face. Farmers in some areas of Bolivia may own several tiny scraps of land: a few hundred square metres on the hilltop; another patch on the valley slopes and perhaps some flatter, better land in the valley bottom. Each of these is a different ecological niche: for example, they have different soil types, frost exposure, danger of flooding and daily temperature range. So, a wide range of potato varieties, planted in small quantities during five separate sowing periods over six months, in mixtures or singly over the range of ecological niches, provides an almost infinite variety of conditions and the widest possible safety net in a risky environment. The aim is to minimize risk: if one type of potato fails, there is usually another type, somewhere else, that produces.

These, however, are the lucky farmers. In many other areas, such as the high, flat altiplano of Bolivia, farmers have one altitudinal niche and a very high risk of frost. In these cases, farming practices such as establishing raised planting beds, can create a new ecological niche which can compensate to a small degree for the lack of altitudinal variability available to these farmers.

Farmers' livelihood strategies are not always obvious. Travelling around the southern Andes you could almost be forgiven for thinking that a lot of the land has been abandoned. Although there are neatly walled fields in places, large parts of the land look uncultivated, covered with short grass, perhaps grazed by sheep or alpaca. But, of course, the agricultural system here traditionally involves leaving the land for a fallow period of anywhere between one and eight years to let it recuperate.

In the 'high climatic risk' Andes of Bolivia and Southern Peru, a series of crops is planted on one piece of land over four or five years. Potatoes are generally the most important crop, both economically and culturally. Usually, as they are planted the soil around them is fertilized. Piles of chicken manure line the roadside, destined for the potato fields. At low altitudes, in the second year, *oca* may be planted, or if there is enough residual fertility in the soil, a second year of potatoes; year three might see broad beans, a legume that fixes some nitrogen in the soil; in year four, perhaps oats, barley or a forage crop; by year five the soil needs a fallow, but increasingly farmers return to potatoes, with more fertilizer. At higher altitudes the rotation is less diverse: one year of potatoes, one year of oats and seven or eight years of fallow. In between these extremes lies a vast range of systems.

In the 'Green' Andes stretching from northern Ecuador through Colombia and Venezuela, the system is very different. Farmers plant potatoes for the market in a high input, high output system. Generally two or three crops of potato are planted in succession, each taking six months to mature. Fields are then used as pasture for three to five years, before beginning on the potato cycle again. There is a heavy dependence on synthetic fertilizers and pesticides to keep potato production high. In a vicious circle, high pesticide use destroys the beneficial insects and birds, encouraging more pest outbreaks, which in turn encourage farmers to apply more pesticides. High rainfall levels permit fast growth of potatoes and allows continual cropping without the necessity for a break between crops. But the combination of continual cropping and market demands for a very few varieties of potato, favours high incidences of pests and diseases.

Land inheritance and population growth, particularly in the southern Andes of Bolivia, mean that land is subdivided at every generation. Where it is common for families to have eight or nine children, the problem of land subdivision is severe. Following the 1953 Agrarian Reform in Bolivia, people in the village of Candalaria near Colomí, each received about 20 hectares of land. Over two generations it has been subdivided and sold: where perhaps half of the original 20 hectares could be cultivated, now families may have only 3 or 4 hectares of cultivable land out of a total of 10 hectares. At Escoma, on the shores of Lake Titicaca close to the border with Peru, we climbed a small hill overlooking the village. The surrounding slopes were divided into a patchwork of tiny fields, separated by stone walls. As Guntar, the director of an NGO based in Escoma explained, the 1992 census calculated that each family had only 0.8 hectares; this is probably now as little as half a hectare each. Often emigration from the area is farmers' only option.

Despite these land pressures, potatoes and other tubers still contribute much to food security and farmers' livelihoods throughout Peru, Bolivia and Ecuador. What is more, farmers still maintain diversity. In some areas, communities may be cultivating between 70 and 100 potato varieties and a typical household may be growing 10–12 varieties.[4] In Candalaria in Bolivia, Don Vicente, a local farmer, shows us his family selection of *oca*, a wrinkled carrot-shaped tuber in a variety of colours and sizes. He burrows into some of the neatly thatched piles dotted around his adobe-walled yard and in minutes retrieves nine different types of *oca*. Each type has a different use, Don Vicente explains: for sale, for soup, for freeze-drying, or because they are highly productive. These nine varieties represent just part of the total 27 varieties of *oca* grown in the Candalaria region. The diversity is stunning.

Don Vicente also grows a number of potato varieties and he demonstrates how he makes *chuño*. He stands in a rough wooden trough, treading an unpleasant-looking mush of small brown potatoes with his bare feet. All around lie little potatoes, spread out on the grass in the sun. *Chuño* is freeze-dried potato, made from specific bitter potato varieties. The fresh potatoes are spread on the ground on frosty nights in June and July to freeze. After a few days the skin puffs up with water inside; the potatoes are trodden in the wooden trough to squeeze the water out and then they are spread on the ground to dry. The resulting *chuño* is black and wrinkly; hard as a rock, it can keep for up to ten years. In the urban market, chuño finds a limited place as a Bolivian delicacy. To the rural farmer in Bolivia, it is not just a delicacy: it is vital for food security.

Still a part of Andean culture

The importance of diversity to farmers' livelihoods is reflected in the fact that the full range of potatoes and other tubers are an integral part of Andean culture. In many areas of the Andes, farmers grow small patches of particular local varieties, known as 'gift potatoes'. These are not for sale: reserved for household use and special occasions, they have an important place as presents for friends and relatives.[5]

In Andean cosmology, everything is a living part of the landscape, and the cultivation of potatoes is central to life. Acquiring new seed involves a ritual 'theft' of the seed from a neighbour because the seed, as a member of the family, would resent being given away.[6] Farmers in Bolivia share the belief that potato seed needs to be treated with respect in order to ensure productivity. 'We don't give [the seed] love or attention like our grandparents used to, so the seed resents it and stops producing', said one farmer at a workshop held by PROINPA in 1997.[7]

Rituals at various times of the year invoke the goodwill of the Earth Mother or *Pachamama*, asking her permission to walk among the crops and for her help with a good harvest. Part of the value placed on the diversity of potato varieties maintained by indigenous Quechua and Aymara farmers in the Andes, may also be linked to a general value placed on diversity per se.[4] Farmers are proud to demonstrate the diversity of potatoes they own, each known, named and familiar.

Although potato diversity has played a vital role in food security and farmers' livelihoods for centuries, and despite the fact that farmers understand the importance of maintaining diversity, some potato researchers and development practitioners are concerned that farmers are now cultivating fewer varieties. The reason for this erosion of diversity, they suggest, is market pressures.

Impact of the market

The demand for improved varieties

In the Andes, seed fairs and local markets developed over centuries have provided a forum for the exchange and sharing of diverse genetic resources and knowledge. However, as farmers are drawn into national and global markets, smallholder farmers react to the demands of these new markets. The fear is that increasing market requirements for consistency and quantity will force farmers to focus on a few varieties of potato at the expense of a diversity of traditional types. But the situation is as variable across the Andes as the range of niches for growing potatoes. In some areas, diversity is clearly being lost as farmers adapt to particular market demands; in others a combination of production for market and for home consumption may be conserving a wide, though unknown, range of varieties.

In the Carchi region of the 'Green' Andes in northern Ecuador, improved varieties of potato are grown for the market. The first improved varieties were introduced in the 1960s, replacing low-yielding, slower-maturing traditional *Andigena* varieties. The newer varieties mature in under six months, allowing faster rotations and quicker returns on investment. They also offer higher resistance to pests and diseases. The tens or even hundreds of native varieties that were planted only one or two generations ago have now been reduced to a handful,[8] occasionally grown in small plots for home consumption.

However, the market can favour native varieties. In Ecuador, the *Chola* potato is native and popular, but has practically disappeared because of its susceptibility to the fungal disease 'late blight'. An improved variety of the *Chola* potato, called the *Superchola* was produced in 1991 by a farmer who taught himself plant breeding. The *Superchola* offers the traditional taste and texture of the *Chola* potato and now accounts for about 30 per cent of the market.

In other areas, however, a different situation is revealed. In the 'Yellow' Andes of Cuzco, Peru, 63 per cent of the area sown to potatoes utilizes improved varieties; this drops to 21 per cent in the 'high climatic risk' Andes of Puno around Lake Titicaca.[9] In Bolivia, improved varieties probably comprise less than 20 per cent of the potato crop area.[10] Here, however, a small number of native varieties (such as *Waycha* and *Imilla negra* potatoes) are highly valued by markets and have become much more cosmopolitan, displacing the local varieties from other areas. Loss of diversity may be occurring, linked to increasing market integration, but not because of the introduction of improved varieties from outside.

So, the picture is not straightforward. While some native varieties in some places are shunned by processors or consumers, others are more in demand than the improved varieties. So why do farmers not concentrate on the highly valued native varieties? One strategy used widely by farmers in Bolivia and Peru is to plant the seed potatoes and native varieties in the higher altitude niches, while the commercial potatoes for the market are planted on the lower, more fertile valley sites with better access but higher disease risk. For example, in the Morochata area near Cochabamba, Bolivia, farmers with land at higher altitudes grow only the native variety *Waycha*. At lower altitudes, where late blight is much more of a problem, the improved variety *Runa Toralapa* is grown for its disease resistance. It is the farmers' choice for disease resistance, rather than market demands, that is promoting improved varieties.

Roberto Valdivia of the Centro de Investigación de Recursos Naturales y Medio Ambiente (CIRNMA) in Puno, Peru suggests that the diversity of tubers grown depends largely on access to the market. He believes that the full range of traditional potato varieties is being used and conserved by the smallest and poorest farmers around Lake Titicaca, but there is little hard data to confirm this. These farmers are furthest from the market and largely produce for home consumption. Roberto points out that understanding the flows and changes in use of traditional varieties is difficult. He has been following the trends in cultivation of the 22 varieties of *oca* identified by farmers in the Puno area. Some varieties appear only very rarely in individual farmers' fields, perhaps only once every ten years. Then they disappear again and no one in his survey group claims to be growing them. Overall in the mosaic of small farms in the region, however, these rare varieties are being grown and conserved, to reappear at intervals on individual farms. When asked where the rare varieties come from, farmers nonchalantly say, 'they just appeared', or, 'we bought them in the market'. Evidently there are many aspects of farmers' decision-making and diversity use that researchers still do not understand.

In Peru and Bolivia, farmers produce four general classes of potatoes: mixed native traditional varieties; selected native commercial varieties; improved varieties; and bitter varieties for making *chuño*.[4] The proportions of each class of potato that farmers grow depends on the markets they supply, the environmental constraints such as frost, hail, late blight and other pests, and the importance of home consumption. While some native varieties, such as the floury *Waycha* in Bolivia, are in high demand in the market for domestic consumption, others may experience no demand at all. The French fries and chips processing markets require entirely different potatoes again.

The proportion of farmers' production which is destined for the market is difficult to assess and, like every other aspect of potatoes, enormously variable. It depends on location and market demand, and will vary between years. But this is probably the key factor in questions of whether diversity in potatoes and other tubers is being lost. In Bolivia and Peru, it is clear that farmers cultivate some specific varieties of potato for the market on part of their land, while simultaneously producing a wide range of native varieties of potatoes for home consumption.[10] Much diversity may be conserved in this way. For instance, in a survey by PROINPA in the Colomí region of Bolivia, researchers asked local farmers to do a 'memory inventory' of all the varieties they used in 1953, a marker year when agrarian reform occurred in Bolivia. This list was compared with the varieties currently being planted in the area. In the first year of asking, 80 per cent of the varieties recalled from 1953 were found to be still in use; by the third year of the study, 100 per cent of the varieties had been found.

An unanswered question is whether the potato varieties are grown in the same quantities, or whether varieties that used to be produced in large quantities are now relegated to a corner of a field for occasional home consumption. 'We don't know', says Franz Terrazas of PROINPA; 'we don't even have the indices to measure the subtleties of diversity, rarity and commonness. What we do know is that in some areas a proportion of farm area in regions of high diversity has been converted from local varieties to those more suitable for the market'.

The market at work: falling consumption

Lunch in a cheap canteen in the Andes is generally a high starch affair. A soup helps take the edge off your hunger, usually a flavoured broth filled out with spaghetti, noodles or sometimes potatoes, along with quinoa. The main course arrives with more carbohydrate: a pile of rice and pasta compete for space with a piece of potato. Admittedly, this is not home cooking, so it does not reflect entirely the staples of the household. But it is notable that the food is not potato-based. Tastes have changed in South America and, 'encouraged' by cheap imports, more and more people substitute rice and pasta for their traditional potatoes. Particularly in urban centres, potatoes (with the exception of French fries) have lost ground.

Potato consumption in South America is falling. In 1985, Bolivia had the highest potato consumption per person in the Americas (94kg/person in 1985, compared to Peru at 67kg/person).[1] By the mid-1990s, in Bolivia this had fallen to 54kg per person, according to the Centro Internacional de la Papa, (CIP),[11] while consumption in Peru remained stable. Consumption in Ecuador is relatively low (32kg per person), and is exceeded by both Argentina and Chile. Marked differences exist between the consumption of potatoes by urban and rural households, being much higher in rural areas. As people migrate from the uplands of Bolivia to the lowlands, for example, traditional highland diets are left behind and rice and wheat figure more strongly.

For the urban population, potatoes are increasingly eaten as French fries. Fast food outlets selling chicken and French fries are the growth industry. French fries require improved potatoes: standard quality, reliable quantities, consistency. Hamburger chains like McDonalds import their French fries frozen. Other retail outlets use nationally produced potatoes. For example, every day thousands of tons of improved potatoes are brought into Lima in Peru from rural areas to make French fries. Native varieties, apart from not having the right texture and taste for frying, nor providing the quality necessary for peeling and chopping, cannot provide the quantities required. So, while consumption of potatoes as a staple in Peru and Bolivia is decreasing, urban consumption of French fries is increasing as the international junk food culture gains ground. Down the line, demand for improved potatoes varieties suitable for frying is on the increase.

In addition, native varieties of potato and other tubers are often regarded as 'third-class food' by the rapidly growing urban population. Their aspirations tend to be emulated by the rest of the country. In Ecuador, says Patricio Espinoza of CIP, tubers such as *oca* are seen by consumers as third-class foods. Farmers do not sow native tuber varieties on a large scale because there is no market: a few rows for home consumption will suffice. But as fewer and fewer people grow food for home consumption, and more and more for the market, the native tubers run the risk of being lost.

Market prices: a roller-coaster ride

In the wholesale potato market in Colomí in Bolivia, women traders are busy negotiating prices for their sacks of potatoes. The men take a back seat in these transactions. Franz Terrazas translates for us from the native Quechua spoken by a woman wrapped in a colourful woven shawl. Dutch improved potatoes are selling at about US$0.03/kg, she says. The native *Imilla blanca* variety is going for about US$0.10/kg, but that is the seasonal price for July. In May, vendors receive only about US$0.05/kg. *Oca*, the native tuber, on the other hand, now sells for US$0.10/kg, but at times it goes up to five times that price.

Prices vary throughout the year depending on the weather, the season, and the number of people cultivating potatoes that year. At harvest time, oversupply causes the price to drop. Farmers who can store their potatoes can extend the period over which they can sell, allowing them to wait until the price begins to recover. Señor Fortunato Carballo, a potato farmer near Cochabamba in Bolivia, shows us his new storage shed which he built following a PROINPA workshop for farmers in Toralapa. The shed is made from local materials: adobe walls, thatched roof and wooden slatted storage shelves. A local grass called *muña* is used to line the shelves because of its insect-repelling qualities. With improved storage he hopes to be able to sell his potatoes and *oca* later in the year. 'We sell about 80 per cent of our potato production and 99 per cent of the *papalisa*,' Señor Carballo tells us. 'If we can store them until later in the year, the price is about twice what we would receive at harvest time.'

In the Carchi area of Ecuador, farmers are heavily dependent on synthetic inputs of fertilizer and pesticides. On average, farmers spray their potato crops seven times in six months; each application is typically a cocktail of three insecticide and fungicide products. Although yields in the area are three times the national average, studies have found that farmers lose money on their potatoes about 43 per cent of the time.[8] This is largely due to the huge fluctuations, by up to eight times, in potato prices,[12] and the costs of inputs to the production system, particularly mechanized land preparation, fertilizers and pesticide costs, which make up some 45 per cent of the production costs.

At times potato prices fall so low that improving productivity may not be the prime concern for farmers if it requires inputs of chemicals or increased costs for improved seed. In Peru, for example, some farmers in Huancayo and Junin abandoned their potato harvest in 1999 because it was not worthwhile investing further labour and chemical inputs for the low price received. However, it is probable that the price in Peru is cyclical.[13] During bad years for production – for example, during the *El Niño* phenomenon – the price of potatoes rises, reflecting their scarcity. The following years, encouraged by high prices, more farmers plant potatoes, leading to oversupply and a fall in prices.

Prices vary regionally too, so a high price in Ecuador often bears no relation to the price in Colombia, Peru or Bolivia. However, as potatoes are increasingly traded between countries, prices are beginning to coincide and in 2001, for example, prices were low throughout the Andes.[10]

Farmers are also confronted with transport problems, which have an impact on the price they receive for their crops. Farms in the Andes are often isolated; roads are poor, public transport lacking and farmers do not own vehicles. In order to get their produce to the market place they have to rely on an intermediary, or pay to hire the transport. In many situations, farmers sell small amounts of potatoes on the local market to the merchants from the city, rather than take a large quantity to the city themselves. Although merchants may offer them a poor price locally, it reduces the risk of arriving with an entire year's harvest at a time of oversupply and low prices.

However, as farmers have found in Escoma, Bolivia, beside the blue waters of Lake Titicaca, the intermediaries who buy their potatoes and take them to La Paz are paying a low price for a mixture of varieties and qualities. The intermediaries separate the varieties out and sell them for a higher price in La Paz. Development projects in the area are providing improved seed and encouraging the farmers to plant their varieties separately, and to separate the produce according to size and quality; to use improved seed for better potatoes for sale and to apply appropriate chemicals (supplied at cost price by the project). The reasoning is that, by so doing, farmers will be able to capture a larger percentage of the final sale price.

The danger of this approach is that encouraging farmers not to mix varieties in their fields may increase their risk of total crop failure. It also promotes the shift away from native varieties, adapted to the severe climatic conditions in the area, towards those for sale. Many farmers in this area produce potatoes for their own consumption. It is important for them to strike a balance between the needs of meeting market demands and the risks that this entails.

The impact of markets on potato diversity is not confined to the demand for a handful of improved potato varieties. There is also the question of what makes 'economic sense' and where limited research money should be directed. When it comes to the allocation of limited financial and human resources, hard choices have to be made and invariably native species with less commercial value suffer. This is particularly the case when it comes to disease control.

Disease control: which varieties do we focus on?

The potato germplasm bank at Toralapa aims to keep the full range of potatoes that exists in Bolivia. Because potatoes cannot be stored for long, every year each potato variety must be grown and harvested in order to preserve the varieties and genetic information they contain for the future. Each variety must be carefully kept separate and identified. To make sure the germplasm bank does not lose a variety entirely to an unseasonal frost or other natural calamity, only half the stock is planted at once. With some varieties the harvest may yield less than the seed used. More complex techniques of vegetative propagation have to be used to bulk up the quantities.

When potatoes begin to yield less and produce deformed tubers, farmers describe them as being tired. 'Of the potatoes which our grandparents managed, many have disappeared in our community, and others are now so tired that they produce little', said one farmer participant in a workshop held by PROINPA in 1997.[7] It often means the potatoes have a virus or other pathogens, which reduce productivity over time. Traditionally, seed exchange systems and farmers' own management of seeds have helped to keep these problems under control, and in some areas they still do.

Seed degeneration occurs faster at lower altitudes where there are more aphids to carry the pathogens. In areas with a high rate of degeneration, farmers may have to replace their seed every year to maintain productivity; at altitudes above 2800 m, degeneration is slow, and above 3500 m, very slow indeed. Seed at these altitudes needs to be replaced less often.[9] Sometimes farmers sow seed of tired varieties at higher altitudes to clean it, and then bring it down again for planting later at the lower levels. This reduces, but does not eliminate viral infection.

Communities in some areas, especially in Peru and Bolivia, are renowned for their abilities to produce high-quality seed of a wide range of varieties. These communities are generally at the higher altitudes where problems of viral infections are less. They sell seed potatoes to the farmers downhill, some of whom multiply it up for their own seed and some of whom simply use the seed potato direct to produce a crop. Some farming practices also have the effect of limiting the impacts of viruses and other pathogens, but these are often not followed. By selecting seed from healthy plants showing little sign of viral infection, the transmission of viruses from one year to another can be reduced. However, it is more common for farmers to select their seed potatoes after harvest, keeping the smallest potatoes as seed. There is every possibility that the small potatoes are in fact those infected with virus, causing their small size. Clearing all the potatoes from the field following harvest removes carriers of disease from one year to the next, but farmers often retain these 'volunteer potatoes' until maturity. Similarly, leaving the fields fallow for a period breaks the hold of diseases resident in the soil, but is feasible only where enough land is available.

Scientists at research stations such as Toralapa have worked on cleaning certain varieties of their viruses, but this is a long and expensive process. Between 1992 and 1994, 24 varieties of native potatoes were selected by farmers and scientists in Bolivia; the potatoes were cleaned of viruses, multiplied up in the laboratory and in the field, and returned to the farmers in small quantities in 1995–96. But this is expensive and does not always work out. Twenty-four varieties represent a fraction of the varieties known in Bolivia. Some of the scientists worry that there is a chance of infecting the potato seed with new viruses during the cleaning process, thus spreading them to new areas. Furthermore, farmers sometimes do not trust the scientists to take away their potato varieties and return them; people fear the theft and patenting of their diversity.

Farmers complain that their traditional varieties of potato are tired and of very low productivity. Often the traditional methods of maintaining seed viability are being lost: farmers themselves lament their poor management of seeds compared to that of their grandparents. One solution to the problem of reduced yields from traditional varieties is to turn to the improved varieties often promoted by agricultural extension agents.

In some Andean countries, particularly Bolivia, soil nematodes are a further factor in reduced yields. According to PROINPA, native potato varieties have resistance to only one of the three types of nematodes endemic to the country. Nematodes affect up to 95 per cent of potato lands,[14] causing yield losses of between 68 and 88 per cent. Researchers at PROINPA, with backing from the British Government aid budget, are working on the development of genetically modified potatoes with resistance to nematode infestation, using a gene imported from rice. Genetically modified resistance to pests and diseases may be the improvement technology of the future; it may also increase the existing pressures on native varieties.

Perhaps the clearest example of the way in which the research agenda affects farmers' use of certain potato varieties is the endemic problem of late blight. In 1846–7, Ireland suffered from a devastating failure of the potato crop, which caused a famine that killed over a million people and prompted the mass exodus of another million refugees across the Atlantic. The failure of the potato crop was caused by a fungus, *Phytophthora infestans*, otherwise known as late blight. It is an integral part of the history of both Ireland and the USA.

Over the past two decades, says Rebecca Nelson at CIP in Lima, there has been a worldwide resurgence in late blight. It has become more pathogenic, more virulent and shows a higher resistance to fungicides than previously. Even the most resistant varieties of potatoes are becoming susceptible to late blight.[15] A recent survey of farmers' problems in Peru, Bolivia and Ecuador found that late blight was perceived by farmers to be their number one problem in production.[16] In a study in 1997–98 in Cajamarca, Peru, 67 per cent of farmers said that late blight was their biggest problem, while 24 per cent said it was their second biggest problem.[17]

The scientific response to this has been to focus on breeding for resistance and a move towards integrated pest management: effective, targeted use of chemicals and management of the crop to give it a better chance against disease. However, there is a limit to the number of varieties that can be worked on at once when breeding for resistance: the priority is the commercial varieties, those improved varieties that farmers grow and sell worldwide. In a global breeding programme funded by international donors, says Rebecca Nelson, how can we justify focusing on the non-commercial, native varieties for home consumption, with their distributions limited to specific niches in the Andes? China alone produces over three times as much potato as all of Latin America, using only a few improved varieties: it is irrelevant to the Chinese whether native potatoes in the Andes have any resistance to late blight.

According to Ramiro Ortega of the Universidad Nacional in Cuzco, Peru, native varieties are particularly susceptible to late blight, but conversely have better resistance to frost than improved ones. While potato breeders have had some success developing resistance to disease in potatoes, they have had less success dealing with drought and frost. In many parts of the Andes, where frost is the major limitation to growing potatoes, late blight is less of a problem.[10] However, in Chimborazo Province of Ecuador, we visited the farm of Manuel Yunda. In a small, sheltered valley above a little stream we walked on the rich brown terraces held up by banks of thick *milin* grass where his 7-month-old potato crop had been frost-damaged the week before. Most of his potato crop is for home consumption, he explains; this is a big investment lost. Late blight occurs here too, so there is a balance to be struck between frost tolerance and blight resistance. For farmers, it is one more factor that they need to understand and take into account when deciding which types of potatoes to plant.

In general farmers combat late blight by spraying fungicides. It may be one of the major reasons for farmers remaining in the market system despite diminishing returns and fluctuating prices: to grow potatoes one needs to spray with fungicides, and to spray with fungicides one needs to sell potatoes. Breaking out of the circle is difficult. On the other hand, in very small areas – perhaps an eighth of a hectare, suggests Daniel Selener of the International Institute for Rural Reconstruction (IIRR) in Quito – with crops changing in rotation every year it may be possible to grow organic potatoes without losing all to late blight.

On a steep hillside in Chimborazo, Ecuador, Mariano Volcar and his wife Mercedes are growing organic potatoes on terraces. The improved *Gabriella* variety is grown for home consumption, and for sale in the local market. If you plant too late, in January, says Mariano, the rains make the plants susceptible to late blight. Evidence of the disease was visible, but perhaps at a level acceptable to a farmer devoted to organic farming. Gabriella potatoes are susceptible to late blight.

'We used to have a lot of native varieties of potato, which tasted good, were excellent for cooking and received a good price in the market. The seed used to sell well, too, because of its resistance to late blight', says Mariano.[18] 'Little by little I learned about improved potato and barley seed, which were fashionable and produced good incomes, but every year the harvest diminished.' Now Mariano aims to do his own experiments with native varieties of potato, recuperating the lost varieties. Different management techniques which Mariano and Mercedes practice, such as crop rotation, seed selection, fallowing and the use of more varieties of potato, will also help him combat late blight.

Displacement of traditional crops

While some researchers and development practitioners are concerned about an erosion of diversity among potatoes and the impact that this has on farmers' livelihoods, others have identified another phenomenon: the substitution of cash crops for the staples of potatoes and other tubers. While these cash crops can be profitable, they are vulnerable to the vagaries of the market. The predicament facing farmers is very clear in the highlands of Peru.

Cuzco was the capital of the vast Inca Empire. The city that enchanted the Spaniards in the sixteenth century continues to attract hundreds of thousands of tourists every year, who flock to see its stunning Inca stonework topped by ornate colonial churches and to visit the nearby ruins of Machu Picchu. They bring with them their foreign money and taste in food. Ironically, the growth of interest in Inca history and traditions of Cuzco and the phenomenal increase in tourism has led to the almost complete disappearance of native tubers from local farmers' fields.

Ramiro Ortega of the Universidad Nacional works with communities around Cuzco. He took us to his project headquarters, a small adobe house in the village of Matinga, some 20 km from Cuzco. Around the village, lining the steep hillsides, are neat, terraced fields which fall away suddenly into the deep valley where tourist buses ply the paved road from Cuzco to the ancient town of Pisac. Villages such as Matinga can easily transport their produce to the urban market in Cuzco.

Twenty years ago, Ramiro Ortega says, when he first started to work with these communities, people used to cultivate a wide variety of native potatoes, as well as other tubers like *oca*, *papalisa* and *isaño*. By 1995 these had all disappeared. They were replaced by introduced onions and carrots, which could be sold profitably to the tourist restaurants in Cuzco. Farmers' diets have changed to include bread, made of imported, subsidized North American wheat and bought with the money made from selling vegetables. But as increasing numbers of farmers caught on to the opportunities of the vegetable market, price fluctuations have become more extreme and now farmers complain they cannot always sell their produce. Overproduction of cash crops for the market has led to falling prices and an incentive to return to traditional crops.

Ramiro Ortega's project aims to reintroduce *oca* to the fields and diets of the farmers near to Cuzco. In the adobe house next to the project office, its yard surrounded by the high, mud wall typical of the region, a woman proudly showed us her store of *oca* seed tubers, which she is multiplying up, with the help of the project, in a rustic plant propagator.

The challenge is that farmers will consider growing *oca* again only if Ramiro and his colleagues can help them control the gorgojo caterpillar (*Microtrypes* sp.), which tunnels through the tubers, ruining them. Ramiro explains that in 2000 the potato crop failed due to disease. Now people are more interested in cultivating *oca* and other tubers again for food security, but not if they lose their crop to gorgojo. It seems that, if it is only marginally worthwhile to cultivate traditional crops for home use, the presence of a serious pest or disease problem may tip the balance. People are more likely to purchase expensive chemicals to protect a cash crop such as carrots and onions, in the hope that the sale price will cover the cost of inputs.

Cheap, non-chemical means of controlling the gorgojo are needed, ones that complement farmers' land, financial and labour constraints. A number of management techniques are available. These include harvesting the *oca* early before the gorgojo really has an impact; taking the chickens into the fields to eat the grubs; allowing more weeds to grow; and rotating crops every year. Although these practices have no financial cost, they do have to fit with labour patterns. Many people from the uplands migrate seasonally to other areas to earn cash: there is no point telling people to harvest early, if everyone is away during the early harvest period. Equally, crop rotation may be sensible, but not if you have insufficient land to take some out of production. Despite these complications, the project is experiencing some success; as farmers learn how to manage the gorgojo, *oca* is returning to the fields of Matinga.

Conservation through use

Where do we go from here?

When we talk about the impacts of the loss of potato diversity, it is important to consider *for whom* it may be a problem. Many concerned analysts and spectators in the developed countries consider that the loss of potato diversity is a problem because of its long-term implications. The Andes is the centre of diversity for potatoes and tubers, with thousands of varieties. In the future, that diversity may form the basis of genetic material from which we may be able to breed further improved varieties, a vast armoury in the constant battle with pests and diseases. Once we lose these varieties, their unique genetic makeup is gone forever. We are, we feel, losing something that may be important to all of us in the future, and farmers should be encouraged to keep using their diversity of crops. Even when not explicitly expressed, this philosophy lies behind much rural development thinking.

So called *ex situ* conservation, which preserves samples within gene banks such as the one at Toralapa, maintains only a small proportion of the genetic variation within each type and runs the risk of losing those varieties that do not grow well in the climate of the gene bank. Furthermore, gene bank collections often fail to capture new resources that are generated after the collection has occurred. These new resources become available because of genetic mutation, recombination and exchange from outside the collection region.[19] For many, *ex situ* conservation is the choice of last resort. The alternative, *in situ* conservation, means working with farmers to conserve their diversity within a living and changing agricultural system.

The issue for many farmers is that they are caught between two opposing pressures. On the one hand are the environmental and cultural pressures to maintain a diversity of potato varieties to insure against the dangers of an increasingly risky world. On the other hand, is the pressure to sell to a market that values consistency of production, quality and adequate quantities of the same product, a pressure that often drives farmers towards reduced diversity. Pest and disease problems may also oblige farmers to move towards improved varieties, particularly in a market-oriented system, as reduced diversity and shorter fallows become common. Decreases in land availability due to population growth and subdivision of farms increases the pressure to intensify production on the remaining portion. Farmers may subsequently reduce fallow periods and turn to more productive, improved, potato varieties, supported by chemical inputs of fertilizers and pesticides.

Is it reasonable for people in the developed world to expect farmers in the Andean countries to conserve the diversity of their native varieties for posterity, unless it makes short-term economic sense to them? And if not, can we find ways to ensure there are adequate short-term incentives for farmers to conserve the diversity of their crops? In some areas, changing markets, lifestyles and environmental constraints are undoubtedly reducing the diversity of crops. However, throughout the Andean countries we encountered dedicated farmers, researchers, NGOs and state-sponsored organizations that are grappling with the issue of how to conserve potato diversity while simultaneously ensuring that farmers' ability to survive in a globalized world is not jeopardized.

Andean farmers are not passive participants in the 'where do we go from here?' debate. Since the Spanish conquest, their crops have been regarded as third class and they have been encouraged to grow introduced crops. However, their agricultural systems have not been destroyed; rather, farmers have adapted and adopted the parts that they want, and ignored the rest. Native varieties of potatoes and tubers have many advantages over high-yielding improved varieties in terms of taste, environmental tolerance and processing or storage qualities. Farmers are not blind to these advantages. Farmers need to find a balance between the environmental risks of growing fewer potato varieties and the risk of not supplying the products desired by the market if they choose to cultivate a diverse range of native potato varieties.

There are alternative approaches that partially resolve the dilemma that farmers face in meeting the demands of the markets, maintaining on-farm potato diversity and achieving an adequate livelihood. The first is to modify the market so that it makes commercial sense for farmers to grow local potato varieties rather than improved or more cosmopolitan varieties. A second approach is to assist farmers to make more money from growing commercial varieties. This aims to offer greater prosperity to farmers; with a more secure livelihood, there may be more opportunity to devote a percentage of the farm area to non-marketable native potato varieties for home consumption. Finally, there is a movement that shuns the demands of the mainstream markets, and focuses on production for home consumption and sales through local, organic markets.

Transformation and diverse markets

In Cochabamba, Bolivia, researchers from PROINPA are working with the food programme of the local university to improve the market value of local potato varieties. It is essential to understand the whole chain, the production system as well as the market, says Franz Terrazas, leader of the project, which will allow researchers and farmers together to look for market outlets and transformation possibilities. The project is working to develop new market niches for a number of tubers grown locally.

Chuño, the freeze-dried potato, is produced mainly for home consumption in this area, with a limited market in town. It is hoped that clean, good-quality and well-presented *chuño* may command a higher price in the urban markets. The project is therefore examining ways to improve the appearance and saleability of *chuño* in order to command a higher price. In a frosty field in Colomí, we looked at chicken wire racks with wooden frames, simple techniques being tried to keep the potatoes off the ground when they are spread out to freeze overnight. This helps to keep them clean and may ensure that they freeze more thoroughly. Other techniques imported from Peru suggest it may be better not to let the frozen tubers defrost during the day; piling the potatoes under a cover of grass keeps them frozen despite the sun.

Other types of freeze-dried potatoes and tubers have potential too. *Tunta* is a white form of *chuño*, often made from bitter white potatoes called *lukis,* which cannot be eaten fresh. The process of transforming potatoes into *tunta* is labour intensive. The potatoes undergo the same 2–4 day freezing process as *chuño* and are trodden in the trough. Then they are soaked in the river for two days to remove the skin and bitter taste. A second freeze overnight is followed by another two-day soak. Finally the *tunta* is dried in the sun. It is a labour-intensive process, but there is a high demand for *tunta*, and it commands a good price in the urban market in Cochabamba. Improving the appearance and quality of *tunta* may substantially improve its market value.

Papalisa is a small, round pink and yellow tuber unrelated to the potato it resembles. While other tubers start to rot once washed, *papalisa* is the only tuber that can be washed before sale, helping it to create an attractive pastel display in the market. *Papalisa* is a very efficient crop: it suffers from few pests and needs few inputs, while providing reasonably high yields. The problem in Bolivia is the market: while in Holy Week the price may rise to US$0.28–0.32/kg, for the rest of the year it falls to about US$0.08/kg. Franz Terrazas and his team believe that drying and slicing the *papalisa* may allow it to be sold year round through the supermarkets; to help introduce it to the urban middle class, recipes are included in the packets. This marketing tactic is more advanced in Quito, Ecuador, where this tuber finds a place in urban homes: a trip round any cosmopolitan supermarket will discover neatly bagged packets of shiny *papalisa*, at prices of US$0.57/kg.

Isaño is a bitter tuber, generally used domestically for fattening pigs. It is so bitter that it needs to be boiled before it can be fed to the pigs. However, the bitterness is thought to repel some pests such as gorgojo, potentially decreasing the costs of protection for adjacent and subsequent potato and *oca* crops. In practically all studies, *isaño* is a non-market crop. However, it might be possible to use *isaño* as a substitute for the relatively expensive maize in intensive pig farms in Cochabamba; dehydrated, it could be easily stored and transported. Nutritional tests are underway.

Another initiative to develop new market niches for native potato varieties is the Papa Andina project, co-ordinated by CIP in Lima.[5] Working with PROINPA in Bolivia, Papa Andina is looking for ways to capitalize on small farmers' knowledge, abilities and the diversity of their potato heritage.

The project aims to help improve small farmers' access to markets for specific potato products. This requires a co-ordinated approach to improving agricultural techniques, training farmers in better farming methods, identifying market niches, helping farmers to organize themselves, developing market channels and securing access to credit.

A specific focus of the Papa Andina project is to identify the market niches where small farmers actually have a competitive advantage. There is little point in encouraging small farmers to enter new markets that will ultimately be taken over by large farms. For example, potatoes which are destined for French fries are subject to stringent demands for quality of non-visible characteristics such as dry matter or sugar content. Small farmers find these particularly difficult to check: the market is likely to be dominated by the larger farmers. Papa Andina aims to identify markets where small farmers have a long-term competitive advantage, because of their location, local knowledge, access to local varieties or crop management practices. For example, they suggest, some market niches require small tubers grown at high planting densities and manually harvested, all of which is much more difficult for mechanized farmers to achieve.

The Papa Andina project has brought together potato producers and local French fry producers in Cochabamba, Bolivia. Both parties have agreed to establish direct links. During the discussions the farmers learnt more about the processors' demands in terms of preferred potato varieties, volumes required and timing of production. The processors, in turn, learnt about the varieties of potatoes that farmers grow and, more importantly, why they grow them. With a greater understanding of the reality faced by both parties, the Papa Andina project is exploring ways in which the processors could utilize potato varieties that have previously been ignored. Meanwhile, it is also working with farmers to ensure that they benefit from these emerging market opportunities without undermining the foundation of their livelihoods, namely potato diversity.

Following the market: the potato chip connection

In Ecuador, projects working with CIP and the Instituto Nacional Autónomo de Investigaciones Agropecuarias (INIAP) have also attempted to make the link between small-scale potato farmers and the processing companies that are becoming increasingly important buyers of potatoes. In these cases, the emphasis is on providing decent prices and an adequate living to small farmers, rather than conserving the diversity of native varieties, but the experiences might provide clues for possible future directions.

Lautaro Andrade works with a small NGO, the Centro Ecuatoriano de Servicio Agrícola (CESA) in Quito, Ecuador. For 33 years, CESA has been working in rural development, mainly in the management of rural credit and irrigation systems. Only in the past few years has CESA begun to conclude that the way forward is not exclusively through increased production, but also through improved marketing. Commercialization is often the bottleneck for farmers.

CESA, working together with INIAP, is assisting smallholder farmers in Ecuador to develop their market with potato chip manufacturers. The potato processors demand quantities beyond the production capacity of individual small farmers; they want quality control and they want specific varieties for frying. CESA has negotiated an agreement between the potato chip processors and the farmers: the processors pay a good price to the farmers (US$0.26/kg at the factory gate), and save themselves money by cutting out the intermediaries. The farmers agree to provide a certain quantity of potatoes: in the first year (2000) this required the co-operation of 86 farmers in 11 communities, each with a tiny plot, some of only 700 square metres. The total area is only 15 hectares. Andrade hopes to increase the number of participating farmers and the area each year, building up to the kind of quantities required by the processor.

INIAP has been providing training to farmers involved in the project on integrated pest management. This can help them manage their crop better, produce potatoes of the required quality, and potentially reduce the costs of inputs like fertilizer and pesticides. Certified seed of an improved variety is sold to the farmers by INIAP. The new variety matures in only five months, so the farmers can harvest twice a year. Farmers need irrigation, but with the short growing season they may be able to avoid some pests and diseases and thereby use fewer chemicals. But to buy the seed from INIAP requires credit, not available to many. Local NGOs are co-operating to provide cheap credit. According to Andrade, the scheme answers a need expressed by the farmers themselves. Years of providing assistance to farmers, helping them to increase yields only to find the products unmarketable, has disillusioned farmers and prompted a revision of CESA's working methods.

There are several drawbacks to the scheme from the point of view of diversity. Small farmers with tiny plots of land may be increasing their risk by specializing in one crop, and with such small areas available they are unlikely to devote a portion to non-market native varieties. The use of one improved variety of potato may leave them susceptible to pests, diseases, frosts and droughts, which might be offset by more diversity. Farmers need to invest financial resources or take out credit to buy the improved seed, leaving them vulnerable to losses if the scheme does not work.

However, according to Andrade, the skills farmers are learning through the scheme will stand them in good stead. Farmers have developed their own standards and procedures for classifying their potatoes and ensuring quality control. The farmers intend to set up a small company, which may be able to contract in further technical assistance when the CESA/INIAP project has finished in two years' time. The processors are providing some technical assistance, which also ensures they are aware in advance of any problems that may be developing. In the meantime, CESA is working to identify further markets that could be supplied by small farmers.

But however hard organizations like CESA may work to develop secure markets for farmers' produce, the power asymmetry between small farmers and large processors leaves farmers vulnerable. The Fripapa provides a salutary example. Fripapa is a potato variety that was developed by CIP, INIAP and the Fritolay processing company, which makes potato chips in Ecuador. The potato has a good resistance to late blight and is ideal for potato chips. It was released by INIAP in 1997 and was well received by farmers. Fritolay came to agreements with farmers to take their production of Fripapa potatoes.

Then, in 1999, an economic crisis hit Ecuador, inflation rose and the currency was devalued. Ecuadorian consumers stopped buying high-quality potato chips like those produced by Fritolay, and switched to those on the street, which are one-third the price. As a result, demand dropped sharply and Fritolay began to reject contracted potatoes, saying that they did not meet the required quality standards. Researchers were adamant that the potatoes met required standards. It is an added danger for farmers where contracts on which they rely may be ignored or cancelled because of factors outside their control.

Perhaps, one day, smallholder farmers in the Andes will be capable of providing the quality, quantity and consistency of potatoes demanded by the big, international fast-food chains. McDonald's currently find it cheaper to import potatoes, while Pizza Hut say the quality of local potatoes is too poor for their needs. The day that McDonald's and Pizza Hut accept locally grown potatoes may herald a new era of success for local farmers, but it may also mean new risks for farmers and new pressures on the native potato diversity.

Subsistence and local sales

A radically different alternative to conventional market approaches is promoted by several other NGOs working in Latin America. Daniel Selener at IIRR in Quito appreciates that almost all farmers in Latin America are involved in the market in some form or other, and that they need access to money for fertilizers, clothes, schools and medicines. However, IIRR is strongly averse to encouraging farmers to enter cash crop markets with monocultures of crops like potatoes, where diminishing returns and high risks mean that they do not make money in the long term. Selener believes that diversity and self-reliance are the answers. IIRR facilitates farmers' experimentation with production systems and their sharing of that knowledge with other farmers. Other organizations like INIAP are also realizing the importance of farmer-based approaches and are helping develop training methods which emphasize farmers' learning and decision-making capacities. The important factor is developing farmers' self-esteem and abilities to manage the world around them.

Back on the hillside in Chimborazo, Ecuador, Mariano Volcar explained about his organic farm. 'You don't get large quantities, but good quality', he said, 'and we don't need to pay for our chemicals by selling the animals'. They plant small quantities, a few at a time, minimizing attacks by the gorgojo and other pests and diseases by rotating the crops. Keeping a range of crops and varieties on the terraces at any one time spreads the risks of losses. If it rains, late blight can be a problem, which they try to avoid by planting early, applying ashes and organic fertilizer. Mariano is now experimenting with native varieties which were lost from their farm in the past. Some varieties, for example, although highly susceptible to late blight, can be harvested in just three months. Combined with crop rotations, these early varieties can be harvested before the gorgojo completes its life cycle and enters the tubers.

One of the problems Mariano points out is that in Chimborazo there is no specific organic or quality market: people want bigger and cleaner potatoes, not organic and good quality. And with such small quantities they cannot provide a consistent supply to the market. This is a problem recognized by several projects. SwissAid provides credit to support the development of organic farms in Ecuador, including Mariano's. Some farmers, supported by credit from the project, have found that better presentation of their organic produce at local markets has helped build up a core of regular customers: selecting the best produce, weighing and packing it, and working with regular orders has helped one family build up to a weekly average of 150 customers.[18]

There is a local demand for organic produce, says Mercedes Barrera of ProBio, an organic producers' association based in Quito. ProBio aims to organize a weekly organic market in Quito, and later, regional markets throughout Ecuador to supply this unmet demand. Local markets have several benefits for producers, she says. Sales are direct to the customer, cutting out the costs of intermediaries and improving contact and understanding between farmers and middle-class consumers. Local markets are also somewhat less demanding of consistency and high quality than other markets, allowing more flexibility for farmers.

Although supplying local markets, the focus of these initiatives is self-sufficiency rather than production for mainstream markets: lower production is compensated by lower costs. Food security is paramount and the maintenance of the family and farm environment are more important than sales and markets. As SwissAid director, Francisco Gangotena says, people think monocultures are more profitable than diverse farms, but often they do not take into account the huge fluctuations in the market. Diversity balances risk.

The way forward

As the cases discussed above show, farmers across the Andes find themselves in a diverse range of situations. There is no single picture of what is happening to the diversity of potatoes and other tubers in the face of increased market pressures. The market itself appears very stratified: potatoes produced for domestic consumption or local markets tend to be of traditional varieties; urban consumer markets for household use favour a particular limited set of commercial native varieties; processors for French fries and chips favour commercial improved varieties. In some areas, such as Carchi in Ecuador, potato diversity has certainly been lost to improved varieties, and farmers have been largely integrated into the market. Farmers' choices of varieties may be constrained by pests and diseases: where late blight is prevalent, improved varieties may be the only option. In other areas, farmers such as those seen in Colomí, Bolivia, manage a whole range of potato types for a mix of market and non-market uses.

What is clear is that there is a need to stimulate market demand for native potatoes and other tubers. As Patricio Espinoza of CIP, Quito says, we need to improve the profile of traditional foods among urban consumers: conservation through use is the only way forward. Promotion of traditional, native or low-cost foods does not work: native varieties retain their stigma as third class. Instead, native varieties need to be reinvented: branding them as organic, low-input and a 'new' flavour can all increase sales appeal. Recipe books and television cookery programmes, as well as the perception that these foods are being exported to the developed world, all help to promote traditional foods to a middle- or higher-income urban consumer.

This challenge is not confined to Bolivia, Peru or Ecuador. In Jujuy Province of northern Argentina, attempts to rescue native varieties of potatoes have revolved around rebranding them with an image that appeals to the urban consumer. Native potatoes from Jujuy are being sold in Buenos Aires under the English name *Inca Potatoes*, to give them an international, exotic image and remove the stigma of native, third-class food.

In Ecuador, Bolivia and Peru, different agencies promote different approaches. The 'conservation through use' approach of PROINPA and Papa Andina aims to develop new markets for traditional varieties, increasing the economic value of native potatoes in order to increase the incentive to grow them. CESA and INIAP have sought to ensure that farmers benefit more from the production of potatoes for mainstream markets and processing. SwissAid and IIRR emphasize the route of organic production and home consumption. The different approaches have different implications for the use and conservation of potato diversity as well as for farmers' livelihoods.

The choice of where to go next belongs to Andean smallholder farmers. They need to be able decide which livelihood options best suit their needs. But they also need the resources to enable them to pursue these options. As well as the technical knowledge to grow potatoes without an excessive reliance on chemical inputs, farmers need management skills. In particular, they need the self-confidence to negotiate with government, NGOs and processing industry representatives; marketing skills to understand the importance of presentation, quality control and consistency of supply; and the business skills to work together in order to provide the quantities demanded by commercial markets.

Providing all these skills is a tall order, but already Farmer Field Schools (FFS), a training approach for integrated pest management, have been extended to help farmers learn about product requirements and negotiation in these new markets. A further extension of this process might well mean that farmers can indeed maintain the diversity of potatoes and other tubers, while simultaneously benefiting from market opportunities. The onus is very much on the development community to support this process.

CHAPTER 5

*Quinoa and food security**

Introduction

THE COLD WIND whips up the hill and the red wool ponchos worn by the inhabitants of Guantug village look increasingly alluring. Overhead, the sky threatens rain that never seems to fall; the rains are very late this year, delaying planting of next year's crops but perhaps saving the small patch of quinoa (known in Spanish as quinua) that was planted earlier in the year and that now clings to the steep hillside. At over 3500 metres above sea level, the small village sits in a landscape of rolling hills covered with tufts of grass and small agricultural plots. The scenery is typical of the highlands of Central Ecuador. It is November and villagers are harvesting onions – the quinoa is next.

The quinoa patch where we are standing is the result of last year's efforts by the extension team from a local NGO called Escuelas Radiofónica Populares del Ecuador. Known locally as Radiofónica, the NGO is based in the regional centre of Riobamba and one of its aims is to increase quinoa production and exports from the area, providing markets for some of the poorest farmers in the country. Sadly, last year the seed was sown late and here, high in the Ecuadorian Andes, the frequent cloud and cold have slowed its growth. The strong winds threaten to scatter the small quinoa grains before they are ready to harvest. And if the rains start before the grain is mature, it will germinate on the plant and be ruined. Although quinoa is a traditional grain in the region, its reintroduction into this community is presenting some serious challenges.

Radiofónica's programme of increasing the cultivation of quinoa in the Riobamba area characterizes some of the issues surrounding this ancient crop in the modern world. Quinoa is nutritious in a land where under-nutrition affects a majority of the population. Quinoa grows in conditions of cold, drought, altitude and salinity, where other crops would perish. The crop has been selected by the Food and Agriculture Organization of the United Nations (FAO) as one destined to offer food security in the twenty-first century.[1] And yet, the quinoa that Radiofónica assists communities like Guantug to plant is destined for export to the USA and Europe. Meanwhile,

* The authors are grateful to Oxfam for allowing us to include material from: Hellin, J. and Higman, S. (2001) 'Quinoa and rural livelihoods in Bolivia, Peru and Ecuador'. Oxford, Oxfam.

many of the Ecuadorian urban and rural poor eat less nutritious bread and cheap pasta made from subsidized North American wheat.

In this chapter we look at the extent to which quinoa can contribute to food security in the Andes and whether its potential can best be realized through production for export, as a contribution to diets locally and nationally, or both. We detail some of the obstacles facing farmers, researchers and development practitioners as they seek to boost quinoa production and consumption levels in the region. And we identify some of the steps that can be taken to overcome these obstacles and ensure that quinoa contributes more effectively to smallholder farmers' food security and rural livelihoods.

Diverse, robust and nutritious

Quinoa (*Chenopodium quinoa*) is an annual plant found growing in the Andean region between sea level and the heights of the Bolivian altiplano, above 4000 m altitude. The two-metre high plants produce striking purple and yellow heads of seeds, which turn brown on maturity. The grain is small, and can be used as flour, or toasted, added to soups or made into bread. Dried, it can be stored for up to ten years. Quinoa has been cultivated in the Andes for over 7000 years and has long been known and appreciated for its nutritional value. For the Incas, it was a staple, known as the 'Mother Grain'. As with the *chuño* (freeze-dried potatoes), quinoa was a light, nutritious food, helping to sustain the Inca army on its long march through the Andes.[2]

As a species, quinoa is a collection of very variable sub-types, which allows the different varieties to survive in an extraordinarily wide range of conditions. In Bolivia, quinoa is found in two main areas. About 70 per cent of the national production comes from the northern and central altiplano, around Lake Titicaca and stretching south to La Paz, where quinoa probably originated. This, however, is almost entirely a subsistence crop, with about 80 per cent of the production kept for home consumption. Here it is produced in small plots of land, in rotation with a variety of other crops. The southern altiplano of Bolivia is a desolate high-altitude plain: dry, cold, windy and frosty. This lunar landscape produces most of Bolivia's commercial quinoa: here 81 per cent of production is destined for sale, and only 19 per cent is retained for home consumption.[3] In Peru, 65 per cent of quinoa is produced in the Puno area, around the northern shores of Lake Titicaca. Comparatively little quinoa is grown in the much smaller country of Ecuador.

Once established, quinoa can survive levels of drought, salinity, hail, wind and frost in which other grains would perish. Near the famous salt lakes of Uyuni in southern Bolivia, quinoa grows in areas that receive only 200 mm of rainfall per year, in saline soils and conditions of frost on over 200 nights per year.[4] During the day the sun dries the air mercilessly. There are few plants that produce a useful crop under these conditions. In such extreme and highly variable conditions quinoa may have relatively low and fluctuating yields, but it is the only crop available to farmers.

Quinoa is variable, too, in the type of grain it produces. In some areas, notably southern Bolivia, native quinoa varieties tend to be large grained and bitter, with rapidly germinating seeds and quick maturation times. Further north, there are more varieties of sweet quinoa, with small grains and a longer growing cycle.[5] Colour of the seed also varies widely, ranging from white through pale yellow, orange, red and black. Says Dr Angel Mujika of the Universidad Nacional del Altiplano in Puno, Peru, about 150 different traditional ways of consuming quinoa have been identified in his research and traditionally a different type of quinoa is used for each one. And yet, this vast array of varieties and uses is barely known.

Quinoa is a source of a wide range of nutrients. The overall energy and protein contents exceed that of other cereals and it contains high-quality protein, rich in particular amino acids which are scarce in other cereals.[6] The quality of the proteins available in quinoa is similar to that of milk products, suggesting that it is appropriate for supplementing the diets of young children. Quinoa is also rich in a range of vitamins and minerals, with a particularly high iron content; it often contains all essential amino acids, making it a food superior to both cereals and legumes.[7] Based on its nutritional properties, quinoa ought to be playing a major role in enhancing food security in the region, and perhaps in other parts of the world. But why is it not doing so?

Quinoa's contribution to food security

Nutritional status of the Andean population

There are varying views on the nutritional status of the Andean population. With almost half of the population below the poverty line in the altiplano areas of Peru,[7] nutritional problems, particularly among pre-school children, are thought to be serious. It is estimated that up to 50 per cent of the Peruvian population does not receive adequate quality and quantity of food.[8]

A large number of the inhabitants of the Andes are stunted in their growth, which is indicative of chronic under-nutrition. For example, in the Ecuadorian Andes, stunting has been reported at levels of 57 to 67 per cent,[9] although acute malnutrition does not appear to be widespread. While some studies from the 1980s and 1990s have suggested that, on average, Andean people's energy intakes range from 80 to over 100 per cent of the required calories,[10] there are indications that food intake among some sectors of the population is inadequate.

The traditional Andean diet, based on high consumption of tubers and a mix of different grains (including quinoa), ensured that on the whole, protein levels were adequate.[11] However, the average adequacy of the diet doubtless conceals severe extremes of nutritional levels. Changing dietary habits, where traditional foods are being substituted by imported foods with lower nutritional values, such as rice and pasta, have been blamed for poor nutrition.

Following the World Food Summit in November 1996, The Rome Declaration on World Food Security was issued. Food security was defined as 'food that is available at all times, to which all persons have means of access, that is nutritionally adequate in terms of quantity, quality and variety, and is acceptable within the given culture'.[8] Traditionally, the focus has been on the problem of ensuring an adequate overall supply of food to the population as a whole. However, while adequate food supply may be available in total, not all members of the population necessarily have the resources or ability to obtain it. Those most at risk from a lack of food security are the marginalized urban poor and the rural population who are either landless or land-poor. These groups of people often cannot supplement their diets with home-grown foods. Hence, in Ecuador, while 65 per cent of the population is now estimated to live in poverty, in rural zones this figure rises to 77 per cent and in marginalized indigenous communities, mostly in the Andean Sierra area, the figure is over 95 per cent.[12]

With such a large proportion of the population lacking adequate nutrition, ensuring food security in the region is essential. Food needs can be supplied by locally produced foods or through imports of cheap, subsidized basic foodstuffs such as wheat. Quinoa is viewed by many as a nutritious grain which can be produced locally, thereby fulfilling twin objectives: to provide basic food for people in need and to provide markets for local farmers' produce. Quinoa's importance to Bolivia, for example, was demonstrated in 1983 when a serious drought led to substantial crop losses in potatoes and barley. Quinoa was barely affected. FAO's choice of quinoa as a crop offering food security in the twenty-first century is unsurprising.

Production and consumption

It was with understandable concern, therefore, that many researchers and development workers viewed the downward trend in quinoa production during the 1970s. In the early 1980s quinoa was a crop in danger of disappearing. Production in Bolivia and Peru fluctuated around 15 000 tonnes per year, while wheat imports increased sharply. In Ecuador, cheap imports of wheat, changing patterns of consumption and the inferior image of native crops pushed quinoa to the verge of extinction.[13] For example, research in three rural communities in northern Ecuador in 1980 demonstrated that in 89 households, only 5 per cent of total meals in a 24-hour period contained quinoa.[11] While in the 1960s quinoa and another indigenous crop, *kañiwa*, were together the eighth most important crops in Peru, by 1996 quinoa had dropped to thirtieth place.[14]

Other studies provide a different picture. Much of the quinoa produced nationally in Peru and Bolivia is destined for home consumption by the farmers. In Peru, 65 per cent of national quinoa production comes from Puno, making up an average of 10 000 tonnes annually. Of this, some 60 per cent is never traded, being consumed within the household. Another 20 per cent is sold at local markets, and the remainder is sold to processing plants in Puno and Cuzco.[15] A survey in 1992 in the Puno region found that 25 per cent of farmers planted quinoa, with 65 per cent of them aiming for home consumption only: average family consumption was 1kg/day. However, another study in the Cuzco area in 1996 suggested quinoa makes up 2 per cent of daily energy intake, with people eating between 0.11 and 0.16kg/day.[8] The figures make confusing reading.

For farmers, quinoa presents some problems because harvesting the tiny seeds, as well as post-harvest processing, is very time-consuming. As Oscar Barea of PROINPA in Sucre, Bolivia, points out, this labour-intensive harvest coincides with annual migration patterns to the cotton, sugar cane, soya and grape harvesting areas in lowland Bolivia and Argentina. It is a disincentive for farmers to produce and process quinoa, particularly for home consumption.

While the urban poor tend to consume potatoes and wheat-based products such as bread and pasta, quinoa still makes a minor contribution to their diets. Surveys of consumers in Lima showed that low- and very low-income families are still more likely to eat quinoa than the medium- or higher-income families. While 15.2 per cent of very low-income families ate quinoa daily, only 3.8 per cent of high-income families did so.[8]

Whatever the patterns of quinoa production and consumption, there is little doubt that increasing trade liberalization has reduced the ability of countries to favour food production within their own borders. In South America, this has been blamed for the reduction in quinoa production. Over the past five decades, the increasing imports of subsidized wheat products from North America have displaced traditional crops and nationally produced foods as basic foodstuffs. Wheat imports to Peru have risen from 400 000 tonnes in 1961 to about 1.3 million tonnes by 2000.[16] The scale of the imports dwarfs the national production of quinoa, which in Peru in 1999 stood at 28 439 tonnes. There is a strong argument that Peru could not feed its population without vast imports of cheap wheat; the flipside is that traditional crops face an uphill battle for markets.

A bitter harvest

Increasing urbanization of the population throughout the region, increasingly busy lifestyles, and the high cost of quinoa products compared to cheap, easily prepared foods like bread and pasta, have all contributed to the decline in consumption of the traditional grain. Another obstacle to increased consumption of quinoa is that the grains are bitter – too bitter to eat without processing. And the processing can be a laborious process.

The bitterness is caused by saponins, a group of chemical compounds found in the outer layers of the seed, and which may make up between 0.1 and 5 per cent of the grain.[7] Quinoa needs to be 'de-bittered' before it can be eaten. Although not actually poisonous to humans, the saponins are distasteful. It can be a tedious process to remove the saponins. At the household level, quinoa is washed several times in water, while rubbing the grains to remove the outer layers. Farmers and their families increasingly work off-farm, leaving them less time for labour-intensive activities like washing their home-produced quinoa. Furthermore, the grains need to be dried again for storage and, in some cases, transport. This increases costs significantly.

Removing the saponins may require more water than is available in the semi-arid highlands of Bolivia, Peru and Ecuador. Also, while washing the grains is relatively efficient in removing most of the saponins, the waste water is toxic and needs to be disposed of, a problem which has yet to be solved. The effluent containing the saponins is poisonous to reptiles and amphibians[7] and also pollutes the water for other people downstream. Saponins do have traditional uses as natural soap for washing hair and clothes, but are not currently used in industrial processes.

The alternative to washing involves the dry removal of the outer layer by mechanically polishing the grains. The outer layers, containing the bitter saponins, are rubbed off, leaving a clean, white grain. However, mechanical cleaning removes only about 80 per cent of the saponin, and it does not work for all varieties of quinoa: with the bitterest varieties, a bitter taste is left. The advantage of mechanical cleaning is that it does not pollute water in the same way as washing, and is cheaper. Nevertheless, the saponin-charged coatings still have to be disposed of safely, not necessarily an easy task in large quantity. There is also limited capacity for mechanical cleaning of quinoa in the Andean region: one of the few adequately functioning plants was developed by the multinational company Nestlé and was purchased by a small private company in Ecuador called Inagrofa (see page 108).

Typically, quinoa which is sold in the local market makes a long journey to urban centres. A chain of intermediaries buys and sells increasingly large quantities of quinoa at area, regional and finally national levels. Eventually, in urban centres, the quinoa is split into small amounts for sale to the final consumer.[17] The chain has many links: transport costs and intermediaries' margins may make up 70–80 per cent of the final price. The mixing of grain from a large number of farmers, from different regions, means that any semblance of quality control is lost along the way. Even if a farmer produces good-quality quinoa, and cleans it of grit, stones and debris, by the time it reaches the consumer it has been mixed with poorer-quality grain. In these circumstances, there is little incentive to produce high-quality quinoa.[18]

The lack of quality control has been partly responsible for the decline in consumption of quinoa nationally. A survey of consumers in six provinces of Peru suggested that, although people were aware of the high nutritional value of quinoa, it contained an off-putting amount of impurities.[15] Urban housewives, increasingly themselves part of the labour market, who purchase dirty quinoa in the market, may not have enough time or access to clean water for further washing. Cleaning and cooking are made more difficult in a food which is already relatively expensive, especially for the poorest households, who are the largest urban consumers.[8]

As populations of the Andean countries become increasingly urbanized and linked to the market, the urban poor have tended to move away from consuming quinoa, and purchase products that are easier to prepare and which are of a more consistent quality, cheaper and less nutritious, such as pasta and rice.[9] For example, at 1999 prices a Bolivian farmer who sold 1 kg of quinoa, without the laborious task of removing the saponin, could buy about 1.8 kg of pasta ready to cook.[19] Not only does this price differential push urban consumers away from consumption of quinoa, it may even provide an incentive for farmers to turn away from eating quinoa and instead sell the quinoa for export, and use the income to buy cheaper, easier but less nutritious foods.

The quinoa which is sold to processors for the industrial removal of the saponins tends to have a shorter chain to market. The quinoa is processed, packed and passed direct to the final distributor. Quinoa sold in supermarkets and subject to quality controls is of better quality. It arrives already cleaned of saponins and impurities, neatly packaged. Ready to eat in 20 minutes, this offers a healthy meal to those who can afford supermarket prices. Although this quinoa is clean and convenient, the price is considerably higher than the subsidized wheat products available, augmented by costs of processing, marketing and in some cases scarcity of supply.[13] The relatively high price puts it beyond the reach of the low-to-middle classes who make up the majority of the urban population.

The picture may appear bleak for quinoa, but the prospects are brighter. A number of researchers and development practitioners, recognizing quinoa's unfulfilled contribution to food security, are working to increase production and national consumption. People know quinoa is good for them: making it accessible and convenient for them, while at the same time providing adequate incomes to farmers, is the challenge that has been taken up by these projects. And it seems that it is a challenge that is being met: in the Andean region, production has risen by 50 per cent over the past five years.[6] This is the result of an increase in the area planted and a modest increase in yields per hectare. Production has been geared for both domestic consumption and the export market.

Focusing on the domestic market

CIRNMA: making the national market work for farmers

One of the many NGOs and companies working to improve quinoa producers' access to markets is the Centro de Investigación de Recursos Naturales y Medio Ambiente (CIRNMA). Based in Puno, Peru, CIRNMA works with about 800 smallholder farmers producing quinoa on some 420 hectares of land. CIRNMA's activities are directed from the half-finished office in Puno, overlooking the turquoise waters of Lake Titicaca. Here, facilities are gradually being installed for mechanical cleaning of quinoa, next door to the women's co-operative producing knitwear for export. The mechanical de-bittering will help add value to farmers' produce, diversifying their market options and improving quinoa's appeal to consumers. As Roberto Valdivia, the energetic president of CIRNMA, showed us around the developing facilities, he explained a little about their programme.

To date, CIRNMA's activities have focused largely on facilitating farmers' access to the national market for quinoa. Good seed and technical assistance have helped farmers obtain yields of 700–1400kg/ha, which considerably exceed the average for the area of only 500kg/ha.[15] The use of consistent seed varieties and quality control have ensured that the quinoa produced is of a high quality.

CIRNMA has also worked to assist in the marketing of the quinoa, through a variety of channels. Market outlets have been sought by directly approaching wholesalers in the capital, Lima, thereby avoiding the long chain of intermediaries normally faced by farmers, and allowing better control of the quality of the final product. Assistance is also provided to small processing plants in the form of credit for modernization as well as technical and business advice; direct links are fostered between farmers and processors by arranging field visits; and processors are helped to develop new and more attractive ways of packaging their products to appeal to urban consumers. CIRNMA also acts as an agent for the smallholder farmers, bringing together adequate quantities of quinoa to allow them to tender for contracts to supply the national and regional food programmes.[15]

In addition to the local market, CIRNMA is considering the development of international markets for locally produced quinoa. In common with other exporters, CIRNMA's small farmers are faced with the challenges of producing adequate quantity, quality and consistency of quinoa. One buyer in Canada showed strong interest in buying quinoa through CIRNMA but required 20 tonnes per month, a quantity which they could not consistently supply with high-quality, clean grain. This is a target to build up to, not something that can be supplied overnight, Roberto pointed out. For now, the focus is on the domestic market where the demand for quinoa has grown as a result of government-supported food programmes.

PRONAA: the Government Food Programme in Peru

Since 1994, the government of Peru has authorized the national food assistance programme, Programa Nacional de Apoyo Alimentaria (PRONAA), to purchase certain agricultural products direct from farmers. Among these products is quinoa, as well as a number of other native Andean grains. The state has become one of the main buyers of native crops in Peru, leading to an increase in the area under their cultivation.

In the early 1970s, only about 14 000 hectares was planted in Peru with quinoa; by 2000, this had risen to almost 30 000 hectares. The biggest increase came between 1996 and 2000, when the area planted rose from about 18 000 to 30 000 hectares. Part of the extra incentive to grow quinoa has come from its use in the provision of school breakfasts and for the *Comedores Populares* (popular canteens) run by the government food programme.

Between 1990 and 1995, the school breakfast programme was based largely on wheat, of which 55–65 per cent was imported. The cost was calculated at approximately US$0.21 per meal. Since 1997, more emphasis has been given to the use of national inputs to the programme, which now account for 70–80 per cent of ingredients: quinoa and other native grains are among these inputs. In 1998, the cost was calculated at US$0.15 per meal and the number of school meals provided rose from 1.45 to 2 million between the period 1990–95 and 1997.[20]

A national food programme, with a deliberate policy of support to national farmers can provide a low-cost, dual function support to food security. On the one hand, farmers benefit from a market for their produce and do not have to compete with subsidized imports such as wheat. On the other hand, some of the most vulnerable sections of the population – children and women – receive good-quality, basic nutrition.

The PRONAA programme inevitably has impacts on other quinoa users and processors. As Roberto Valdivia, president of CIRNMA explained, PRONAA requires good-quality quinoa from farmers, and offers a high price of about US$0.60/kg. Although CIRNMA has tendered for some PRONAA contracts, they also supply other parts of the market at lower commercial prices. The price offered to farmers by PRONAA exceeds the price CIRNMA can afford to pay – approximately US$0.43/kg. Farmers are aware of the price being offered by PRONAA and are reluctant to sell to another buyer for a lower price, even though the food programme cannot buy all their production.

CIRNMA, which is trying to develop other markets for quinoa, cannot afford to compete with PRONAA by offering farmers anywhere near US$0.60/kg. This also affects the development of an export market: overseas buyers demand a regular supply of quinoa, which CIRNMA cannot guarantee if farmers periodically withhold their produce in the hope of extracting a higher price. Hence, while PRONAA has been successful in promoting the production and consumption of quinoa in Peru, it may be jeopardizing other efforts, such as CIRNMA's, to involve Peruvian farmers in the production of quinoa for sale in local commercial markets or for export.

The other critical question is what happens if government-funded initiatives such as PRONAA are discontinued in the future. If this were the case, alternative markets for quinoa would be needed. One such alternative is the demand for quinoa in Europe and the USA.

An Andean grain goes global

Meeting rich countries' demands

Quinoa has been discovered as a nutritious, versatile healthfood in the developed world. Markets have grown in the USA, Japan, Germany and other parts of Europe for products containing quinoa. The health food market in the northern countries offers a growing opportunity for quinoa produced in the Andean region, to be marketed as a healthy, environmentally-sound and possibly fair trade product.

A number of projects in Bolivia, Peru and Ecuador are attempting to do just this, although it may seem that there is an inherent contradiction between producing a highly nutritious grain in a region where undernutrition is widespread, and then exporting it to the rich developed world to sell in health food shops. In fact, there need not be any contradiction: many current research and development efforts can be seen as two-fold: to encourage the production and national consumption of quinoa within Andean countries and to encourage its production for export, providing a much-needed cash income to rural families.

The export market for quinoa from the Andean region is growing. For example, Bolivia's exports have risen from 378 tonnes in 1997 to about 2000 tonnes for the year 2000. However, internal markets in Bolivia and Peru are currently far more significant than the export markets. In Bolivia, exports in 2000 accounted for approximately 8 per cent of production;[16] in Peru, less than 1 per cent of production was exported in 1998.[21]

Increased sales for export should mean greater incomes for farmers living in some of the most extreme conditions in South America. Greater income, in theory at least, allows farmers to purchase the foods and other goods that they need, raising living standards and indirectly improving food security through more secure livelihoods. Nevertheless, projects that encourage farmers to produce quinoa for the market, either national or international, do not automatically have beneficial impacts on the nutritional status of the family. Much depends on whether any increase in income is spent on nutritious food, and how the increased quantity or quality of food is distributed among family members. In general, the more control women have over income, the more expenditure tends to be on food, health care and education. Involving and empowering women is an essential part of development.

One study in Ecuador, which examined the impacts of an agricultural development project to reintroduce quinoa in the highlands, concluded that it was not clear that quinoa cultivation necessarily improved the nutritional status of families, especially of women.[9] One of the problems was that, in the study, households that adopted quinoa production also had more land and grew a wide range of crops. The experimental design used in the study was such that no relationship between quinoa production and improved nutritional status could be established.

ANAPQUI in Bolivia

The Asociación Nacional de Productores de Quinua (ANAPQUI) represents about 5000 of the perhaps 20 000 quinoa producers in Bolivia. ANAPQUI has its head office in La Paz and seven regional offices in the departments of Oruro, Potosí and La Paz, each covering 20 or 30 communities. Farmers need to be affiliated to a local association to be part of ANAPQUI, ensuring that they are organized and therefore easier to reach, for both delivery of technical assistance and purchasing. ANAPQUI has a processing plant near Uyuni in Southern Bolivia, allowing them to de-bitter the quinoa and process it into quinoa flakes.

The Salar de Uyuni in southern Bolivia is the second largest salt lake in the world, and at almost 4000 metres altitude, it quite literally takes your breath away: a thick sheet of hard white salt that stretches to the horizon. Further south is a series of snow-capped volcanoes, where pink flamingos stalk the thermal lakes and barren, salt-encrusted soils. The area is raw, inhospitable and stunningly beautiful. Extraordinarily, and seemingly against all the odds, a number of villages are dotted around the landscape. On the outskirts of each village, walled fields have been constructed to keep out the foraging goats. Within the walled enclosures are patches of tall quinoa stalks, each with a head of ripening grains. This is where the best quinoa grows, *Quinua Real,* and it is the focus of Bolivian hopes for an expanding export market.

ANAPQUI's objective, explained Juan López, the organization's president, is to improve the living conditions of its member producers by paying a fair price for their quinoa. Increasingly, ANAPQUI is looking towards the relatively small but growing export market. In 1997 it absorbed only 1.4 per cent of Bolivia's quinoa production, rising to 4 per cent in 1999 and almost 8 per cent in 2000.[22] The increase is almost exponential and the figures do not include the substantial amount of quinoa which is smuggled out of Bolivia and sold in Peru and Ecuador as nationally produced.

In an attempt to ensure a stable livelihood for their producers, ANAPQUI usually offers a fixed price for the year, based on the previous year's price and an increase for inflation. The price is set before farmers sow the seed, which leaves ANAPQUI vulnerable to fluctuations in the free market price, caused in the main by the size of the harvest. At times it is difficult for ANAPQUI to compete with the larger private buyers, who have no fair trade element to their pricing.

ANAPQUI faced a difficult year in 2000. Average annual quinoa production in Bolivia between 1987 and 1993 was 22 000 tonnes;[23] an excellent year for quinoa in 2000 meant that production nationwide of over 40 000 tonnes was expected.[24] ANAPQUI faced a dilemma: the market price dropped sharply due to oversupply. Commercial buyers in the open market were offering about US$0.28/kg of quinoa, a good deal lower than the price ANAPQUI had promised to its participating farmers prior to the harvest. To abandon their producers in a bumper harvest year would be a set-back in building trust and expanding markets, but when even the international fair trade buyers requested a review of the price, ANAPQUI had no choice but to offer farmers less than they had been promised.

Demand for organic quinoa is increasing worldwide and it commands an international price some 10–15 per cent higher than conventional quinoa. The high altitude of the Bolivian altiplano means there are relatively few pests and diseases, making quinoa a good choice for organic production; further north, with increasing humidity, mildew becomes a greater problem. In this respect southern Bolivia has a natural competitive advantage over Peru and Ecuador. Many of the farmers who are affiliated to ANAPQUI have qualified for organic certification, ensuring that approximately 80 per cent of the association's production is organic. Recognizing the opportunities that this offers, ANAPQUI hopes to build a new processing plant in El Alto on the outskirts of La Paz in order to produce good-quality pasta and cookies based on quinoa for export.

What does ANAPQUI mean in terms of food security? The organization offers a link to national and international markets, provides technical assistance to farmers and access to processing. Together, ANAPQUI's farmers can produce enough quinoa to market it in quantity, thus meeting one of the key obstacles to securing a niche in export markets. Through its extension network, ANAPQUI can also provide adequate quality control to ensure it meets market requirements. Many farmers who produce quinoa for ANAPQUI have expanded their farms and some have mechanized their production. Quinoa has brought relative prosperity to the harsh and poor southern altiplano of Bolivia. This has allowed children to go to school and farmers to have an unprecedented level of prosperity. The fair price paid to farmers means that the extra income can be used to increase household food security.

Increased quinoa production has, however, also led to serious environmental problems. Mechanization and the expansion of production into marginal areas and lands previously used for grazing have contributed to severe soil erosion. In some areas, yields have fallen since 1990, caused by low rainfall, eroded soils and increasing pest problems.[4] ANAPQUI encourages farmers to return to less mechanized production methods on the traditional growing areas, particularly as part of its organic production programme, even though production costs may be higher.

As the harvest in 2000 showed, quinoa yields may fluctuate wildly depending on variation in conditions in the areas where it grows. It is difficult in the face of such uncertainty to develop a sustained supply of quinoa to meet market demands.[25] Under such circumstances it is also hard for an organization such as ANAPQUI to offer a fixed price to producers before knowing the level of the harvest and the consequent market price at harvest. On the other hand, the increasing market demand has undoubtedly contributed to higher living standards for many communities in the southern Altiplano areas of Bolivia. In a climate where little else will grow, quinoa provides an unparalleled economic opportunity for many small farmers who have few other options.

Escuelas Radiofónica Populares del Ecuador

In the highlands of Ecuador, the bustling town of Riobamba is a commercial centre for agriculture in the steep surrounding mountains and upland valleys. Radiofónica, a community radio station based here, is perhaps an unlikely candidate for a development organization. But when Juan Pérez explains the history of the station it becomes clear why they are developing one of the largest quinoa exporting networks in Ecuador.

Radiofónica started life as a basic education and literacy radio station some 40 years ago. Insufficient funds to finance the radio led them to start their own four-hectare farm in the late 1980s. They decided to focus on organic production. As Radiofónica started to broadcast about their own experiences of organic agriculture in the area, more and more people began to ask for advice and assistance. Without their own agricultural technical staff, this was difficult: poor advice based on their own limited experience might cause more harm than good. But once Radiofónica started to promote its own organic produce through trade fairs in Germany and Costa Rica, it became evident that there was an international demand for organic produce, which could be filled by small farmers around Riobamba.

Radiofónica's role has evolved to form the link to international markets for local quinoa producers. The aim is to improve the standard of living for the marginalized indigenous, mixed (*mestizo*) and urban populations, in an area where the average land holding is only 0.8 hectares and yearly income only about US$230. In 1997, Radiofónica received its first concrete order from the USA; they worked with 220 families to sow quinoa and harvest it in June and July 1998. By 1998, Radiofónica had secured funding from international donors: three years of funding in which to set up a self-sustaining quinoa production and export business. Suddenly quinoa became big business in Riobamba, and by 2002 they aimed to involve 4000 families in the production of 700 tonnes of quinoa. This would almost double Ecuador's current production of 938 tonnes per year.[16]

Radiofónica aims to expand its market from the USA into Europe, as well as trying other crops, such as the grain amaranto and the nutritious lupin seed. Participating farmers have been certified as organic producers. This is particularly important because many countries will accept only organically certified quinoa, especially as much of it is sold through health food stores.

As with ANAPQUI, Radiofónica sets its offer price for producers before sowing, but the margin within which they can vary it is defined. Each community that wants to be involved must provide a list of members and areas to be planted; Radiofónica provides the seed and some technical advice. The radio helps to promote quinoa, provide basic training and motivate people to join the programme. From each year's harvest, Radiofónica allocates a proportion for the farmers' food needs, a proportion for next year's seed and the rest for sale to Radiofónica at the price fixed prior to sowing. In this way, Radiofónica hopes to improve farmers' food security by providing a nutritious crop for home consumption and a cash return from export sales.

The washing and cleaning of the grain is done by Radiofónica. Although they buy the uncleaned quinoa from farmers for US$0.63/kg, they will also purchase clean quinoa from farmers at a better price of US$0.73/kg. As with ANAPQUI, Radiofónica can find themselves paying considerably more than the market price, in this case about US$0.43/kg. Radiofónica's cleaning of the quinoa is also a matter of concern to environmental groups, who claim the effluent from the processing plant is poisonous with saponins. It is an issue that is unlikely to go away, as Radiofónica doubled the capacity of its processing plant in 2000.

Despite the best efforts of Radiofónica's teams of dedicated extension agents, increasing quinoa production in line with predictions has not been easy. In 2002, only 490 of the target 700 tonnes production was achieved. In 1999 and again in 2000, the weather conspired to confound production in the harvest. Planting was late in some villages under Radiofónica's scheme in 1999, as some villages were slow to organize into groups, and extension teams did not manage to get out into the field early enough for sowing. Climatic factors played a part in low production in 2000: high rainfall early in the growing cycle, frosts, little sun to help ripening, and strong winds may all have had an effect. In 1999, 1 kg of seed produced 30–40 kg of quinoa at harvest; normally production of 100 kg would be expected, rising to 200 kg in some areas.

Radiofónica's extension agents are also learning on the job. We stand around the patch of quinoa in the village of Guantug near Riobamba and the farmers and extension agents discuss why the grain is not growing as well as had been expected: perhaps it was planted too high up and is too exposed to the winds; perhaps the seed was poor quality or the soil too heavy; perhaps a different variety of quinoa would be more suited to the conditions in Guantug? 'Next year you should try further down the hill where there is less frost and sandier soil, and fewer problems with flooding', the extension agents suggest. But some of the farmers are demoralized by their lack of success, and organizing them into a group for planting more quinoa is difficult.

We wait for people to gather in the village hall in Guantug for a talk about growing organic quinoa. Somewhat reluctantly, people file in: tomorrow is market day in the town of Guamote and people need to harvest their onions. Following the meeting, the villagers offer us lunch in the school room: steaming plates of rice, spaghetti and tinned sardines are carried in. It appears that locally produced foods are still considered inappropriate for visitors.

Organization of the communities into groups of at least 20 people is important to Radiofónica. This minimum group size makes their training and extension visits to remote villages cost-effective, as well as facilitating collection of the harvest. Furthermore, the scheme is more likely to be sustainable in the long run if the farmers are organized. Where fewer than 20 people are interested, advice and seed may be provided on an occasional basis, but Radiofónica makes no commitment to provide regular assistance.

The project has three years in which to establish itself. Extension workers are enrolling farmers as fast as possible to meet the target numbers of people and communities predicted for the project, and by which the funders will judge the success of the project at the end of the three years. By necessity, extension techniques are traditional and top-down: lack of time, long distances between communities and a large number of communities per extension team mean that the extension agents do not have enough time to develop the experimentation and management abilities of farmers in a more participatory way. Radiofónica is constrained by the three-year project cycle set by the donors.

Although more participatory extension techniques would lead to greater farmer empowerment, they take time and resources that are not always available. In the long term, this may make the project and its contribution to farmers' livelihoods less sustainable. We return to the issue of farmer empowerment in Chapter 10, Conclusions: the need for aid and trade.

The export market: increased income, increased risk?

Diversity and the organic conundrums

The experiences of CIRNMA and ANAPQUI have illustrated some of the problems of growing quinoa for export, especially with respect to maintaining the quality and quantity of production. Quinoa is generally not irrigated and is susceptible to climatic variation, particularly during the early stages of germination and growth, and in the final stages when the grain is ripening on the plant. Depending on conditions, yields can vary between years by almost 100 per cent.

The intensification of production methods, the focus on monocultures of improved varieties, expansion to marginal areas, and perhaps even the move to organic production, may in themselves increase risks for farmers and threaten their livelihood security in the longer term. For many farmers, diversity of quinoa is intricately linked to food security. In the Bolivian altiplano, farmers traditionally cultivate three or four varieties of quinoa, which include some with high productivity in good years, and others with high resistance to frosts, pests and other environmental pressures that yield a minimum production even in a bad year.[26]

Quinoa fulfils very different roles, with a focus either on production for sale or on subsistence production for home consumption. Both may be fundamentally important to farmers' livelihoods, but their needs are likely to be different. With the demands of quality and quantity imposed by the market requiring careful consideration from the start, it is no longer optimal to grow a crop for home consumption, sending any excess to market. Farmers now need to consider from the outset market requirements for type, quality, timing, and so on.[27] In the past, farmers have often been excluded from conservation and research projects. As a result, markets, research projects and biodiversity conservation initiatives may neglect farmers' environmental and social constraints and opportunities.[26]

Commercial production of quinoa often requires farmers to produce a single variety of quinoa, of a type that is generally large seeded, white and often low in saponins. Low saponin levels, however, make quinoa more susceptible to pest damage. Farmers are, therefore, encouraged to cultivate particular quinoa varieties with good market value, while native varieties are lost, potentially increasing the social and ecological vulnerability of rural communities. The more farmers rely on a single variety of quinoa, the higher the risk they take of losing their crop to pests and erratic climatic factors.

The focus on production for the export market may increase farmers' income, but it is also likely to increase their risks. This is particularly the case when the demand in the USA and Europe is for organic quinoa. In this context, there is an apparent contradiction for farmers who are trying to produce quinoa for the organic market as well as producing other crops as part of their normal agricultural system.

Farmers often reduce pest problems and achieve greater food security by crop rotation and diversification. However, rotating quinoa with potatoes one year, followed by barley and then back to quinoa, may well compromise the organic status of the quinoa. While some pest and disease problems in potatoes can be partly managed by rotation, others are extremely difficult to control without chemical applications. In Ecuador's relatively humid climate, fungal diseases such as late blight make organic potato production unrealistic on a commercial scale. Hence, while the quinoa itself may be grown organically, it would not pass a certification assessment if it was grown on a plot of land that had, one or two years previously, been sown with potatoes and treated with chemicals.

Hence, rather than being well-suited to small farmers' conditions, organic farming of quinoa for the export market may in fact exclude them. It is a challenge that research institutions are aware they need to address: how can organic quinoa be produced within a sustainable farming system, rather than as a stand-alone crop?[28]

There is undoubtedly a compromise between maintaining a diverse production system (including quinoa) for food security at home and the demands of organic quinoa production for the external market. This raises the fundamental questions as to whether a choice has to be made between these two approaches and, if so, should development efforts be targeted at quinoa production for the export market or quinoa production for national consumption? And if the focus is the export market, how secure is it?

The case of Quinova: could increased world demand bypass Andean farmers?

At the University of Westminster in London, a research team directed by Dr John Hedger has come up with an interesting scientific discovery. Hedger and his team have discovered a means of making a fermented quinoa product, which they have named 'quinova'. Currently at a pilot stage, they are trying to find a commercial backer for the process, with the prospect of producing a rival for the vegetarian staples of 'tofu' and 'quorn', with high levels of protein derived from the quinoa. If 'quinova' took off, the international market for good-quality, organic quinoa might expand rapidly, as processed quinoa could be included in a wide variety of processed foods.

It is unclear whether Andean farmers would benefit from a huge increase in demand sparked by quinova. As John Hedger points out, quinoa entering the fermentation process used for producing 'quinova' must be of consistently good quality. It needs to have been harvested at the right time, to be a consistent variety with a low saponin content and to be clean and free of debris. Working with small farmers in the Andes presents problems in controlling all these aspects: farmers often prefer to use their own varieties of quinoa, from seed collected the previous year; traditional quinoa varieties mature at different rates within one seed head, so harvest tends to produce a mixture of ripe and immature grains, and strict control needs to be exercised over the cleaning of the grains post-harvest. In addition to these problems, productivity of quinoa in the Andes is relatively low, with production levels often 0.5–1t/ha. When quinoa was grown on a trial basis in Portugal for the quinova processing, productivity was around 5t/ha, of clean, consistent, cheap grain.

Hedger, who has worked in Ecuador and whose sympathies lie with the Andean farmers, believes that the crop has potential as part of an agricultural diversification programme within the European Union. Research trials are underway to test a number of varieties of quinoa under European conditions.[29] Fast and uniform maturation as well as high yields are desirable for quinoa destined to be grown in Europe: conventional plant breeding has not yet produced the appropriate variety for commercial production but is not an unlikely development.

Added to this are problems of quality control in the production process for quinova, which requires careful control of microbial contamination during the fermentation and packing processes. This may be seen to be more easily controlled in the more developed countries. Recent advances in pasteurization techniques do, however, allow the quinova to be stored and transported, which enhances the potential to process quinoa in South America and transport it to markets in developed countries. In the event that quinova becomes a widely used product, it remains unclear whether the demand for quinoa will be met by smallholder farmers in the Andes or by large-scale production by European farmers.

Protecting the genetic heritage

The contribution of quinoa to food security in the Andes (and worldwide) is also dependent on local people's ownership of the genetic property rights of quinoa, the enormous variable pool of genes that allows quinoa to grow in such a diverse range of conditions. At the Universidad Nacional del Altiplano in Puno, Peru, Dr Angel Mujica is directing an international trial supported by the FAO, to compare the growth of 24 varieties of quinoa in experiments repeated in 25 countries. The objectives of the trial are to provide researchers with new varieties of quinoa which may be suited to marginal areas other than those found in the Andes, to develop management techniques, and to develop inter-institutional co-operation between research agencies in Europe and those in North and South America.

This type of research is much needed, but there is also the need for safe-guards to avoid the type of unscrupulous behaviour periodically demonstrated by research organizations. In October 1996, Colorado State University (CSU), which had been co-operating with the Bolivian research institute PROINPA on the collection of quinoa seed in Bolivia, took out a patent called the 'Apelawa patent' (USA Patent No. 5,304,718).[26]

The patent was named after Apelawa village on Lake Titicaca, where CSU first collected the seed samples. It covered a method of hybridizing quinoa which CSU claimed to have invented, but which also covered another 43 traditional varieties of quinoa found throughout the Andes. Potentially, Andean exports of quinoa to the USA and Europe were threatened by enforcement of this patent, and even local production might have been affected. After a 14-month struggle by ANAPQUI, supported by the Rural Advancement Foundation International (RAFI), a USA-based NGO, and Oxfam, CSU quietly allowed the patent to lapse in 1998.[30]

In this instance, the piracy of Bolivian farmers' traditional heritage has been defeated. But farmers may now be more suspicious and reluctant to work with researchers who wish to experiment, improve and work with 'their' quinoa varieties. The possibilities for genuine development may have been narrowed by the action of one international partner. If quinoa is to play a role in the food security of the Andean countries, and particularly in an export market for Andean producers, the patent taken out by CSU could have had a potentially devastating effect. There is a growing international demand for regulation of this type of bio-piracy.[31]

Ways forward for an ancient grain

Focusing on the national market

Quinoa has been rescued over the past two decades from a slow slide into extinction. Much research and extension work has been directed at increasing the area of quinoa, both to provide a nutritious food crop for domestic consumption, and as income for farm families from the sale of quinoa, for both the national and international markets. Given the propensity of export niche markets to be rather fickle, several researchers believe that a focus on the development of the national market is the first priority, with sales on the international market being a secondary objective.[14] Their vision is increasingly shared by the private sector: one example of this is the Ecuadorian company Inagrofa.

Inagrofa: a business with development aspirations

Rodrigo Aroyo is a businessman in Quito, the capital of Ecuador. He is urbane, casually dressed and speaks fluent English. His business interests cover a range of commodities: when we met him he had just returned from a trip to China to learn how to make parquet flooring from Ecuador's abundant bamboo supplies. For many years now Rodrigo's company, Inagrofa, has also been buying and selling quinoa.

It was in 1987 that the Quito businessman sold his first two tonnes of quinoa to Germany, securing a niche, he says, on a health food market which has been developing for the past 20 years. The Swiss-based multinational Nestlé also saw this market opportunity and spent considerable sums of money – at one stage about 60 per cent of its annual research and development budget in Ecuador – on quinoa. For a variety of reasons, Nestlé dropped out of the market in 1997, and Rodrigo bought their mechanical processing plant. There is little doubt that this cleaning system is better for the environment than processing which relies on washing the grains.

Between 1987 and 1994, Inagrofa sold quinoa to both the USA and Germany, but with increasing concerns among consumers in the developed world about health and the environment, the market began to demand organic quinoa. Rodrigo was not in a position to supply certified organic quinoa and his contract lapsed.

For the past few years Rodrigo's company has increasingly focused on the national market in Ecuador, with small exports to Colombia. He now sells 400–500 tonnes of packaged quinoa a year on the national market. Since 2000, the company has again been in a position to sell on the international market because it now has access to organic quinoa. Rodrigo buys quinoa from about 35 small to medium-scale producers in Ecuador, some of whom are organic farmers, and for whom he has arranged certification. The cost of the certification is split between farmers and the company, with Inagrofa bearing the largest part.

For export-quality organic quinoa, Rodrigo needs good-quality production and he needs to be able to predict the quantities available each year. Yields of quinoa are highly variable; production fluctuates wildly between good and bad years, as evidenced by the problems of a 'good' year facing ANAPQUI in Bolivia. Excess rain or drought at the wrong time will severely affect the harvest. Rodrigo explains that international buyers check the exporter's stock to ensure that they have sufficient stores to assure the buyer of consistent supply: they will require the exporter to have at least 50 per cent of expected production in store, so that there is a fall-back in the event of a disastrous harvest. The implication for the small-scale exporter is the need for credit, to buy up sufficient supply and store it as a guarantee against a poor harvest, as well as for financing the organic certification of the farmers. These are both costs that the national market route can avoid, but until recently this showed little sign of growth in Ecuador.

With the recent development of the Ecuaquinua project (see page 113), however, the national market now also looks set to grow. And as the project gets underway, the opportunities to expand exports regionally to Colombia and beyond to the USA or Europe, are expected to fuel a second phase to the project.

Improving the grain

There are a number of barriers to increasing the local consumption of quinoa in the Andean countries. Quinoa is relatively expensive in the markets. It is seen by consumers as poor quality, it is inconvenient to prepare, and it maintains something of a third-class image. If the national consumption of quinoa is to be increased, as well as the potential to export, the issues of quality, processing, image and market access need to be addressed. This is precisely where research, extension and marketing expertise is being directed.

The Patacayama research station sits on the bleak space of the northern Bolivian Altiplano, just outside La Paz. The facilities are shared between the Bolivian State University of San Andrés, and PROINPA. Alejandro Bonifacio, a researcher with PROINPA, shows us their collection of quinoa seed from all over Bolivia: tiny seeds stored in neat plastic tubes with red stoppers. With over 2700 different seed samples, this represents one of the largest collections of quinoa in the world. These samples can be used for breeding improved types of quinoa: PROINPA has put much effort into developing varieties with larger, sweet grains, or white grains, that are desired by the export market. Recently, more effort has been put into developing faster-maturing (precocious) plants, prompted by shorter rainy seasons.

Exporters are particular about the quality of the grain they will buy: large, white grains are the preferred type. While the national market may be more tolerant of a range of different grains, only in some specialist markets do darker grains, and even wild varieties, find a use. Sweet quinoa offers the added advantage that it can be cleaned mechanically, though this advantage is offset by the greater losses to birds, which are attracted to the sweet grains. Consistency of ripening is a problem, and some of the improved varieties have been bred to ensure that all the grains on a plant develop at the same pace. Differences in resistance to pests and diseases, drought, salinity and frost can also be bred into improved varieties. Traditional plant breeding for improved varieties can address many of these issues, though a lack of understanding of the genetic markers that would allow farmers and scientists to recognize easily the different varieties makes breeding quinoa particularly complicated.

In part because quinoa has been a forgotten, third-class crop, it was only recently that work on developing improved varieties has really got under way. This partly explains why the yields are so low and production costs relatively high in comparison to better-known and more highly 'improved' crops such as wheat and barley. And during the scientific process of developing improved varieties, sometimes farmers' real needs have been forgotten, says Alejandro Bonifacio. Growing sweet, white grains may not be farmers' top priority, if they really need varieties that will produce in extreme environmental conditions of drought, salinity and low temperatures.

Government programmes to promote large, sweet, white grains to farmers were rejected, says Alejandro, because birds are attracted by the sweet grains and losses were too high. Often too, researchers have been poor at disseminating the results of their research: improved varieties may be available at the research station where they were produced, but unless they are distributed through markets or local networks, farmers may not know they exist or see any benefit in planting them.

Bringing quinoa to a more prominent position in a national food security role and as a high-quality export crop, requires grain of a consistent variety and of consistent quality. Plant breeding techniques can help achieve this potential if they are designed in such a way as to make them accessible and appropriate to the small farmers who need to use the new varieties. In addition, researchers stress that new uses need be found for traditional varieties, as increasing markets for certain varieties of quinoa are leading to the genetic erosion of traditional varieties. It is important for research to be appropriate, not only to the demands of the high-profile export market but also the local market, and that the research results should be appropriate to farmers' conditions.

A major focus of research on quinoa in recent years has been the improvement in productivity needed to ensure locally produced quinoa becomes more efficient and competitive, and grows in more marginal sites. Productivity of quinoa has remained relatively low, despite many years of work on crop improvement. Average yields in Bolivia have risen slightly during the 1990s from 0.4t/ha to 0.64t/ha, while in Peru they have risen from similar levels in 1990 to 0.9t/ha by 1999.[32] In theory, it should be feasible to increase yields considerably.

The use of improved varieties of seed that mature faster, have better resistance to pests and diseases, drought, salinity and low temperatures, has been shown in experimental sites to improve yields. Similarly, different agricultural practices may improve productivity. Experiments in Peru commonly resulted in yields of 2–4t/ha and in one case of 6.6t/ha.[21] Ensuring that these technologies are really appropriate for farmers, and within their capabilities to put into practice, as well as the mechanics of providing the know-how to farmers, is a challenge in itself. But this research is essential for helping farmers produce better-quality grain, improving yields and, in theory at least, increasing returns.

Post-harvest management

It is not only improvements in the agricultural part of the process that are needed to improve the profitability of quinoa for farmers and its desirability for consumers. Good-quality grain can be spoiled by its post-harvest management. Perhaps bigger gains can be made through improvements to the post-harvest processing and a marketing strategy that focuses on fulfilling the needs of the national market.

Much of the post-harvest processing of quinoa is carried out by traditional methods. Once harvested, quinoa is dried for one to two weeks, threshed to separate the grains from the stalk, winnowed to remove impurities, dried again in the field for several days, stored and finally de-bittered. Each of these processes, frequently carried out by hand or using animals, involves losses of significant amounts of harvested grain. Some producers are beginning to mechanize these processes, but these technologies are often justified only on a larger scale. Mechanized harvesting, for example, is worthwhile only on areas greater than 10 hectares.[14] While farmers in southern Bolivia may be included in this category, it is beyond the means of individual small farmers of the northern Altiplano.

CIRNMA in Puno, in Peru, estimates that post-harvest losses may amount to more than 40 per cent of the total harvest, compared to losses of between 10 and 37 per cent for cereals.[14] The use of manual processing increases losses at every stage and lowers the quality of the product reaching the market. Poorly dried quinoa increases the incidence of mould and insects; badly threshed grain tends to break and is susceptible to insect attack; poor storage conditions encourage mould, insects and rodents. Field drying leads to considerable contamination from rats. Threshing the quinoa immediately after harvest in the field, and drying it afterwards in a clean location significantly improves quality, but requires facilities. It is difficult to produce consistently good-quality, clean quinoa without adequate technology and management.

Organizations like CIRNMA are working hard to improve the post-harvest management of quinoa by providing technical and business assistance to small rural processing industries, providing credit for machinery and helping small companies to improve the presentation of their products.[15] This assistance is particularly important for local companies that wish to supply PRONAA, the national food programme in Peru, which is required to ensure certain standards are met.

A better image, a better way to market

Surveys of quinoa consumption, particularly in the cities of Peru, reveal that it is regarded as one of the most nutritious and natural foods available.[15] It is also regarded as dirty, containing large amounts of stones and grit, and therefore is considered unhealthy. It is not cheap, or easy to prepare, nor is it always available. The grain has intrinsic qualities on which its market appeal can be built, but there are significant disadvantages to its use which must be overcome.

About 92 per cent of quinoa sold in urban areas in Peru is bought loose in the market. It is generally dirty and although de-bittered, it needs to be cleaned of impurities after purchase. The challenge to improving the market appeal of quinoa, is to present it as a clean, washed product, ready to use. Moving to such a ready-packaged presentation of the product has implications for the part of the population that is targeted. Sales of clean, relatively expensive grain, conveniently packaged and easy to prepare need to be focused on the richer strata of Andean society.[15]

One of the difficulties facing quinoa in the Andes is that the urban rich who can afford quinoa are not its traditional consumers. Very low-income families are almost four times as likely to consume quinoa daily as high-income families.[8] The crop still maintains something of its third-class food status. Changes in the image of quinoa are being brought about in the urban population through promotion of recipes, programmes on television and through the fact that quinoa has become an export crop, symbol of wealth and health. Lima, for example, now supports a restaurant in the expensive Miraflores District which specializes in high-quality local produce such as quinoa. There is some evidence that as quinoa begins to be seen as a food favoured by middle-class Andean families, the urban poor will mimic their eating habits and quinoa consumption will increase. But this takes time, and in order to ensure that quinoa does contribute more to food security in the short term, the focus needs to be on providing nutritious food direct to those who cannot afford to buy it.

Food security revisited

Pulled back from the edge of extinction, quinoa is promoted as both a means of promoting food security at home and generating export earnings abroad. Quinoa does offer a high-quality protein source in the diet, and if the national consumption of quinoa is to be increased the issues of quality, processing, image and market access need to continue to be addressed.

However, quinoa can be made to contribute more rapidly to food security in the Andean region. The example of PRONAA in Peru demonstrates that production and consumption can be significantly increased as part of a government-sponsored food programme. Since 1997, companies in Peru that supply the various food programmes have been encouraged, or required, to include native Andean foods in the meals they supply. The programme has led to a sharp increase in the area of quinoa planted and to its use in the food support programmes.

The beneficial impact of a PRONAA-like programme has been recognized by other governments, development workers and some private companies in the region. A new project in Ecuador proposes to follow a similar dual purpose path, utilizing quinoa as part of a food support programme, whilst strengthening production, processing and marketing capability among small producers. Quinoa is not widely produced in Ecuador: in 2000, only 938 tonnes of quinoa were produced in the country, compared with some 25 000 tonnes in Bolivia and 30 000 tonnes in Peru.[16] The new project, *El Proyecto Nacional de Quinua en Ecuador* (Equaquinua), has the backing of the World Food Programme, along with NGOs, international and national research bodies and private companies including Inagrofa.

The project aims to improve quinoa production to provide simultaneously an income to poor rural farmers in the Andes, and to improve nutrition through inclusion of quinoa in the World Food Programme's School

Breakfast programme. The World Food Programme can guarantee a market of 3000 tonnes per year for the first five years. At present, faced with lack of supply in Ecuador, the World Food Programme needs to import quinoa from Bolivia. The project hopes to build on this opportunity to improve Ecuadorian farmers' productivity and profitability, as well as improving the quality of the quinoa produced. Over the longer term, it is hoped to build on this capacity, promoting the consumption of quinoa nationally and perhaps developing regional and international markets for Ecuadorian quinoa. The contribution of quinoa to food security looks set to grow and is likely to continue to do so in the context of a policy environment which supports public and private interventions in quinoa production, processing and marketing.

CHAPTER 6

Coca eradication and alternative development

Introduction

CARMEN SPREADS OUT the small, pale-green coca leaves on the slate floor of the drying area known as a *cachi*. In the distance behind the adobe walls surrounding the yard, are the steep treeless hillsides dotted with small coca fields where the half-metre tall coca plants are grown densely on carefully constructed terraces. We are in the Yungas, one of two coca-growing areas in Bolivia. Coca-growing in the Yungas is legal: the government allows farmers to cultivate 12 000 hectares of coca for traditional uses such as chewing the leaves and drinking coca tea. Coca is harvested three or four times per year and Carmen is drying the most recently harvested leaves in the sun prior to taking them to the legal coca market in La Paz. Carmen and her neighbours are well aware that the Bolivian authorities, under pressure from the USA government and the EU, are seeking to reduce the area of coca in the Yungas. They have every reason to be concerned about the impact on their livelihoods of any coca eradication campaign.

Mention coca and most people will think of Colombia, cocaine, drug barons and narco-terrorists. However, the USA and EU-supported *Plan Colombia* is only the latest phase in the long-running war on drugs in Latin America. What is less well known is that over the past decade coca eradication and alternative development have been enthusiastically pursued in the Chapare, Bolivia's second coca-growing region, and in the Quillabamba region in Peru.

Unlike the Yungas, coca-growing is illegal in these two regions. A major focus of this 'alternative development' is the promotion of licit agricultural crops and the provision of improved road and farming infrastructure, as well as marketing skills for farmer associations. Assistance is directed at replacing family incomes derived from coca with incomes generated by the sale of licit agricultural products to national and international markets.

While few would deny that the Bolivian government has been successful in eradicating coca in the Chapare – coca was officially eradicated from the region at the end of 2000 – the success of the alternative development programme, in terms of the social and economic impact on ex-coca growers, is questionable. Despite some success stories, many farmers have not seen the benefits of alternative development that they had been led to expect. They complain about the lack of markets for their produce, oversupply, price fluctuations, and the lack of reliable transport. These are the classic problems faced by farmers seeking to exploit local, national and global markets.

This chapter examines the importance of coca cultivation in the Andes. It looks at the history and mixed results of coca eradication and alternative development in the Chapare. The Chapare demonstrates the challenge of 'persuading' farmers to switch to crops that are very unlikely to be as profitable as coca and the need for considerable donor funding and farmer participation. Lastly, alternative approaches are discussed, ones that if followed in the Yungas and other parts of the Andes, may well avoid some of the social and economic turmoil engendered by the coca eradication and alternative development programme in the Chapare.

A long history

Coca's cultural roots

Coca (*Erythroxylon coca*) is a robust shrub that flourishes in the eastern lowlands of the Andes where the sunny climate and acidic soil conditions increase its alkaloid content.[1] Although the coca leaf is the source of cocaine, this is a relatively recent development. Chewing coca and drinking coca tea have a very different effect from using the refined powder and there is no evidence that it is harmful. Coca acts as a mild stimulant and alleviates the effects of altitude sickness, tiredness and hunger. It enables people to walk long distances and work long hours. It has also been a part of Andean culture for centuries.[2]

During the pre-Columbian era, coca played an important role in the region's barter economy. After the arrival of the Spanish conquistadors, the Catholic Church identified the consumption of coca as a pernicious and pagan custom. This condemnation did not, however, prevent the Church from collecting a 10 per cent tax on its sale.[1]

Coca leaves are still traditionally chewed by indigenous people from the Kogi and Arhuaco people in the Sierra Nevada de Santa Marta in northern Colombia[3] to as far south as northern Argentina.[4] In Bolivia, chewing coca is ubiquitous. For example, the miners working in the 500-year-old mines at Potosí chew coca as they toil in medieval conditions. Coca is so important to them that offerings of the leaf are made to statues of their gods that are found deep inside the mineral-rich mountain at over 4000 metres above sea level. In this context, coca eradication campaigns are often seen as an assault on Andean culture.[5]

Migration and coca in the Chapare, Bolivia

The Chapare, east of the capital La Paz, lies in the sub-humid tropics at the foot of the eastern range of the Andes. At approximately 150 metres above sea level, it has an area of about 2.5 million hectares and annual rainfall ranges from 4000 to 7000 mm. After the Second World War, governments in Peru, Bolivia and Colombia identified the Amazon basin as an area that could absorb population groups and alleviate land pressures in the highland areas. In the case of Bolivia, thousands of highland farmers migrated to the Chapare, a process exacerbated by the agrarian reforms of the early 1950s.[6] However, soils in the area are relatively poor with only about 32 per cent of the area suitable for permanent agriculture.[7] Therefore, following the first wave of migration to the area, introduced crops such as coffee and cocoa did not bring the benefits originally expected.

At the beginning of the 1980s, the Bolivian tin industry collapsed, its economy foundered, and unemployment soared. Impoverished farmers and ex-miners migrated from areas such as Potosí in the highlands to the Chapare in a second wave of migration. Between 1981 and 1985, the population in the Chapare rose from 80 000 to 120 000. The second wave of migration to the Chapare coincided with a boom in the international market for cocaine.[8] Coca has been cultivated in the Chapare for centuries[9] but in the late twentieth century, the combination of inward migration and burgeoning demand for cocaine led to a rapid increase in the area planted with coca. Coca was also an attractive crop because it could be grown relatively easily by ex-miners who had little experience of lowland agriculture.

Unlike the introduced crop species such as coffee, coca is well-suited to the Chapare. Coca does not require fertilizer, it suffers from few pest problems, it grows well in impoverished soils, it can be harvested three or four times a year, it is easy to transport and despite price fluctuations it can bring in a good reliable income.[10] The second wave of migration to the Chapare led to the colonization of land that was not suited for permanent agriculture. In this context, coca became the one crop that enabled farmers to escape abject poverty, and its cultivation was a rational choice in the face of economic collapse.[11]

While the majority of the 12 000 hectares of coca grown in the Yungas region is used for traditional purposes, most of the coca from the Chapare was processed into cocaine paste and taken to Colombia to be further refined and then sold abroad. Moreover, the dollars brought in by drug trafficking in the Chapare were welcomed by the Bolivian central bank in order to ease the foreign exchange shortage in the country. By 1989, the area of coca cultivation in Bolivia peaked at 52 900 hectares,[12] of which approximately 41 000 hectares were in the Chapare.

Other farmers in the Andean region had also been busy reacting to the market forces of supply and demand. The increased demand for cocaine in the developed world coincided with the suspension of the International Coffee Agreement (ICA) in 1989, and a 50 per cent reduction in the world price of coffee by 1993. That reduction has continued to this day, leading to a 30-year low in international coffee prices (see Chapter 3, Niche markets: a solution to the coffee crisis?). The sharp fall in coffee prices had, and continues to have, an adverse impact on the livelihoods of coffee producers in Peru and Colombia. The explosion in the late 1980s and early 1990s in the area planted to coca in Bolivia also occurred in Peru and Colombia. As part of the West's war on drugs, something had to be done. That something was a two-pronged approach: coca eradication and alternative development.

The first steps in coca eradication and alternative development

Coca eradication and alternative development began in the Chapare in 1987 following legislation in the United States that not only approved funds for alternative development but also began the process of certification, whereby countries that were not deemed to be adequately fighting the war on drugs were blocked from receiving funds from the World Bank, the International Monetary Fund (IMF) and the United States Agency for International Development (USAID).

In 1988 the Bolivian government approved Law 1008. This recognized two types of coca: coca for traditional purposes, and coca linked to the production of cocaine. The law approved of the former and sanctioned 12 000 hectares of legal coca in the Yungas region. The second type, found predominantly in the Chapare region, was declared illegal and was earmarked for eradication in conjunction with alternative development initiatives. Much of the funding for these initiatives has come from USAID, the EU and the FAO.

Initial attempts to persuade smallholder farmers to replace profitable coca cultivation with alternative crops proved much more difficult than first envisaged. Initially, coca eradication was voluntary and farmers were compensated for each hectare of coca eradicated. However, few farmers voluntarily eradicated their coca despite the fact that in 1994 compensation levels were increased to US$2500 per hectare.

A variety of licit annual and perennial crops were promoted as viable alternatives to coca, but were not suited to farmers' situations or prevailing markets.[9] Furthermore, many species were promoted on the basis of results from on-station trials at a research station in the Chapare and were not representative of on-farm conditions. This is a mistake that is not unique to the Chapare.[13] Early results from the alternative development programme were limited, largely due to the long period without income between planting and first harvest (e.g. macadamia nuts and natural rubber), low yields (e.g. coffee), and disappointingly small markets (e.g. star fruit and turmeric). This engendered a feeling of mistrust towards outsiders on the part of many farmers. Farmers argued that the alternative crops did not provide a decent livelihood.

Approximately 25 000 hectares of coca were eradicated between 1988 and 1994, but it became clear that farmers were accepting compensation for coca eradication on the one hand, and then establishing new coca plantations with the money. By the end of 1994 there were still 36 000 hectares of coca in the Chapare,[12] only 5000 hectares less than in 1989. Bolivia's government began forcible coca eradication in 1995 after being warned by the USA that it was on the point of being decertified.[10]

Pressured by the USA and to a lesser degree the EU, the Bolivian government introduced the *Plan Dignidad* with the twin objectives of coca eradication and alternative development. The Plan began in early 1998 and set targets to reduce the total area of coca in Bolivia to 7000 hectares within a five-year period. This would clearly require eradication efforts in the 12 000 hectare traditional coca-growing area in the Yungas (see page 132). Individual compensation for eradication was replaced by communal compensation and the amount has been progressively reduced on a yearly basis.

Despite the shortcomings of the alternative development initiatives in the early 1990s, alternative development was identified as a central pillar of the *Plan Dignidad*. Since the early 1990s technical assistance and marketing support have focused on a smaller number of crops deemed to be suitable to the Chapare, even though much of the land is not suitable for permanent agriculture. These species include banana, pineapple, palm heart, and to a lesser degree, passion fruit and black pepper.[14]

Much of the alternative development is being funded by USAID through a project called the Consolidation of Alternative Development Efforts in the Chapare (CONCADE). In addition, the United Nations Drug Control Program (UNDCP) funds the Jatun Sach'a Project, which is implemented by FAO. Jatun Sach'a (literally 'Big Tree' in Quechua) promotes diverse agroforestry systems which incorporate licit agricultural crops, including some promoted by CONCADE. Jatun Sach'a also has a forest management component, which is discussed in more detail in Chapter 9, Forestry and livelihoods: making trees pay.

Alternative development and farmers' livelihoods

Measuring success?

The Bolivian government's efforts to eradicate coca in the Chapare have been a success. By the end of 1999 there were fewer than 10 000 hectares of coca in the Chapare[10] and by the end of 2000, the last remaining coca was officially eradicated.[15] Legal commercial crops now cover over 100 000 hectares in the Chapare, almost three times as much as in 1986.[10] Some farmers in the Chapare, however, continue to plant some coca among rows of rice and yucca so as to avoid detection by satellites.[16]

Quantitative data on the amount of coca eradicated and the area planted to licit crops are, however, only one criterion for measuring the 'success' of alternative development. Of great importance is the impact of the alternative development initiatives on farmers' livelihoods. CONCADE uses a number of other indicators, including: annual farm-gate value per CONCADE-assisted family of licit agricultural products; the number of agri-businesses that regularly buy Chapare licit products and/or supply farm inputs; and the value of private sector investment in the Chapare. But these criteria seldom measure farmers' attitudes or expectations. What are needed are qualitative criteria that capture farmers' assessments of the changes in their quality of life.

With considerable amounts of development money and with a cadre of dedicated extension staff, there has certainly been the will to make the alternative development efforts work. Alternative crops have been grown and the development of a transport and marketing infrastructure means that farmers in the Chapare have better access to markets. However, access is no guarantee that the markets will function as envisaged. As early as 1991, development specialists stressed that one of the critical issues that needed to be addressed was the opening of market opportunities.[8] Ten years later, smallholder farmers are still plagued by the lack of markets for their produce, oversupply, price fluctuations, poor quality of produce and, in some cases, lack of reliable transport.[16]

In the late 1980s, unfulfilled promises of the alternative development initiatives engendered a feeling of mistrust towards outsiders on the part of many farmers. In many cases this feeling has grown rather than diminished. In the past few years, there has been much social unrest in the Chapare, illustrating farmers' discontent with enforced eradication and alternative development. In 1998, coca farmers' unions closed roads in protest at the compulsory eradication programme and there were more road blocks in September 2000.[17] Meanwhile, according to some sources, the population in the Chapare has already fallen by as many as 50 000 to 100 000 people.[10] An analysis of alternative development in the Chapare demonstrates both the challenge facing farmers seeking access to global markets and the type of development assistance that they need.

Coca eradication has also had several unexpected consequences. Reports indicate that some of those migrating from the Chapare have returned to their land in the highlands. These farmers are now engaged in growing potatoes, one of the few crops that can be grown in this harsh environment. Partly as a result of this, potato production in 2000 rose dramatically and the market price for this staple subsequently dropped, threatening the livelihoods of another section of Bolivian society. Additionally, with fewer coca- and cocaine-derived dollars in the economy, house building in the thriving city of Cochabamba has almost come to a standstill. The sustainable management of forests is another component of alternative development in the Chapare; Cochabamba is seen as one of the key markets for the Chapare's timber. As demand for construction timber drops the market for another well-meaning alternative to growing coca is undermined (also see Chapter 9, Forestry and livelihoods: making trees pay).

Alternative development planners and practitioners have undoubtedly made mistakes, but there is also growing evidence that fundamental lessons have been learnt. The learning process is on-going and it has, at times, been a painful one. The successes and failures are best illustrated by a handful of licit crops including pineapple, oranges, coffee and bananas.

Pineapple and oranges: recurring market saturation

Pineapple is one of the main alternative crops offered to farmers in place of coca. In the Chapare, pineapple has been plagued by the harsh reality of the rules of supply and demand. In 1986 there were 338 hectares of pineapple. Between 1990 and 1995, there was a stable national market for pineapple, along with a small export market to Chile, Argentina and to a lesser degree, Uruguay. In the Chapare, pineapple was increasingly promoted, and approximately 3.5 million pineapple plants, of the Smooth Cayenne variety preferred by the export market, were distributed to farmers in the Chapare. A credit system was used whereby farmers received five plants and, after a period of two years, were obliged to contribute six plants to the farmers' association. These were, in turn, provided to other farmers.

By 1997 there were 3804 hectares of pineapple. The principal difficulty with pineapples is that there is only one harvest per annum. This occurs between September and December and because pineapples are perishable, they must be harvested and moved direct to market when they are ripe. Overproduction and a collapse in the national market price meant that farmers received as little as US$0.20 per ten pineapples during sporadic national market saturations. The crisis was exacerbated because it coincided from 1995 to 1998 with the imposition by Chile of stringent phytosanitary requirements that Bolivia could not meet. Farmers reacted to the collapse in the market by reducing the area cultivated. By 1999, the area of pineapple had dropped to 1660 hectares.[14]

Doña Marina was one of those farmers who used to grow pineapple. She has a diverse eight hectare farm and has received assistance from the Jatun Sach'a and CONCADE projects. For her, the low market price for pineapple was exacerbated by disease problems. In 1998 she had some 8000 pineapples; now she says, she is not bothering to grow the fruit. The over-supply problem is not confined to pineapple, she adds. She has several orange trees but far too many other people grow oranges and the middle-men who come to her farm to buy the fruit are offering less than US$0.30 per 100 fruits. She says that for this price it is not worth picking the fruit and many are left to rot on the ground. It is sadly a phenomenon seen elsewhere in Latin America and the Caribbean.

Extension agents working with Jatun Sach'a explain that the project has now started working with a group of women to make marmalade from the excess oranges. While this may provide Doña Marina with more income, she has decided to focus on palm heart, one of the other main crops promoted by CONCADE. Doña Marina's children are all attending school and her husband, Don Gerardo, is trying to get a job elsewhere in a factory. She needs to grow something profitable, with low labour requirements. As we leave her farm, she smiles and says that she really wants to grow a legal product that is as profitable as pineapple was in its first years, but she shrugs her shoulders and says '*no hay*' – there isn't one.

This does not mean that some farmers cannot make a living out of pineapple. Three farmer associations are successfully growing and marketing pineapple. They have received assistance in the establishment of a packing plant, technical advice in post-harvest care and they have access to credit. This is also the type of development assistance that a handful of banana-producing farmer associations have received (see page 125).

Repeating mistakes?

During our visit to the Chapare, there were occasions when it seemed that the gulf between extension agents and farmers was so great that it did not bode well for many alternative development initiatives. In one village, a group of approximately 25 farmers' leaders had gathered for a meeting. As the extension agents delivered their presentation on the virtues of their path of alternative development, the farmers sat around listening nonchalantly. Periodically the farmers plucked coca leaves from their small plastic bags and added them to the semi-masticated ball of coca leaves that they kept lodged in the side of their mouths.

At the end of the presentation, one of the farmers stood and after thanking their guests, somewhat defiantly pointed out that promises about markets had been made before. He added that the farmers here had tried growing passion fruit and palm heart but they had either not grown or there had been little market for them. He added that another problem is that the farmers see a rapid change over of extension agents and that none of the agents takes responsibility for any previous advice that time had shown to be inappropriate. These farmers had made up their own minds they were going to grow bananas. He had a point, but it was also clear that the extension agents were in an impossible position. They were being asked to promote crops that they knew were not necessarily the answer to the development issues that had to be met.

Another local leader did not mince his words when asked if he might be interested in growing coffee. Since his coca was eradicated, said Don Herman, he had tried macadamia nuts which extension agents had promoted, but after three years of work they did not produce. He went on to explain that passion fruit grows well, but there is no market for it; palm hearts may grow, but prices are poor. 'The problem is the lack of markets,' he complained. 'We'd sell the stones from the river if there was a market.' Now, he continued, farmers have no confidence or trust left in the crops promoted by the extension agents because there is never a market for them.

Extension agents have been further placed in a very difficult and uncomfortable position by being asked to promote crops that failed when they were tried over a decade ago. The current emphasis is on coffee and cocoa. Despite assurances from extension agents in the Chapare that there are guaranteed markets for cocoa, most farmers we met in the Chapare had little confidence in these crops or their markets. Past failures are attributed by extension agents to poor management, who believe better results are possible. However, the wisdom of promoting coffee at a time when coffee prices are so depressed is highly questionable. Even if farmers were able to grow coffee, can they realistically earn a decent livelihood from this crop when the majority of coffee growers in Central and South America are unable to cover their production costs?

While farmers can receive higher prices for good-quality organic and fair trade coffee (see Chapter 3, Niche Markets: a solution to the coffee crisis?), experts point out that agro-ecological conditions in the Chapare are such that the coffee produced will not be of sufficiently high quality to be sold in these niche markets. In fact coffee producers in Caranavi, the main coffee growing region of Bolivia, voiced concern at the attempt to promote coffee in the Chapare. They argue that there is an urgent need to improve the overall quality of Bolivian coffee and that poorer-quality coffee from the Chapare will jeopardize this endeavour.

On one occasion a village leader in the Chapare repeated a message that we had heard several times that day: 'We tried coffee before: it doesn't grow well'. On the wall behind him was an election poster for the local mayor.

The candidate was from the *Movimiento al Socialismo* and one of his election promises was to protect people's right to grow coca: it was referred to as *la hoja sagrada* (the sacred leaf). Trying to encourage these farmers to grow coffee will be very difficult.

Bananas: showing the way forward?

There are success stories in the Chapare and bananas are seen as one of these. Bananas have traditionally been grown in the Chapare, for the local market. Since 1991, commercial varieties for the external market have been introduced and there are currently about 13 000 hectares of bananas, of which approximately 1000 hectares are planted with export varieties. Banana production in the Chapare is approximately 800–1300 boxes/ha per year. This is low compared to Ecuador (see Chapter 2, Green gold: Ecuador's banana producers).

Farmers' experiences with bananas have, however, been mixed. In 1997, the leaf-browning fungal disease caused by *Micosphaerella fijensis* (and known locally as *sigatoka negra*) was inadvertently introduced to Bolivia. As a result, local banana varieties were decimated and Bolivia lost the comparative advantage of being a disease-free banana producer. Production of bananas now requires regular spraying to control the disease and, hence, production costs have risen. There are also fears that too much spraying will result in increased resistance by the leaf-browning fungus.

Those farmers who have benefited most from the introduction of new banana varieties tend to be members of eight farmer associations that have managed to secure a niche in the export market. There are three banana export companies in the Chapare. In addition to having their own plantations, the companies buy bananas from the eight farmer associations. The largest export market is Argentina. Although Argentina imports approximately 15 million boxes of bananas each year, less than 1 per cent of these are supplied by Bolivia. According to banana exporter, Carlos Flores, his company could sell 10 000 boxes of bananas each week in Argentina, but currently exports only 3000–4000 boxes/week. The major obstacle to increased banana exports, cited by Carlos Flores and confirmed by Charles Foster, a marketing expert with CONCADE, is the lack of adequate transport, rather than production per se.

Banana exporters complain that in order to reach Argentina, they have to use a 130 km section of road, parts of which are in very poor condition. Charles Foster explains that the banana exporters are reluctant to invest in refrigerated trucks, which cost US$65–80 000 each, if they run the risk of damaging them while transporting fruit to Argentina. As a result, there is a shortage of transport and the market niche in Argentina is not being exploited. The road was being improved during 2000 but it is unclear whether the Bolivian government is committed to road maintenance, which is often far more costly than initial improvements.

Charles Foster also explained that the problems facing banana exporters had been exacerbated in early 2000 by sharp falls in the banana price in Argentina. This had been caused by the import of cheap Ecuadorian bananas, following the massive currency devaluation in that country. Recognizing the predicament faced by the banana exporters, USAID via the CONCADE project encouraged the three companies to purchase bananas from small farmers and their associations by paying the companies a start-up incentive of US$0.25 per box of farmer-produced export bananas. What was not clear at the time was what would happen if or when the financial incentive was removed. When questioned about this, a marketing specialist in the region smiled wryly and shrugged his shoulders.

In fact, CONCADE continues to offer modest incentives to three Chapare-based banana exporters to buy from the farmer associations. The objective has evolved from one of encouraging ever-greater purchases of bananas for export from the smallholder farmers and their associations to one of laying the foundations for a more permanent contract farming relationship between exporters and farmers.

USAID has also invested heavily in the eight banana associations. This investment has taken the form of technical advice, training in administration, accounting and marketing, and substantial assistance in infrastructure, such as packing sheds, wells and cable lines. The banana associations have been brought together under the 'umbrella' of a federation known as the Unión de Asociaciones de Bananeros (UNABANA).

Another feature of these associations is that farmers have consolidated individual 10–15 hectare holdings to form large blocks of over 100 hectares. Some degree of economy of scale is achieved and the large blocks also facilitate control of *sigatoka negra*, which is most effectively done by aerial spraying. If farmers cultivate small blocks of bananas that are separated by patches of forest, spraying has to be done by hand which is less effective.

One of the associations is the Ingavi B Banana Growers' Association. This represents 115 farmers. As we look out over a green sea of banana plants, Jaime Caballero, founder of the Ingavi B Association, explains that the farmers have amalgamated their land holdings and there are now 340 contiguous hectares of good-quality bananas. The area is divided into four large blocks that can be fumigated by air. Other banana associations gave up when *sigatoka negra* arrived, he tells us, but Ingavi B has made the effort to make things work.

From the look-out tower, we can see another reason why Ingavi B can produce good-quality bananas: cable lines criss-cross the dense green plantations. Bananas can be harvested, attached to the cable lines and transported to the packing shed without mishandling and bruising the fruit. The association says that exporting bananas is the key to their success and this in turn relies on their producing good-quality bananas. All harvested bananas are graded into four quality categories and only the best can be exported. The Association is responsible for checking the quality of the bananas produced by its members.

The Ingavi B Banana Growers' Association exports 1000 boxes of bananas per week but Jaime confirms that this represents only 10 per cent of the number of export bananas that could be produced. Like the banana exporters, he cites poor road conditions as an obstacle to Bolivia securing a bigger niche in Argentina. However, since our visit to the Chapare, the situation has changed. Argentina's economy has imploded, with good and bad consequences for the Chapare banana producers. On the good side, most of the competitors from Ecuador and Brazil have withdrawn from the Argentine market, leaving Bolivian bananas as the only game in town. Orders are actually increasing from established buyers in Argentina. On the down side, Bolivian exporters are finding it more difficult to get paid. Given the restrictions on transferring dollars out of Argentina and the fluctuating exchange rate for Argentine pesos, Bolivian exporters must travel to Argentina or the Bolivian–Argentine border to receive payment in cash from their buyers.

Whatever the outcome of the economic crisis in Argentina, the farmers attached to Ingavi B in the Chapare know that they are the lucky ones: they received external assistance early in the alternative development programme and have a head start over other aspiring banana producers. What is not at all clear is whether newer farmers' associations can ever emulate Ingavi B. Is the market large enough to accommodate more banana associations and is the Bolivian government, along with the USA and EU, committed to providing the long-term support that is needed?

Making alternative development more effective

Benefiting the few or the many?

In 1998, 70 per cent of farmers in the Chapare depended on coca for 60–100 per cent of their income.[18] Those promoting alternative development acknowledge that it is almost impossible for alternative licit crops to match the income that coca can provide, but are adamant that alternative development can still deliver a decent livelihood to ex-coca farmers.[19]

'Decent' can be interpreted in several ways. Officials rightly argue that when coca production is linked to cocaine production it brings in its wake credit and cash, but also violence, corruption and disorder. In this context, alternative development does indeed provide a decent, law-abiding liveli-hood: the Chapare is no longer the lawless region it once was. 'Decent' can also mean an 'adequate' family income and there are data to suggest that licit agriculture provides a superior income when compared with the national average. In 1998, the United Nations Office for Drug Control and Crime Prevention (UNODCCP) cited a report by the USA Department of State on the international narcotics control strategy, which referred to alternative development in the Chapare as having been 'highly successful' in providing farmers with viable, legal alternative crops.[20]

Development practitioners and officials in the Chapare are not as san-guine and admit that while it may benefit the few, in its present guise alter-native development is unlikely to deliver a decent livelihood to the majority of ex-coca growers. An official working with the Dirección General de Reconversión Agrícola (DIRECO), the organization charged with certifying areas as 'coca-free', admitted that alternative development will benefit only a minority of ex-coca producers. He added that many of the ex-coca farm-ers would have to find non-agricultural work such as eco-tourism, though examples worldwide demonstrate that the beneficiaries of eco-tourism are often outsiders rather than locals.

Meanwhile, it has been reported that only 20 per cent of ex-coca grow-ers in the area are likely to become successful farmers, with another 20 per cent being forced to migrate and the rest surviving on odd jobs and mar-ginal farming.[10] This should not come as any surprise. The DIRECO offi-cial we interviewed cited a widely-available report dating from the beginning of the 1980s which pointed out that the greater part of the Chapare is not suitable for permanent agriculture.[7] The reality is that if farmers are not allowed to grow coca, there really are no licit crops that can support in the long term the number of people who have migrated to the Chapare since the 1950s. It is, therefore, disingenuous to claim that alternative develop-ment can provide a decent livelihood for the majority of ex-coca growers in the Chapare. That having been said, it can be made to work for more ex-coca growers.

Improving quality and focusing on the domestic market

The example of the successful banana associations demonstrates that where alternative development has worked in the Chapare, much of the success has come from substantial investment and price support. While recognizing the importance of this type of support, Charles Foster of CONCADE also stresses that alternative development could benefit a greater number of farmers if more emphasis is given to ensuring that produce is of high quality and that farmers fulfil contracts with respect to delivering on time.

Foster shines a different light on the over-supply crisis that affected pineapples. An additional problem with the export of pineapple from the Chapare, he says, is poor quality. He maintains that markets exist in Chile and Argentina, but that up to 50 per cent of shipments from the Chapare have been rejected on quality grounds, particularly because of interior browning, which can be avoided by improved management at the farm level or by pre-cooling after harvest. Product rejection at export destination represents a substantial financial risk to exporters and is a key obstacle in developing a stable set of satisfied customers. Hence, while farmers believe the market does not exist, it is partly that they are not producing the quality necessary to fulfil an existing opportunity.

Milton Pereira agrees with the need to focus on quality. He works for an NGO called Proyecto de Asistencia Técnica para la Producción y Comercialización Organizada (CIAPROT). This is part of the CONCADE project. CIAPROT offers farmers technical assistance, particularly with respect to producing high-quality produce. Like Charles Foster, Milton is convinced that the pineapple market will grow if farmers produce the quality of product that consumers want. CIAPROT is working with 1000 families divided between 22 farmer associations. There are plans to introduce a certification scheme so that consumers have the confidence that they are buying good-quality fruit.

At the same time, CIAPROT and the 22 farmer associations are exploring different management techniques which mean that the pineapple harvest can be staggered so as to avoid huge over-supply between October and December. As a further challenge, market research has demonstrated that people in the Bolivian cities of La Paz and Cochabamba prefer different varieties of pineapple. Farmers are now producing the correct varieties for each city. There is little rocket science involved in this, and from a marketing perspective it makes sense. What is encouraging about CIAPROT's work is that outside assistance is being used to dismantle some of the obstacles that farmers face when trying to benefit from markets.

There remain a series of unknowns. How big is the potential pineapple market in Argentina and Chile? How many pineapple producers in the Chapare will these markets sustain? Will outside assistance continue until the farmer associations are able to stand on their own feet? With respect to the size of the international markets, Yuri Maldonado from Consultores del Campo (CODELCA), a private company working with CONCADE, cautions that taking into account the demand in Argentina and Chile, the realistic export potential of pineapple from the Chapare is approximately 5000 boxes per month during a five-month harvest period. This translates as the production from a mere 10 hectares. The three pineapple farmer associations that have received substantial external assistance already have

150 hectares. Furthermore, Bolivia's ability to take advantage of market opportunities in countries such as Argentina is heavily determined by the competition from economic giants such as Brazil, where economies of scale mean that production costs are lower than in Bolivia.

It is this uncertainty that had prompted advisers such as Charles Foster to focus on generating greater internal demand for agricultural products from the Chapare. This is partly a question of improving the internal transport infrastructure in terms of road conditions and more refrigerated trucks. Largely as a result of improved quality, national demand within Bolivia is steadily growing and fresh pineapples are reaching more markets beyond Cochabamba and Santa Cruz. For example, in September 2000, Chapare producers signed a contract with a wholesalers' association in La Paz to sell 8–10 truckloads (7000–9000 units of fruit) of pineapple per week during the September to December harvest.

Another tactic is to persuade the Bolivian authorities to use Chapare-grown pineapple and bananas in the school meals that are provided throughout the country by the municipal authorities. Foster has calculated that if 50 per cent of school breakfasts included bananas from the Chapare, there would be sufficient demand for all the bananas produced in the region.

The need to rely less on international markets and to boost internal demand has become clear since early 2002. The consequences for Bolivia of the economic turmoil in Argentina are still unclear. Although banana exports have not been jeopardized, palm heart exports have been affected (see page 130) and it would be surprising were the crisis in Argentina not to have more detrimental impacts on those farmers in the Chapare whose produce is exported to Argentina. Banana and pineapple producers in the Chapare will need assistance in securing a niche in national markets. There is some urgency in this because if Chapare farmers suddenly find that export market opportunities disappear, it will be all too easy to lay the blame at the door of development officials and to claim that, once again, it is the farmers who have been led up the garden path.

Building farmers' trust: encouraging transparency

The Chapare is a region riddled with mistrust. The army, the government, the farmers, the aid agencies, and the exporters are suspicious of each other's motives. This is the legacy of forced coca eradication together with alternative development initiatives that have often failed to bring the benefits that farmers had been 'promised'. In this context, farmers often feel that they are being exploited by the buyers of their produce. This feeling of persecution is not unique to the Chapare but that is little consolation to those outsiders who are trying to encourage better relations between farmers and buyers.

Milton and his colleagues at CIAPROT are trying to reduce the degree of mistrust that exists between farmers and buyers. Attention has been focused on palm heart, which is one of the most commercially important crops in the Chapare. Cultivated palm heart (*Bactris gasipaes*) is grown in dense single-species plantations. It takes two years to reach maturity and can be harvested every three months, giving an advantage of continuity of supply to the market. Only the growing tip of the palm is utilized. This is canned in a solution of salt and citric acid. Between 1994 and 1999, the area under palm heart in the Chapare increased from 309 hectares to 3000 hectares. The majority of farmers sell their produce to four local processing plants, which have markets principally in Argentina, Uruguay and Chile.

The price of palm heart on the international market has dropped substantially over the past two years, due to currency devaluations in Brazil and Ecuador and oversupply worldwide. The major effect of this has been a sharp reduction in farm gate prices for Chapare farmers, who are receiving about half the price that they expected. Palm heart producers do not understand the reasons for the reduction in the prices they are offered by the two local processing plants and feel that they are being cheated. This acts to confirm their suspicions that alternative agriculture is not to be trusted.

CIAPROT aims to counter this by encouraging greater transparency in the relationship between producers and buyers. The idea is to encourage the two parties to meet, discuss market conditions and agree on prices every two months. While it is not a panacea, some of the anger that farmers feel at being 'cheated' by the buyers could be reduced if they were informed why the buyers are unable to pay the amount expected before world oversupply led to a drop in prices.

CIAPPROT's efforts have been helped by the fact that world prices for canned palm heart are cyclical and during the first quarter of 2002, prices started to move upwards. Furthermore, recognizing the threat that the collapse of the price of palm heart represents to the Chapare, CONCADE has been prepared to offer short-term support to the palm heart exporters, during an economic downturn, to enable them to offset some of their losses and maintain a steady flow of purchases from smallholder farmers at favourable farm gate prices.

This provision of periodic support continues. The economic crisis in Argentina has meant that, as is the case with the banana sector, the palm heart exporters are not being paid on a regular basis. The normal 30-day terms of payment have been extended to 120–150 days. This leaves the four Chapare-based palm heart processors without sufficient working capital to continue operations. CONCADE is making US$200 000 available in the form of interest-free loans to the processors, repayable in six to 12 months.[21]

Encouraging farmer participation

There is a more fundamental critique about the type of alternative develop-ment generally being promoted in the Chapare. The issue is less whether the components of the programmes per se are appropriate, but more whether they can contribute in any meaningful way to 'development'. Development is a process of empowerment in which farmers learn to take charge of their lives and solve their own problems by way of participation and innovation.[22] It is the opposite of the type of paternalism that is characteristic of many development efforts worldwide, including the Chapare. Several develop-ment workers in the Chapare commented that the early stages of the alter-native development programme were characterized by too many hand-outs, and that this has fostered a climate of dependency.

It is too easy to portray coca growers as both villains and victims of the drugs trade. The danger of this is that heavy-handed eradication efforts (which deal with the coca producer as villain) are combined with develop-ment alternatives that are imposed on the farmers. These alternatives are designed to 'help' the farmers (the producer as victim) but a critical com-ponent is absent from these efforts, namely active farmer participation.

Active participation in problem identification and subsequent project for-mulation and implementation is now recognized as one of the critical com-ponents of rural development.[23] The only way to avoid the growing dependency associated with paternalism is to motivate farmers to do things for themselves.[13] The driving force behind participation is enthusiasm, and the enthusiasm comes from programmes that address farmers' priority problems, work with farmers as partners, and bring about early recognizable success. As farmers participate in programmes, they gain self-confidence, pride and the satisfaction of having made significant achievements.[13]

The confidence that comes from participation increases farmers' ability to learn and experiment. Innovation is part of development and is vital because agro-ecological, social and economic conditions continually change. Farmers need to be able to adapt to these changing circumstances. In the absence of genuine farmer participation, it is debatable whether altern-ative development (as it is generally practised) can make a meaningful contribution to human development.

It needs to be recognized, though, that the situation in the Chapare is both complex and problematic. Encouraging and fostering farmer partici-pation in a development process is a tall order at the best of times; doing so in a context in which farmers' main livelihood option, coca, is forcibly eradicated is a Herculean task. Furthermore, donors understandably want to see results and, what is more, ones that can be easily measured. Therefore, development workers are often under pressure to meet targets with respect to the number of farmers engaged and the area of alternative crops planted. Active farmer participation is all too easily sacrificed in the race to meet these targets. Development workers often find themselves between a rock and a hard place.

Coca-free first, development assistance second

At the start of the eradication process in the Chapare, there is no doubt that many farmers took compensation money for the eradication of their plantations, and then established new coca fields. Following this initial failure to encourage voluntary eradication, the Bolivian government began to require farmers to be certified as coca-free before they could receive any alternative development aid. This conditionality was finally eliminated at the end of 2000. Farmer participation in alternative development efforts and overall trust in the process would almost certainly have improved had the conditionality been relaxed or rescinded earlier. Farmers often have to wait several years before the alternative crops start producing marketable goods, and even then there is no guarantee that the products will command a reasonable price in fickle markets.

A more logical alternative approach would have been a process of gradual coca eradication, accompanied by effective alternative solutions decided upon by the farmers and outsiders. The risk to the farmer is reduced and if the experiment is successful they will continue to eradicate the coca themselves.[24] Insisting that farmers be coca-free before they are able to receive any assistance was seen by many farmers as indicative of outsiders' inability to appreciate the predicament they face and also of the West's obsession with eradicating coca irrespective of the social and economic repercussions. This issue is starkly brought to the fore in the other coca-growing region of Bolivia: the Yungas.

The Yungas: coca and coffee

Now that coca has been largely eradicated in the Chapare, attention is being directed at the Yungas. This is despite the fact that coca has been grown in the Yungas since before the Spanish conquest and the Bolivian government recognizes 12 000 hectares of coca as legal. In terms of its traditional use for chewing, coca from the Yungas has a sweeter taste and is superior to that from the Chapare. The government claims that there are 14 500 hectares of coca and hence an eradication programme of 2500 hectares can be justified. Local coca growers bitterly dispute this figure, claiming that there are only 9000 hectares. They are adamant that officials have misinterpreted satellite images by including abandoned coca fields.[10] Furthermore, reports cited by government officials indicate that coca consumption in Bolivia has fallen and that there is no longer any justification for growing 12 000 hectares of coca in the Yungas. The producers, while accepting that consumption may have dropped, claim that the reports grossly exaggerate production figures and that demand can be met only by continued cultivation of the 12 000 hectares.

The coca-producers have good reason to be concerned about an eradication programme. They explain that in the late 1980s, the UN tried to introduce alternative crops such as coffee and citrus fruits in the Yungas. These crops did not grow on the steep and impoverished slopes where the hardy coca shrub thrives. There is, understandably, deep suspicion of further attempts to eradicate coca. This is exacerbated when, despite evidence to the contrary, the UN continues to claim that coffee is a viable alternative to coca.[18] The only evidence of successfully introduced coffee varieties is in the Caranavi area which lies 80–100 km north of the designated 12 000 hectare traditional coca-growing area.[25]

We visit the coca fields around the town of Arapata in the Yungas with a group of local farmers. Swaying perilously in the back of a pick-up truck, clinging to the vertiginous dry hillsides on the way to Arapata, the farmers are nonchalant about road hazards. They are keen to express their disquiet at the possibility of a coca eradication programme and to demonstrate the importance of coca to their livelihoods.

Carmen grows coca. When we arrive at her house she is drying recently-harvested coca leaves on the patio or *cachi*. Carmen wants to show us one of her coca plots on the outskirts of the village. Like many of the farmers in the Yungas, she owns approximately three hectares of land divided into several dispersed fields. She has two *catos* of coca, which total about 0.35 hectares. The remainder of her land is in fallow and she also grows a little coffee and various fruit trees on the better-quality soil. On-farm diversity is part of the indigenous Aymara culture: a form of security should any one crop fail. However, her most important crop is coca.

Coca's value is reflected in the way that the plants and the land are cared for. Coca plants are grown densely on carefully constructed terraces. We had been led to believe that this hardy species flourishes with very little management. However, growing coca in the Yungas is a labour-intensive process. The crop is weeded by hand every three months, terraces are repaired after heavy rains, pest problems are treated with a combination of natural and artificial insecticides, plants are pruned to about half a metre, and every few years they are cut back to a short stump. After 25 years the land is left in fallow for a few years and then the cycle starts again with new planting stock from a nursery. The heaviest labour demands are at harvest time. There are three harvests spread across the year and each time all the leaves are carefully picked and then taken to the *cachi* to be dried. The harvests are staggered so that friends and family can work on each others' land.

Farmers like Carmen produce about 330 kg of coca each year and, depending on the quality, they can earn US$1200 per year from two *catos*. This represents a reasonable income for the 10 000 families in the Yungas who grow coca. Carmen and the other farmers are adamant that coca is three times more profitable than alternative crops such as coffee. Even assuming that it could be grown in the Yungas, alternatives such as coffee would be more attractive were the international price to increase dramatically. However with huge oversupply of coffee, a big recovery in coffee prices is unlikely.[26] In addition there is immense competition among smallholder coffee producers worldwide to secure a niche in the more lucrative fair trade, organic and gourmet coffee markets.

It would be disingenuous to claim that coffee has no role in alternative development programmes. Coca eradication and alternative development programmes have also been implemented in Peru since the mid-1980s. In the Quillabamba region in Peru, many of the farmers who are now members of the successful coffee co-operative COCLA used to grow coca (see Chapter 3, Niche markets: a solution to the coffee crisis?). Some still do, but on a far smaller scale. Their mainstay is coffee, and they receive relatively good prices for their coffee because COCLA has been successful in securing a foothold in the organic, fair trade and gourmet coffee markets.

Roberto, Augusto, Carlos and José are members of COCLA. In a meeting room at COCLA's factory they explain that they are the lucky ones. A substantial minority of ex-coca growers were unable to grow coffee because their land was not suitable. As Roberto explains, 'You can grow coca where coffee grows, but you can't always grow coffee where coca grows'. Faced with coca eradication programmes, farmers with poor-quality land became more impoverished or migrated to the Peruvian Amazon. Similarly, in Bolivia a coca eradication campaign in the Yungas, in conjunction with the promotion of coffee as an alternative, is likely to exclude many farmers with unsuitable land.

Coca growers in the Yungas are adamant that the link between coca and the trafficking of cocaine was confined to the Chapare. Coca cultivation in the Yungas, they argue, is different to the Chapare. Here, the entire process is regulated. Coca-growers are registered, the volume of coca taken to the legal market is recorded with the details checked by roadside government officials. Finally coca is sold in the legal coca market in La Paz only by licensed vendors. Like any other marketable crop, farmers strive to produce good-quality coca. We visit the coca market in La Paz. The sweet smell of coca hits us as we approach the market from the busy side street. In a large room people mill about while they grade the coca into four quality categories. A similar control exists in Peru, where the state-owned *Empresa Nacional de la Coca* (ENACO) oversees the legal production and sale of coca.

That said, it is difficult to regulate and control all of the coca grown in the Yungas. Undoubtedly some of the coca from this region is being sold in places other than the legal market in La Paz. The figures that we were given on the amount of coca sold annually in La Paz did not square with rough estimates of the amount of coca produced in the Yungas.

Whether or not large amounts of coca from the Yungas are being sold illegally, the reality is that coca growers see no justification for an eradication programme in the Yungas. The use and cultivation of coca in Andean society is seen as a central part of Aymara and Quechua culture and tradition. Coca growers see any attempts to eradicate coca in the Yungas as an assault on Andean culture, a ploy to homogenize society, and an attempt to divide communities. Sergio, another coca grower, articulates their fears. 'If the government decides to eradicate several thousand hectares of coca, how are they going to choose which villages to target, and how are they going to select the coca areas within those villages?' he asks. 'The government is trying to divide us and set neighbour against neighbour'.

While to some this may seem an extreme interpretation, it reflects farmers' perceptions and any outside interference will be interpreted from this perspective. The coca producers are well organized and are prepared to resist attempts to eradicate their coca. If the Bolivian government decides to start eradicating coca in the Yungas, the challenge is to learn from the experience in the Chapare and make sure that mistakes are not repeated.

More fundamentally, perhaps, the developed world needs to reappraise its obsession with coca eradication. It also has to ask itself whether, in the context of coca eradication, it is genuinely committed to providing farmers with viable alternatives.

Uncomfortable truths

The commitment from the developed world

A seasoned marketing specialist working in the Chapare commented that: 'agricultural development in Third World countries is an immense challenge, involving a complex inter-locking system of agricultural inputs, improved planting material, technical extension, packing, processing and marketing activities. Add to this the theme of coca-eradication and the challenge is all but overwhelming. The final outcome here depends heavily on whether alternative licit crops will satisfactorily replace the income and employment generated by the growing of coca. Assuring that this happens will require the active participation of the Bolivian government, as well as abundant support from the developed countries.'

As First World leaders argue about debt reductions for developing countries and as aid budgets hover well below UN targets, observers could be forgiven for questioning their commitment to agricultural development in the developing world. The reality is that since the early 1980s, and as aid budgets have been cut, the percentage of Overseas Development Assistance (ODA) directed at the agricultural sector worldwide has declined from approximately 17 per cent to 8 per cent.

The substitution of licit alternative crops for coca exposes farmers to the risks and opportunities of globalization. The vagaries of agricultural markets are hard to cope with unaided, even for farmers in richer parts of the world. Where alternative development has worked in the Chapare, much of the success has come from targeted technical assistance in licit crop management, the fostering of direct links between producers and buyers, and from substantial donor investment in rural roads, productive farming and food processing infrastructure. Even though it is not a panacea, alternative development could be made to work for more ex-coca growers. The question is whether the developed countries are genuinely prepared to offer far greater numbers of ex-coca farmers in the Andes the type of support that they need.

In some cases the support needed may, in the short and medium-term go beyond what has been offered to date. An extension agent in the Chapare pointed out that Bolivia produces only half the amount of black pepper that it needs. There is a market opportunity here, but the question that remains unanswered is whether farmers in the Chapare can produce pepper more cheaply than foreign producers. In this context, a leader of one of the coca growers' federations in the Chapare explained that farmers will readily stop growing coca if the Bolivian government guarantees them a minimum price for their produce and a secure market.

Neither CONCADE nor any other development agency working in the Chapare offers price support in the sense of guaranteeing the purchase of a product at a fixed price if the farmer is unable to sell their production for more. And nor are they likely to do so. But is this idea so far-fetched? Is the concept really so different from the some of the price and production-based subsidies paid to farmers in the USA, EU and Japan? In the context of wildly fluctuating prices for agricultural produce, it is particularly difficult for smallholder farmers to establish themselves. The salutary fact is that some sort of price support may well be needed to wean farmers away from growing coca. And after all, growing coca is simply a response to market forces of supply and demand.

Supply and demand

A policy that emphasizes eradication rather than social development cannot be effective because it does not address the roots of the drug problem: poverty in developing countries and demand for drugs in developed countries.[27] It may be too painful for the USA and European governments to grapple with why there is a demand for cocaine. However, it is an issue that eventually needs to be addressed because it is the key to why farmers grow coca other than for traditional uses. No eradication or interdiction programme in the past 35 years has had any serious impact on the supply of illegal drugs to the USA. Military intervention cannot repeal the laws of supply and demand.[28]

There are numerous examples of where successful supply suppression in one area has led to crop production or drug refining activities being moved elsewhere. This is known as the 'balloon effect': squeeze in one place and the bubble transfers elsewhere.[29] Between 1995 and the end of 1999 the total area of land under coca in the Andes fell by 15 per cent. More detailed examination of the figures makes interesting reading. While the area of coca in Bolivia and Peru fell by 55 per cent and 66 per cent respectively, much of the coca migrated north and coca cultivation in Colombia increased by 141 per cent from 50 900 ha to 122 500 ha.[10] Between 1999 and 2000, over 50 000 hectares of coca was eradicated in Colombia[30] but by the end of 2000 the area of coca had risen further to 163 000 hectares.[31]

In Colombia, coca is now being systematically eradicated as part of the *Plan Colombia*. This is a comprehensive and integrated response to Colombia's economic and societal problems, the internal conflict, and the narcotics business that fuels it. The programme will cost $7.5 billion to implement, with Colombia paying most of the cost itself. The USA agreed to provide a US$1.3 billion assistance package. Coca eradication and alternative development are components of the *Plan Colombia*, with funds for the latter making up just over 10 per cent of the USA's contribution. However, American officials have admitted that although coca is being eradicated, the aid for alternative development projects has been slow to arrive.[32]

Now that coca is being eradicated in Colombia and, faced with continued demand for cocaine in the West, the 'balloon effect' continues. There are reports that coca is making a comeback in the Peruvian Huallaga Valley, an area where coca had been 'eradicated'.[33] It has spread to the Colombian Amazon[34] and may even spread to the Brazilian Amazon, which in the eighteenth and nineteenth centuries was a traditional growing area. The cruel irony is that in parts of Peru, farmers are abandoning coffee promoted by alternative development programmes and have started growing coca again,[35] while in Colombia, the collapse in coffee prices is driving thousands more farmers into coca production.[36]

According to Rolando Vargas (representative of one of the coca-growing organizations in the Chapare), some farmers who eradicated coca and cultivate licit alternatives in the Chapare are now so disillusioned that they are increasingly returning to coca cultivation. The rules of supply and demand dictate that the temptation to cultivate coca will remain whilst the demand for cocaine exists and the alternatives are not seen as viable.

Coca's good for you

Coca eradication also raises the embarrassing issue of apparent Western hypocrisy. Coca producers, NGOs and companies that produce coca tea in the Andean region are angered by the double standards of the developed world. Their argument is based on the fact that, unbeknown to the millions and millions of daily users, coca leaves are still used in the manufacture of the world's 'favourite drink'.[37] Bolivia and Peru legally export annually 70 and 45 tonnes respectively of coca leaf to the USA.[38] The coca is refined at the Stepan Chemical Company in New Jersey and a decocainized flavour essence from the coca leaves is used in the manufacture of Coca Cola. In addition, the Peruvian state-owned company ENACO has a laboratory in Lima that produces high-grade cocaine base which is exported worldwide for use in pharmaceuticals.

If the US government permits the import of coca for use in a product consumed daily by millions of people, then there are grounds for arguing that some of the millions of US dollars that go towards coca eradication efforts could be redirected to research on additional uses of coca. There are a multitude of traditional uses of coca. In Bolivia, coca has been used for centuries in tea. Local NGOs in Bolivia have suggested that the consumption of non-addictive coca tea, as a substitute for coffee and tea, could be encouraged in more countries. In addition, chewing coca suppresses appetite. With obesity levels on the increase in the USA and Europe, there is enormous potential for research into the use of coca leaf to suppress appetite. New licit markets for coca could at least absorb some of the coca currently grown in the Andes and provide a decent livelihood for farmers in place of eradication and alternative development programmes that in many cases have not been as successful as originally expected.

Alternative agriculture: which way forward?

The final issue is less an 'uncomfortable truth' and more a fundamental question about approaches to smallholder agriculture. Marketing specialists in the Chapare argue that more farmers could take advantage of market opportunities if they were to follow the example of the more advanced banana associations and move away from atomised farm plots of a few hectares towards larger consolidated holdings (essentially monocultures) which have the potential to be economically sustainable. By consolidating the agricultural activities of dispersed farmers into production and marketing centres, farmers could reduce their costs through shared equipment and volume buying of agricultural inputs, and justify the expense of a permanent staff of administrators and marketers. Charles Foster refers to these large blocks as potentially 'economically sustainable units'.

However, while large blocks of single species may, in some circumstances, be economically sustainable, are they environmentally sustainable? Are economically sustainable units going to be sustainable in the long term or will pest and disease problems and price fluctuations undermine their viability? Other development efforts in the Chapare, such as Jatun Sach'a, stress the importance of agricultural diversification at the farm level and promote diverse agroforestry systems incorporating licit agricultural crops. These programmes stress the importance of diversity in reducing risk – not putting all your eggs in one basket.

The Jatun Sach'a approach in turn raises a number of questions. Even if diverse plots prove to be environmentally sustainable, can an agriculture based on this type of mosaic survive in a globalized economy or is it a recipe for poverty? Is it possible to compete effectively only by specializing in large-scale, single-species agricultural units? These questions are relevant to farmers throughout Latin America and the rest of the world as they try to integrate themselves in global and national markets. We discuss these issues in more detail in Chapter 10, Conclusions: the need for trade and aid.

CHAPTER 7

*Wine and Pisco: success or sour grapes?**

Introduction

L YING ON THE eastern fringe of the Andean mountain chain is the elegant Argentine city of Mendoza. From the balcony outside the Norton vineyard reception room, we look out across a series of flat fields of vines, to the brown hills beyond, capped by the snowy peaks of the Andes in the distance. Although Argentina is the fifth largest producer of wine in the world, less than a decade ago it did not even merit an individual mention in The World Atlas of Wine.[1] Instead, in 1994 Argentina was just another one of those countries, lumped together in the South America section. Now Argentine wine is everywhere: aggressively marketed, good quality, well priced wine. The established winemakers of Argentina have followed their Chilean neighbours and embraced globalization with alacrity, turning it into their own success story. What has lead to this explosion of Argentine wine on to the international scene and who has benefited from it? And what has happened to the traditional internal markets which previously consumed Argentina's copious production?

Across the jagged spine of the Andes in Chile, and 12 hours to the north, poking into the fringes of the Atacama desert, lies the magical Elqui Valley. The valley snakes up from the coast into the foothills of the Andes, an extraordinary river of green vines among the sandy brown hills, where the sun shines for 360 days of the year and agriculture survives only by virtue of irrigation from the Andean snowmelt. The Elqui Valley is the source of Chile's pisco brandy, best known in its cocktail form, when mixed with lime and sugar into a 'Pisco Sour'. Two huge co-operatives dominate the production of pisco in Chile and dwarf their competitors in Peru, the only other country where pisco is made. Ownership of the name, pisco, is hotly debated between the two countries: meanwhile Chilean pisco is marketed internationally while Peru languishes in obscurity. How have the Chilean smallholder producers managed to capture this market and capitalize on their success?

This chapter looks at wine and pisco production in Argentina, Peru and Chile. Small producers have entered into global markets that prize distinc-

* This chapter owes much to the help the authors received from Javier Luciano Aguerre at the Instituto Nacional de Vitivinicultura in Mendoza, Argentina, for which we are deeply indebted.

tiveness, brand-marking and consistency, where quality is not an optional extra, but a prerequisite for market entry. These are markets where tastes are changing rapidly and farmers need to keep up with consumer demands, or disappear. How do the smallholder producers fare in this new world?

Some history

The conquistadors

It should come as no surprise that South America has a long tradition of winemaking. The conquistadors, arriving from Spain in the mid-sixteenth century, brought with them their priests, missionaries and church traditions. The sacrament demanded wine; raisins and wine provided sustenance for soldiers and settlers. Vines, introduced to Peru in 1531, were established in Chile within 20 years and, just six year later, across the Andes in Argentina. Naturally good climatic and soil conditions were supplemented by the construction of irrigation channels to bring the meltwaters from the Andes. Mendoza, now the centre of Argentine wine production, became a green oasis in a sea of semi-desert. Altitudes of up to 2400 metres above sea level, combined with the dry air, kept diseases to a minimum. In these favourable conditions, the settlers sowed the seeds of a whole new industry.

In Argentina, successive waves of immigrants brought their expertise and tastes for wine with them. Production increased from self-sufficiency for a small and isolated community to a trade in a product which was sought after and transported thousands of miles across the *pampas* to Buenos Aires, Tucumán and into neighbouring Paraguay. Winemaking really took off in Mendoza on the back of the railway which connected Mendoza to Buenos Aires in 1885, bringing Italians, Spanish and French to the area. These immigrants brought expertise from home, as well as a culture and taste for wine that enshrined it in the national palate. The great expansion of Argentina's irrigated vineyards had begun.

On the other side of the Andes, Chilean vineyards were early entrants into globalized markets. By the late eighteenth century, they were so successful that Spain became concerned at the extent of their inroads into world markets and prohibited the sale and shipment of Chilean wines.[2] War in Europe, followed by independence for Chile put paid to any plans to suppress the export of Chilean wines. Over the next century, fashion-conscious mining magnates poured money into the Chilean vineyards, emulating the elegance and sophistication of their European counterparts. When Europe's vineyards were devastated by the ravages of the *Phylloxera* louse after 1863, Chile and Argentina were unaffected.[2] Instead, South America benefited from the exodus of unemployed winemakers from Europe, who arrived to continue their trade in South America.

The Argentine success story

After almost 450 years of growing grapes and producing wine, Argentina is blessed with a huge area of vines, to which it owes its status as the fifth largest wine producer in the world. In 2000, Argentina's vineyards comprised over 200 000 hectares, and even this is a considerable reduction on the all-time high of 350 000 hectares in the 1970s. Most of Argentina's vineyards are strung out along the eastern flanks of the Andes, stretching from the city of Salta in the north, 2000 km south to Rio Negro in Patagonia in the South.

The vast majority of the vineyards cluster around Mendoza City. This is an elegant town of tree-lined boulevards and stylish sidewalk cafés, the perfect setting for a centre of fine wines. The climate is excellent for grapes, with plenty of sun and good, dry mountain air. Mendoza is effectively an oasis in a semi-desert region, but irrigation is possible with water from the Andes. Only the occasional summer hail, which can ruin a grape crop, spoils the idyll. With some 143 000 hectares of vines,[3] Mendoza Province hosts about 70 per cent of Argentina's vineyards, as well as the Instituto Nacional de Vitivinicultura (INV) which is charged with carrying out research to improve Argentina's wine industry.

By many measures, Argentina's wine industry has been an extraordinary success over the past decade. Unknown at the start of the 1990s, suddenly Argentine wines exploded on to the international market towards the end of the decade. They began to win prizes and international recognition, the dream of any wine producing country. Between 1990 and 2000 there was an increase of 788 per cent in the quantity of wine exported by Argentina, while the value of exports rose by 1134 per cent to an annual total of US$125 million in 2000.[4]

Argentina's launch on to the world market has required a leap in the quality of their wines, an increase in sophistication which might have seemed impossible a decade ago. A combination of factors, running all the way from the planting stock in the vineyard to complex processing and marketing links, has played a role in the process of moving from cheap table wine for the masses, to fine wines for a discerning world audience. But the first step in the process had to be producing good wines.

Improving quality

What makes a good wine?

We sit in the vaulted cellar of the Weinert Bodega (winery), surrounded by old barrels, which are now kept only for show, and sip the proffered sample of wine. Deeply red and smooth, this is a joy to drink. But what is it that makes this wine so good?

Winemaking, as everyone knows, is an art and Weinert is developing an international reputation as a fine artist. The flavour of the wine is shaped by a vast range of variables: climate, soils and altitude; grape variety; cultivation technique and harvesting methods – all affect the quality of the grapes. Then there are the winemaking, ageing and bottling processes, also fundamental to the flavour of the final product. The mysteries of the winemaking art are well beyond our abilities to describe here. However, a few points are useful in understanding Argentina's wine industry and its entry into the globalized world.

Grape varieties and locality

Grapes, the raw material for making wine, come in a bewildering array of types. Different grapes suit different locations and produce different flavours of wine. In Argentina, the variety of grapes reflects the origins of its people: French, Italian, and Spanish grape varieties abound.[5] However, for the main part Argentina's vineyards have been dominated by the descendents of the original grapes brought by the Spanish in the sixteenth century, known as *Criolla grande, Criolla chica* and *Cereza*. These so-called 'common grapes' produce prolific quantities of fruit and are generally destined for cheap table wine.

More recently the demand for better-quality wines, both for export and home consumption, has undermined the dominance of the common grapes. So-called fine wines, made from recognized varieties (such as the red wine grapes *Cabernet Sauvignon, Malbec* and *Merlot*) have become the focus of winemaking, supplying an increasingly discerning market.

Site conditions of a particular locality – the soils, its aspect and altitude, the climate and rainfall patterns – all influence the flavour of the grapes. The high altitudes of some of Argentina's vineyards, for instance, ensure that night-time temperatures regularly drop low enough to give well-flavoured, deeply coloured grapes.[6] Not only is the locality of a vineyard important from the point of view of the grapes it produces, locality can be used to emphasize the distinctiveness of the wine for marketing purposes.[7]

Although some aspects of the location of vineyards in Argentina promote good quality, absence of disease and availability of irrigation water also promote vast yields of grapes. In general, high yields tend to produce poor-quality wine. In good conditions, yields need to be restricted in order to produce good-quality wine.

Cultivation techniques

Traditional techniques of grape production in Mendoza aimed, above all else, to produce large quantities. Apart from the use of the prolifically fruiting *Criolla* vine, the cultivation techniques in the vineyard can have a huge impact on yield.

Vines are climbing plants, and they need to be given a structure to grow on. A long-standing technique in Argentina is the use of high frames, known as *parrales*, which allow the vines to form a pergola with a dense canopy of leaves on top and bare stems below. With wide spacing between the plants, lots of irrigation until the grapes are harvested, and minimal pruning, the vines are exuberant and produce vast yields of grapes, of as much as 40 000kg/ha which translates into approximately 26 000 litres per hectare.[2] By contrast, vineyards such as Concha y Toro in Chile, producing a medium-price wine for export, claim yields of only 9000kg/ha, producing about 6600 litres of wine per hectare. Average yields from Argentina's vineyards are approximately 8800 litres per hectare.[8]

Techniques of growing vines that have been used in Europe for centuries aim to produce lower yields of better-quality grapes. The frames are lower, the vines closer together. Irrigation is stopped a month before the harvest, preventing the vines taking up water, and thereby intensifying the flavour. Pruning of leaves allows sunlight on to the ripening grapes; fruit may be pruned to reduce the overall yield, and the harvest is delayed as long as possible to fully ripen the fruit.[7] In vineyards in Mendoza, summer hail represents a significant threat to the grape harvest. Netting stretched over the top of the vines provides some protection, but at a cost beyond the means of many vineyards.

From grapes to wine

The process of turning grapes into wine is, of course, one of the main factors affecting the quality of the product. In Argentina, production of wine in bulk has also led to poor quality. Old-fashioned materials and processes, such as fermentation in large wood barrels, where the process is difficult to control, make the production of good-quality wine almost impossible, regardless of what variety or quality of grapes you put into the process. Traditionally, wines in Argentina have been aged in huge vats made of a local wood, *Rauli*. While the flavour that *Rauli* imparts to the wine may be a taste acquired by generations of Argentines, it does not sell on the 'quality' market. Modern techniques of wine production involve fermentation in temperature-controlled stainless steel vats, and ageing of wines in small barrels of European or American oak.

It seems to be a truism of winemaking that quantity and quality do not go hand in hand. High-yielding varieties of grape do not make good-quality wine. Highly productive cultivation techniques do not make good wine. Winemaking techniques based on mass production and storage in huge vats do not make good wine. This would seem to be an industry where smaller really is better, but perhaps not in ways that benefit smallholder farmers.

The nation's favourite drink

Wine's competition

Sitting at a small table in our favourite canteen in the city of Salta in northern Argentina, we find ourselves surrounded by working men eating good, solid, meaty fare, and obsessively watching football on the large television screen in the corner. As soon as we sit down at our table, the waiter appears with the customary jug of table wine. This is not fine wine, but is perfectly drinkable for the thirsty non-connoisseur. For years it has been the standard produce of Argentina's vineyards: cheap, cheerful and sold in bulk. But looking around, it is evident that wine is no longer the predominant beverage. A few others are drinking wine, but Coca Cola and beer bottles abound.

This observation is borne out by the statistics. In the 1970s, Argentines drank an average of 70 litres of wine per person every year. By the year 2000, this had fallen to under 38 litres per person, almost half the consumption of 25 years ago. Wine has increasingly been replaced by fizzy drinks, beer, fruit juice and mineral waters.[9] And the demand which does exist for wine in the country is rapidly moving towards better quality, like elsewhere in the world. Whereas in 1990, average consumption of fine wines in Argentina was 6.9 litres per person, by 2000 this had increased to 10.2 litres.[9] People in Argentina are drinking less, but better wine. It is partly this change in consumption patterns that has pushed the Argentine wine industry to make wholesale changes over the past decade.

Boom and bust among the grapevines

Ever since the railway was built between Mendoza and Buenos Aires, the expansion of Argentina's vineyards has kept pace with the expansion of its population. Only in the 1930s did severe price fluctuations cause a sharp switch from wine production to other products such as olives. By the end of the 1930s, however, wine production was on the increase again and by 1977, the area of vines was 280 per cent higher than it was during the 1930s.[10] But it was not only demand that caused a vast increase in the area under vines.

In line with government policies of support and protection in many sectors, the 1960s and 1970s saw considerable support provided to the wine industry. From the beginning of the twentieth century, tariff barriers of up to 100 per cent of the import price had ensured that the local producers were protected from foreign competitors.[7]

At the same time, production was encouraged by provincial legislation providing grants for the expansion of vineyards, with no regard to the quality of the product. Small producers were guaranteed a buyer of last resort, with prices fixed for the season. The absence of any significant difference between the price paid for common grapes and that for fine wine varieties ensured that there was little incentive to produce grapes for good-quality wine. When differences in yields between different grape varieties are taken into account, the logic of growing common grapes is evident.

The use of *parrales* to encourage abundant growth, copious irrigation and productive grape varieties led to extremely high yields, compared to the fine wine varieties and 'quality' production techniques. When the grapes were sold by weight, and there was only a 5 per cent premium for fine grape varieties, it is no wonder that farmers opted for mass production. In fact, many small producers who had traditionally grown a range of fine wine varieties were, in the 1970s, encouraged to rip them out and replant with high-yielding varieties which produce poor-quality wines.[10]

In 1977 the area of vineyards in Argentina hit its highest point, with a total of 350 680 hectares. A surplus of grapes and poor-quality wines meant that farmers were sometimes being paid considerably less than the officially set price. Although Argentina was the fourth largest wine producer in the world, the quality was dismal. And then, during the 1980s, consumption of the copious Argentine table wine began to fall.

Argentina's wines entered a crisis. Two factors precipitated the crisis, which really began to hit in the late 1980s. Wine prices collapsed, as supply far outstripped demand, and the official provincial winery in Mendoza went bankrupt.[7] Then, in the early 1990s, President Carlos Menem's government embarked on a path of economic liberalization. Argentina sought to prepare itself for entry to the regional trade block, Mercosur, and opened its markets to foreign investment. Barriers to imports were vastly reduced, while exports were encouraged. Reduced tariffs encouraged outsiders to invest in Argentine industries and the winemaking business was no exception.

The rise of the fine wine phoenix

Between 1982 and 1992, approximately 115 650 hectares of vines were eradicated in Argentina, comprising about 36 per cent of the previous total.[11] Much of the eradication was old vineyards of common grape varieties. With the economic liberalization of the early 1990s, the way was open for better wines to be imported into Argentina, as well as for Argentina to consider wine exports. Economic stabilization encouraged investment, both nationally from other sectors, and internationally, with numerous foreign

146

investors putting substantial amounts of money into the Argentine wine industry.

There has also been planting of new vineyards using better-quality planting stock. Hence, while the area of vineyards in the Mendoza region has stabilized at approximately 143 000 hectares, the figure conceals the fact that over the past six years, the area has increased by some 35 000 hectares in the Valle de Uco, where good-quality wines are produced. There has been a corresponding reduction in the areas where poorer-quality wines are produced. Vines are also being planted in the north of the country near Salta, where a reputation for good wines is being achieved.

Local and family-run wineries were acquired by foreign companies and reductions in import tariffs on equipment and machinery allowed investors to bring in new winemaking equipment, such as computerized irrigation systems, at low cost. For many of the larger wineries, this meant that they had the potential to exploit the world market for better wines. But equipment alone was not enough. Fine grape varieties were also needed to ensure that the wines produced were of sufficiently good quality. Hence, during the 1990s over 35 000 hectares of vines were replanted in the country. Of these, 30 640 hectares were fine wine varieties. Argentina's wine industry was set to rise from the ashes. Fine grape varieties now comprise 42 per cent of the country's total vine stock.

The Weinert Bodega is tucked away in the residential district of Lujan de Cuyo some 25 km from Mendoza. This is one of Argentina's top-quality wineries, established in 1890. The Brazilian-born owner, who bought the winery in 1975, foresaw long ago the way the market was going. Weinert was one of the few wineries to cut its production levels in order to improve the quality of its wines.[12]

When we visited, Hubert Weber, the company's Swiss winemaker, told us that about half of Weinert's production is now exported. The 40 hectares of vineyard Weinert owns provides about 35 per cent of the grapes needed to produce its annual 700 000 bottles of wine. The company still needs to buy in 65 per cent of its grapes. This is a company that is aiming for high-quality wine and to do so it needs to ensure that the grapes it buys are of fine varieties and have been cultivated to exacting standards. Despite the huge change in planting of grape varieties over the past few years, with the focus on new plantings of fine wine varieties, there is still a shortage of fine wine grapes on the market.

The Weinert Bodega is developing a new way of working, to help get round this shortage. It is introducing long-term contracts with its grape suppliers, giving a premium price for high-quality grapes. The contract offers Weinert more control over the cultivation of the grapes, allows it to decide when to harvest, and even to send its own teams to do the harvesting. This type of contract farming is not dissimilar to the arrangements between the independent banana producers and the buyers in Ecuador (see Chapter 3, Green gold: Ecuador's banana producers). In the case of Weinert's suppliers, although the price is set annually, the contract offers growers stability, and at least some guarantee of a market. The company has about 35 suppliers, whose vineyards vary in size from 0.5 to 40 hectares.

For both Weinert and the suppliers, this type of contract offers some protection from risk. For Weinert, having a variety of suppliers in a range of locations spreads the risk of production. Meanwhile, the larger suppliers spread their own risk by selling to a range of wineries and the smaller suppliers reduce risk by having a predictable market. In addition, says Hubert Weber, Weinert cannot afford to buy up more land for its own production. Lujan de Cuyo, one of the best wine producing locations in Argentina, has become such a popular residential area that land prices have spiralled over the past few decades, making purchase of new land for vineyards too expensive.

Weinert's strategy, therefore, is to supplement its own supply of grapes by buying in high-quality grapes from smaller producers who do not have their own winery. Quality control of the grapes is done by Weinert's own technicians; conditions are set out in the contracts. The situation is favourable to those smaller producers who have fine grape varieties to sell. They are the lucky ones who did not pull out their low-yielding, fine wine varieties in previous decades and replace them with high-yielding, low-quality grapes.

This type of relationship between the winery and the producers is a new development in the Argentine wine industry. Until the 1990s, the relationship was mutually antagonistic.[9] A good year for the wineries was a year of abundant harvest and low grape prices; the vineyard owners preferred low yields and high prices, particularly if someone else had the low yield. The pursuit of quality changed that relationship. Entry into globalized markets and the increasing quality demands of the domestic market have forced vineyards and wineries to develop new relationships that focus on quality, from the grape vine through to the final product.

Working together, farmers and processors can meet the demands of the market and increase their market share. At the moment, Argentine wine represents approximately 1 per cent of total wine imports into the USA and UK (Argentina's two largest foreign wine markets). Chile, which produces about half the wine that Argentina does, accounts for 4 per cent of the wine imported to the USA. This is partly due to some aggressive and deft marketing.

Analysts say Argentine wines are bound to be competitive over the long term because of improving quality and because land and labour costs are much lower than those in Europe, Australia, New Zealand and the USA. However, a fundamental question is to what extent are the new market opportunities open to all? Are some farmers, particularly the smallest, able to join in the bonanza and produce the high-quality wines that the international market demands?

The growth of the integrated company

In contrast to the long-term contract route taken by Weinert, several Argentine wineries are choosing an alternative strategy: to increase their own production of grapes and reduce their reliance on grapes purchased from third parties. Norton, a well-established winery in Mendoza, already owns four vineyards in the Maipu area and another in Junin, making a total of 680 hectares of vines. Despite this vast area, Norton still needs to buy in some 15 per cent of the grapes it requires.

This situation is unlikely to last for long. Norton owns a further 420 hectares of land, currently used for other crops. But, explained our guide Anabel from the delightful balcony overlooking a sea of green vines, if you want quality control, you need to own the grapes. The other crops are destined for conversion to fine wine grapes, gradually replacing any need to buy grapes from smaller producers. A proportion of Norton's land is undergoing a trial for organic grape production. It is an investment that only a big company could make, and organic production would need careful management, most easily assured by direct management.

Many other established wineries have also increased their area of grapes in recent years, or plan to do so in the near future.[13] While some wineries, such as Weinert and Chandon, have adopted the strategy of assisting independent farmers to supply them with good-quality grapes, many others have taken the same route as Norton towards greater integration of grape and wine production. This route further marginalizes smallholder vineyard owners.

Can smallholder farmers make the change?

Adjusting to change

The reality is that many smallholder farmers are unable to meet the new market demand for fine-quality grapes. For smallholder farmers, replanting their vineyard with new varieties of grape is a huge investment. Not only do they need to bear the costs of the new vine stock, building the supports, and laying new irrigation systems, they have to wait five years before their vines begin to produce grapes. In the meantime, the vines need to be carefully pruned and trained: cultivated for quality. This is investment which many small farmers can ill afford to make. Even when the vines do reach maturity, yields will be considerably lower than the yields of the common grapes to which they were accustomed. There is little credit on favourable terms available to smallholder farmers to help them reinvest and restock.

Vineyards that were unable to make the change have progressively been pushed out. Since 1982, the total number of vineyards in Argentina has decreased by almost half, from 52 999 in 1982, to 25 180 by the year 2000. The first sharp fall came between 1988 and 1990; over the following decade numbers slowly but surely continued to drop. The fall is most apparent among the smallest vineyards. In 1990, there were 26 173 vineyards of less than five hectares in size, which made up 75 per cent of the total number of Argentina's vineyards. By 2000, this figure had dropped to 15 886 vineyards.[14] The biggest fall came in the very smallest vineyards: those smaller than half a hectare decreased in number by 67 per cent.

Prior to 1990, a farm household could survive with a vineyard of under five hectares, supported as they were by state subsidies, guaranteed prices and protected markets. Now, farms under 11 hectares in size are simply not viable any more[15] unless, of course, they are the lucky few that have already made the switch to fine variety grapes and that can meet the quality demands of the wineries such as Weinert. At the other end of the scale, there has been a marked increase in the number of large vineyards. Those over 50 hectares in size increased in number from 406 in 1990 to 532 by 2000, a rise of 31 per cent.

The smallest farmers certainly seem to struggle to make the necessary changes and meet new market demands. It is not only lack of money to invest in reconverting vineyards to fine grape varieties which hampers small, traditional farmers. This group often finds it more difficult to adapt to new techniques of vine cultivation. As very small enterprises, they lack both the ability to access the new markets and the power to negotiate with the big players in the market and to secure contracts with the wineries. And finally, the lack of a small farmers' co-operative or association leaves them unable to work together to compete with the larger wineries.[16] When it comes to investment, adaptability and quality control, being small does not bring an advantage.

Smallholder farmers, therefore, find themselves in a precarious situation. In response to the difficulty of making a living from full-time farming, there has been an increase in part-time farmers who rely on off-farm work to supplement their income. Hired workers from Bolivia provide extra labour on the farm and are 'cheap substitutes' for family members who are better paid elsewhere. Stripped of state support, farmers either sell grapes to the bigger wineries if they can, or sell up. Creeping urbanization around Mendoza, and especially in sought-after areas such as Lujan de Cuyo, offers a tempting alternative for these small plots of land with poor-quality vine stock.

Slowing the change in Uruguay

The fate of the Argentine small vineyards is in stark contrast to neighbouring Uruguay, where 80 per cent of producers have fewer than five hectares of vines.[17] Here, the state has deliberately continued policies of support for the smallest producers, negotiating exemptions from Mercosur's free trade zone and, until 2010, restricting imports of wine to Uruguay to containers of less than one litre. This ensures the existing national market for cheap table wine sold in demijohns (or *damajuanas* as they are appealingly called), temporarily continues to be supplied by the national producers. Meanwhile, the state provides assistance and cheap credit to small farmers with fewer than ten hectares of vineyard, to convert to fine wine varieties. Up to 90 per cent of the cost of conversion is covered by the state, financed by a specific tax on wine sales.

In effect, Uruguay's small producers are being given time and credit to adapt to the new market. In 2010, they will have to face the results of the Mercosur free market, but perhaps by then they will be able to compete on an even footing. Even before Argentina's economic crisis in 2001, small producers were not being offered such assistance. The trend in Argentina was rather the opposite: the enlargement of the larger and the slow demise of the small.

The story elsewhere

Fine wine or Inca Pop? The Peruvian experience

Argentina's fortunes are mirrored to some extent in the small wine industry of Peru. Here, pre-Columbian civilizations carved green oases out of the parched Atacama Desert that runs the length of the southern Peruvian coast, using meltwater runoff from the Andes. Later, the same irrigation channels were used by the conquistadors to water their vineyards, which were established in the Ica Valley as early as 1563. The vineyards of Ica, a small town some 20 km from the Pacific coast, are surrounded by sand dunes and grey desert, surreal patches of green in the grey heat. Only 100 km to the south of Ica lie the mysterious Nazca Lines, huge drawings etched in the sand some 2000 years ago, which can be seen only from the air. The Nazca area itself is so dry that the lines have never been washed away by rain. Around Ica, occasional floods make agriculture somewhat less reliable, but without irrigation there would be no vines in this desert.

Local farmers here tend to produce sweet grapes, which can be sold either as table grapes or for distillation into the local brandy, pisco. Despite Peru's long history of winemaking, it is a minority occupation here. Sweet grapes offer more flexibility to the farmers: if it looks like being a glut year, they can sell the grapes early for table consumption. Left to mature slightly longer, they may sell larger quantities for a lower price to a winery for distillation into pisco. Rather like the dual purpose sheep of Patagonia (see Chapter 8, Sheep in Patagonia: blown by the winds of change) sweet grapes offer the farmer more flexibility, but may offer the consumer indifferent quality.

There are only three large wineries in Peru (Tacama, Vista Alegre and Ocucaje), while perhaps a hundred more small wineries exist, dotted around Ica. The big wineries produce both wine and pisco, leaving the smaller wineries to focus exclusively on pisco. Most small wineries have grape varieties suitable only for pisco or sweet wines, and lack the equipment and management capacity to produce wine.

The absence of larger wineries is striking in comparison to Argentina. The reason is partly historical, explained Señor Calderon, manager of the Tacama Winery. Agrarian Reform in the 1970s broke up the large vineyards and redistributed the land among smallholder farmers. Tacama itself negotiated to keep 150 hectares of its original 900 hectares. With its remaining area, Tacama produces enough grapes to supply its winery, and even sells some to other wineries. Only in this way can Tacama produce wines made from fine grape varieties, making it the only Peruvian winery to achieve international recognition.[12]

Others were not so lucky: Vista Alegre lost all its extensive lands in the Ica Valley and was allowed to keep only the winery itself. Since then it has bought back 60 hectares of its original land, but it still needs to buy in grapes from local producers, or grape juice from Argentina. Two or three relatively large producers supply the winery with grapes each year. Smaller producers tend not to have appropriate grape varieties for making wine, so they generally sell their grapes to the small pisco wineries. And in any case, the more suppliers the winery has, the more expensive it is to check their production and quality before they buy. Here, though, there is no long-term relationship with producers: the suppliers may change each year, depending on conditions.

The Agrarian Reform created a large number of small farmers, many of whom replaced their vineyards with cotton. Those who still grow grapes do not have the resources to invest in winemaking equipment or the ability to control the quality of their produce. Wine and pisco-making is an uphill struggle in Peru.

As in Argentina, taste is another major influence on wine production. National consumers in Peru prefer sweeter drinks – rum, soft drinks and beer. The equivalent of the Argentine national consumer base for wine does not exist in Peru. Wine is expensive too, and receives no assistance from the state. Until 1989, Peru's markets were protected from imports, although even then contraband Chilean wine found its way across the border. Following liberalization in the early 1990s, wine from all over the world flowed into Peru. Tacama sells 60–70 per cent of its production on the national market, but is operating only at 65 per cent of its capacity. Vista Alegre operates at about 10 per cent of its capacity, unable to sell the wine and pisco that it already has. Peru's rocky economy does not encourage demand for high-price, luxury goods like wine.

While wine remains a minority interest for most Peruvians, pisco is the national drink. But ironically, pisco is not particularly popular among Peruvians either, not sweet or cheap enough perhaps. Small wineries in the Ica area produce tiny quantities – perhaps 2000 litres per year each – and sell it via their local networks, or through on-site shops to visiting tourists. Several small wineries offer tours of their artisanal processing facilities, where grapes are still crushed manually and distillation is carried out in copper vats heated by wood fires. The result is wildly variable quality between wineries and between batches. Only in the larger wineries, such as Tacama, is the pisco of consistently high quality.

To start addressing the quality problem, a new technical college, the Centro de Inovación Tecnológica (CIT) is being established in Ica with Spanish government funds. The CIT aims to help small pisco producers select the best grape varieties for cultivation, increase production and standardize quality. Only by working together to produce pisco of homogeneous quality and in adequate quantities will Peruvian pisco producers ever be able to enlarge their market. Perhaps then Peruvian pisco could develop an export market.

What's in a name?

Peru faces one further problem with exporting pisco, and it lies to the south: Chile. Both countries claim pisco as their national drink for historical reasons. Chile is convinced that Chilean pisco acquired its name first because the liquor was originally exported to Peru and entered the country via the Peruvian port of Pisco to the south of Lima.[2] Peru, meanwhile, lays claim to the name with the justification that some nationally made pisco was itself exported via the same port of Pisco. Peruvian producers complain that it is difficult to market their national drink abroad because of an inability to give it a national identity. Tequila, they say, is well known to be Mexican and is branded and marketed as such. With the origin of pisco in dispute, that national branding does not work.

This is not, however, a problem that seems to have hindered the Chilean pisco producers in the Elqui Valley in northern Chile. For 70 years the co-operative Pisco Control has been producing consistently high-quality pisco.

Aptly named, Pisco Control was established in 1931, in an attempt to escape from the control of large private distillers to whom small grape farmers sold their produce. The aim was two-fold: to produce high-quality pisco under the guidance of pisco's own system of *Denominación de Origen* (equivalent of the European *Appellation d'origen controlleé*) and to make modern technology available to small farmers.[2]

Pisco Control has been spectacularly successful and now counts about 700 smallholder producers among its members. Its main rival is another co-operative, Pisco Capel, with some 1500 members. Together they control 95 per cent of the pisco market. Pisco Capel alone produces about 270 000 litres of the distilled liquor annually, with 30 per cent exported to other parts of Latin America, the USA and Europe. Peru's tiny artisanal producers pale into insignificance in comparison.

Size, infrastructure and the strict application of quality control allows the Chilean co-operatives to dominate. But are there further lessons that we can draw out of this quick taste of South America's wines?

Success for small farmers?

The wine industry has features in common with many other markets in agricultural commodities. However, it goes beyond some of the demands made on other producers discussed in this book. Globalization has led to differentiation in the wine market, and not to standardization. Demand increasingly focuses on good-quality wines, and those in the industry have to pay much more attention to image and market recognition. Wine is a branded consumer good[18] and the wine industry operates in a market where the links between farmer, processor and marketing are much tighter, where consumer tastes are paramount and changing, and quality at reasonable price is at a premium. Wine is a product of the farmer and the winery: consumers identify a product on the basis of both factors.

There is no doubt that small farmers producing grapes for the wine market are struggling to cope with the changes necessary to meet the new market demands for fine wines and good quality. It is also evident from the history of Argentina's wine industry, that subsidies, guaranteed prices, and protected markets are not the answer in the long term. As Argentina demonstrates, it is not feasible to keep supporting farmers who produce poor-quality goods that consumers do not want. In a world of open markets, consumers can simply purchase what they do want from elsewhere.

Smallholder producers who want to benefit from new market opportunities face some monumental hurdles. They can provide high-quality grapes that are in demand, but only if they can acquire credit to help them make the transition from poor to good vine stock. And it is more than just money that is needed for small farmers to adapt. Technical know-how and market information are essential for small farmers to understand the ways in which they need to change. The long-term contracts developed by some of the winemakers in Argentina provide one model for linking small farmers into the processing system. The pisco co-operatives in Chile provide another.

It can be argued that smallholder farmers merit some degree of state assistance to enable them to carve out a niche in the export market but, with the exception of producers in Uruguay, there is little prospect of producers in South America getting that support. While their European counterparts are supported by a complex web of subsidies and price supports spun by the Common Agricultural Policy, farmers in countries like Argentina have no such state assistance. Furthermore, the current economic crisis in Argentina is likely to lead to further consolidation in the wine industry: the bigger exporters with capital outside the country will be able to continue importing items such as steel vats, while those with their money tied up inside the country will find it increasingly difficult to do likewise. So far the established wineries have not been much affected by the economic crisis because they can reach foreign markets with cheaper exports and many of them had already invested in winery equipment.

In order to survive, therefore, smallholder farmers need to be linked into a system that provides them with incentives and information to work effectively in the market. They need to be linked to the bigger wineries via mutually respected contracts. Small may be beautiful, but not necessarily when it comes to the wine industry in South America.

CHAPTER 8

Sheep in Patagonia: blown by the winds of change

Introduction

W E GLIDE THROUGH the maze of watercourses, our big ship squeezing through impossibly narrow passages between jagged rocks and soaring cliffs. These myriad fjords, islands and inlets make up the western coast of Chilean Patagonia. Here the opportunities to lose oneself among the windswept islands are endless. The German cruiser, the *Dresden* availed itself of this opportunity and hid from the desperate pursuit by the British for ten long weeks during the First World War.[1]

Our ship, the *Puerto Edén*, has no such plans of evasion. We are approaching the end of our journey in Last Hope Sound, 1460 kilometres south of the town of Puerto Montt, which is itself regarded as southerly by most Chileans. Below us on the cargo deck, several truckloads of tightly packed, seasick sheep are waiting to disembark on dry land at Puerto Natales. Wedged into trucks four floors deep, the sheep have been nervously chewing each others' wool for the past three days. Balding and sick, they do not look as if they will be welcome additions to Patagonia's sheep flock.

And why bother to bring sheep here? Patagonia already hosts millions of sheep. Is this not like bringing coals to Newcastle? It is only when we happen to find our flock's future 'shepherd', south-east of Puerto Natales some weeks later, that we discover the reason for their great journey. The sheep industry in Patagonia is in crisis, and the sheep on the *Puerto Edén* may be part of the solution. New blood is needed if the industry is to survive.

The semi-desert conditions of the windswept grasslands of southern Chile and Argentina offer few alternatives to sheep farming. However, plummeting world prices for wool, over-grazing, and land degradation have led to a crisis. Sheep farmers have historically supplied two markets – wool and meat – from a 'dual purpose' local sheep breed, which provides both products but is specialized to produce neither. Farmers are having to adapt rapidly to changing conditions. The recent collapse in the world wool market has pushed some farmers into bankruptcy while others are trying to carve out a niche in fickle world markets. The larger farmers, those with access to capital, are bringing in new sheep varieties to specialize in meat production. The sheep on the *Puerto Edén* are part of this process: they are breeding stock for one of the large farms known as *estancias* in Chilean and Argentine Patagonia.

Sheep farming in Patagonia is a very different business from many of the land uses further north in Bolivia, Peru and Ecuador, discussed in other chapters. A smallholder here might own a few thousand hectares of land and hundreds or thousands of sheep. And yet, changes to world markets, new demands for quality, and environmental pressures result in some familiar challenges for farmers in this part of the world. Sheep farming is in crisis, but how viable are the alternatives? What can farmers do to improve their returns from sheep farming? And to what degree are those who continue in the sheep industry hampered by restricted access to international markets (for example in Europe) by demands that local abattoirs meet stringent health and quality requirements? We start, however, with a look at the history of sheep in Patagonia, setting the stage for current choices.

The flock from the Falklands

It was in 1876 that Diego Dublé Almeyda, the governor of the southern Chilean region of Magallanes, travelled to the Falkland Islands and returned with 300 sheep.[2] The governor sold his sheep to an Englishman, Henry Reynard, who placed his newly acquired flock on Isabel Island in the Magellan Straits that separate the land mass of continental South America from the vast island of Tierra del Fuego.

The sheep flourished and, suitably inspired, other pioneers brought more sheep over from the Falkland Islands. By 1890, in only 14 years, 25 000 sheep had been imported from the Falkland Islands.[3] Sheep ranching in Patagonia was a risky business though, and many of the early ventures failed. Much of the area claimed by prospective sheep farmers was poorly known, and vast areas were occupied by indigenous groups such as the Tehuelche and Ona. Like the Tasmanian aborigines, the indigenous peoples were hunted down and exterminated as the sheep ranchers expanded their activities.

In 1884, eager to support the colonization of southern Patagonia, the Chilean government auctioned 570 000 hectares of land north of the Magellan Straits. This was followed a few years later by the leasing of almost one and a half million hectares of land in Chilean Tierra del Fuego. Sheep ranching became the domain of the large landowners, dominated by a handful of people. These included José Noguiera, José Menéndez and the brother and sister partnership of Sara and Mauricio Braun. Together they formed a company called La Sociedad Explotadora de Tierra del Fuego (SETF). When Sara Braun married José Noguiera, and Mauricio Braun married the daughter of José Menéndez, the SETF was truly consolidated.

During the early years, sheep commanded a high price in the Chilean town of Punta Arenas, but start-up costs were very high, not least due to high sheep mortality rates during the passage from the Falkland Islands and the expense of installing many kilometres of fencing. The technology associated with raising sheep was brought in from Britain and the Falkland Islands. Along with the necessary equipment came administrators and overseers, principally from Scotland and England, but also from Spain, Germany, France and Australia.[3] Once settled, the new colonists established their own farms.

At the end of the nineteenth century, the Argentine government encouraged the SETF to expand its activities into Argentine Patagonia and facilitated the process by repealing import taxes. In comparison with Chilean Patagonia, which is made up of the Magallanes region and includes the Chilean section of Tierra del Fuego (17 per cent of the country's total area), Argentine Patagonia covers approximately 700 000 km,[2] stretches further to the north, and encompasses five provinces.[2]

Boom and bust

The rise and fall of the dual purpose sheep

The early sheep ranchers focused primarily on wool. Together with cotton and linen, wool was one of only three textile fibres then available. Merino sheep, raised primarily for wool, became dominant in the more arid north of Patagonia. Once the sheep reached 7 years of age they were uneconomic as wool producers and were slaughtered for meat. The local market for mutton was limited, however, and was unable to absorb the huge supply of meat from the great flocks of Patagonia. Alternative markets were needed.

The development of the meat-refrigerating industry, and the introduction of the refrigerated ship in 1894 for the transport of meat to the United Kingdom, provided a further impulse to the sheep industry.[2] Corriedale sheep (a cross of Merino and Lincoln breeds) raised predominantly for wool but also providing good-quality meat, were introduced from New Zealand in 1907 and became dominant in southern Patagonia. The improved-quality wool and meat could be packaged and shipped to Europe.[3] At the beginning of the twentieth century, the United Kingdom was one of the most important markets for Chilean wool, taking 75 per cent of wool production in 1907 from the Magallanes region in Chile. Evidently, global markets are not new to Patagonian sheep farmers.

The high demand for wool and meat encouraged more and more sheep. Marginal lands were increasingly used for stocking. These areas had sparse forage and stocking densities were, therefore, lower than on the better-quality land. Good-quality land could bear one sheep per 0.8 hectares, while marginal land supported only one animal per two hectares.[3] Production costs were also higher on the marginal lands because more fencing material was needed. But as long as the price of wool was high, sheep ranching remained profitable.

By 1910 the Patagonian rangelands in Argentina alone supported 12 million sheep, a phenomenal increase from the 300 imported in 1876. During World War I, the price of wool tripled and sheep numbers in Chilean and Argentine Patagonia spiralled. More refrigerated plants opened in both countries in order to meet the increased worldwide demand for meat.

For the first half of the twentieth century, the SETF dominated the sheep industry in both southern Chile and Argentina. Walking around the windy streets of Punta Arenas, mainland Chile's most southerly town, the one-time wealth of SETF is still visible. Around the central square stand the beautiful and elegant houses of its wealthy owners. Here is Sara Braun's Palace, built by a French architect, using only materials imported from Europe. Nearby the Braun Menéndez Palace was also decorated with European furniture, even the portrait artist being imported from France. Central heating, installed in 1903, ensured the family lived in warmth as well as style.

Until the opening of the Panama Canal at the beginning of the twentieth century, Punta Arenas was one of the most important towns in South America. The Panama Canal provided a waterway between the Atlantic and Pacific Oceans, but before it was built ships had to pass around the southern tip of South America, either through the Magellan Straits or around Cape Horn. Punta Arenas, located by the Magellan Straits, prospered as a result of all the commercial sea traffic. The town's cosmopolitan nature at the time is further demonstrated by the fact that in its heyday it boasted an array of foreign-language newspapers, including English and Serbo-Croat, that reflected the diversity of its inhabitants.

From the 1940s onwards, however, the vast *estancias* began to lose their hold on Chile as successive governments granted land to new settlers. In the 1960s the largest *estancias* in Chile were finally expropriated and subdivided; further division of land occurred in the early 1970s prior to the military coup against President Allende. Smallholder sheep farmers were to have their turn.

In 1952 the sheep population in Argentine Patagonia peaked at 22 million. Since then it has declined to fewer than 13 million.[2] Numbers have also fallen in Chile. In 1966 there were 2.8 million sheep in the Magallanes region in Chilean Patagonia. Thirty years later this was down to 1.9 million. Magallanes region accounts for approximately 51 per cent of Chile's sheep flock.[4]

Numerous interconnected factors have contributed to the decline in sheep farming. These include declining demand for wool and meat, land degradation, and increased production costs.[5] Furthermore, in August 1995 a harsh, cold Atlantic wind struck Patagonia unexpectedly. Exposed sheep flocks were buried under heavy snowfalls. More than 375 000 sheep were killed in Chile alone in the so-called *Terremoto Blanco* (white earthquake). With farmers already facing low wool and meat prices, many decided not to restock.

Falling demand, falling prices

Although the sheep are dual purpose, wool has always been the mainstay of Patagonian sheep farming. The industry is thus particularly sensitive to world price fluctuations. As demand for wool fell worldwide, so the price went down with it. As one disgruntled sheep farmer pointed out to us, we rarely wear wool nowadays: synthetic fibres offer warmth with easier care and lighter weight. The economic crisis in Asia in 1997, followed by that in Russia, compounded Chile's and Argentina's market woes.

Fluctuations in the price of wool are nothing new. In the 1920s, a slump in the wool price and subsequent wage cuts by owners of the *estancias* led to economic crisis in Patagonia.[6] In Argentina, rising tensions between the English-origin landowners and their labourers exploded in 1921 with the launch of an anarchist uprising and its bloody suppression by the Argentine Army.[7]

Degrading the land

In Tierra del Fuego, there are two immigration posts called San Salvador, one on the Argentine and one on the Chilean side of the border. They are separated by approximately 12 km and reflect the one-time acrimonious relationship between the two countries. We stop cycling on the road in 'no-man's land' and gaze at the degraded grasslands where the thin, golden grass barely conceals the loose sandy soil of the gentle hill slopes. The ferocious wind snatches the breath from our lungs, constantly buffeting and blasting. There is very little vegetation here to hold the fragile soils together but, despite the poor grazing, sheep abound like white, fluffy boulders.

Most of Patagonia is arid, lacks a well-defined rainy season, and vegetation consists of tussock grasses and shrubs. The grassland area is known as *pampa*. Unsustainable rangeland management, especially decades of continuous grazing on marginal lands, has led to soil degradation and a reduction in suitable forage. In turn this has led to a decline in livestock health and a lowering of productivity. Although reduced worldwide demand has contributed to declining sheep numbers in Patagonia, a substantial reduction in the quantity and quality of forage is also to blame.

About 94 per cent of Argentine Patagonia has been classified as degraded, which includes some with 32 per cent of severely or very severely degraded land.[2] In many cases, overgrazing has led to a reduction in plant cover and desirable grazing species. These degraded grassland areas have been invaded by perennial weeds such as *Hieracium pilosella* and dwarf shrubs that are not palatable to sheep. The problem is not a recent one and has been a concern for decades.[3] Furthermore, soil has become compacted and soil erosion rates in the fierce wind are high.

The harsh conditions found in much of Patagonia – little rain, strong winds and short growing seasons – are not conducive to abundant plant growth and this means that natural regeneration is slow. Even in areas where there are no longer any sheep grazing, recuperation of the land may take decades. In Chilean Patagonia, some 750 000 hectares are degraded beyond the point of recuperation.[8] In both Chilean and Argentine Patagonia, there are also areas where degradation is so advanced that there is no hope of achieving sustainable land use based on sheep.[5]

Crisis in the sheep industry

Land degradation and stocking densities: caught in a vicious circle

Land degradation in Patagonia is acknowledged to be a problem: both the Argentine and Chilean governments have encouraged alternative production strategies to try to reduce the degradation. One option is to plant improved forage, introduce irrigation and fence off areas in need of protection. Another common response has been to suggest drastic reductions in stocking rates of up to 40 per cent. However, a major obstacle to better land management is the size of landholdings. In Argentine Patagonia, 61 per cent of landholdings are smaller than 1000 hectares, though in total they cover less than 2 per cent of the total land area. In contrast, 10 per cent of landholdings are over 10 000 hectares, occupying 63 per cent of the land area.[2]

In Argentina, economists have calculated that a minimum of 6000 sheep is needed in order for a ranch to be economically viable. Given the current carrying capacity of Patagonian rangelands of about 0.3 sheep per hectare, this requires a minimum landholding size of 20 000 hectares. In Argentine Patagonia only 5 per cent of landholdings are greater than 20 000 hectares. Those with less land, which is the vast majority of Argentine Patagonia's 13 000 ranchers, often respond to declining wool prices and lower productivity by overstocking their holdings.[2] Although overstocking may seem the best way to meet immediate needs, it accentuates land degradation. Smallholder farmers are caught in a vicious circle which they often find very difficult to break out of.

Repeating history: concentrating ownership

Rodrigo Alvarez at the Ministry of Agriculture in Punta Arenas explains the land degradation problem in Chile and the impact that this is having on farm ownership. In the case of Chile, economies of scale are different to those in Argentina. According to Alvarez, 3000 sheep is the minimum that is needed for a ranch to be economically viable. In the past, one hectare of very good quality land could support five sheep. Due to land degradation, the same area can now support only one sheep, and often less.

This raises the question as to whether some of the co-operatives established in the 1960s and 1970s can be profitable. Alvarez says that in Chile about 10 per cent of sheep farms are still in the hands of co-operatives. However, co-operatives are definitely less profitable than the larger *estancias*, and some have been forced into bankruptcy. This has led to a concentration of land in fewer hands. In some cases, land ownership patterns are similar to those prior to land expropriation and redistribution in the 1960s and 1970s. And in the current economic climate, it is not clear what the future holds for the remaining co-operatives.

Near Puerto Natales in Southern Chile, we met Eduardo Montoya, a Chilean sheep farmer. Eduardo owns 22 000 hectares of land, a sprawling expanse of *pampas*, stretching to the low hills in the far distance. His family have been sheep farmers here for two generations and Eduardo now has 18 000 sheep. Land redistribution in the 1970s saw his father's huge *estancia* broken up and given out to the workers. Eduardo believes that confiscating and redistributing land in the early 1970s was a folly. In his view, ownership and management were suddenly passed to groups of people who had no experience of managing a farm. As the smaller farms failed, he was gradually able to buy back all the land that had been originally confiscated.

In Puerto Natales, Dolly Gibbons and her husband Oscar, voiced similar sentiments about the land reform. Dolly was born on a huge *estancia* at Cerro Castillo, just outside the Torres del Paine national park. With 120 000 sheep, this was one of the farms owned by the SETF. Dolly's father was an Englishman, one of the managers imported by the SETF to administer the farms. Dolly's husband, Oscar, worked as a shepherd on the *estancia*. Each shepherd looked after some 4000 sheep from his *puesto* or post. Dolly and Oscar were nostalgic for the old days of the big *estancias* and explained that when the SETF was broken up in Chile, the small Chilean farmers did not know how to manage their farms. Dolly and Oscar saw their claims to land passed over in favour of people from other parts of the country and looked on in dismay as many of the co-operatives soon fell apart.

The novelist Isabel Allende described some of the, perhaps, unforeseen consequences of land reform in Chile during her uncle's presidency.[9] 'Farmers who had lived for centuries obeying orders, joined together in co-operatives, but they lacked initiative, knowledge, and credit. They did not know how to use their freedom and many secretly longed for the return of the patrón, that authoritative and frequently despised father who at least gave clear orders and in times of trouble protected them against natural disasters, crop blight and epidemic diseases among their animals. Farmers did not have the courage to enter a bank, and even if they did they were unable to decipher the small print on the papers put before them to sign. Neither could they understand what the advisers sent by the government were mumbling about, with their big words and city way of talking'.

Whether it was poor management through lack of resources or lack of initiative, many of the small *estancias* have failed. But in some parts of Patagonia, while some sheep farmers are selling their land, even this is not always an option. There may be no buyers. Dotted all over Argentine Patagonia, and before the economic crisis of early 2002, even large *estancias* sat empty, with padlocked gates. Farmers' livelihoods throughout the region are under threat, and national and regional governments recognize that something has to be done.

Which way forward?

Changing direction: an option for the few?

When we visit Eduardo Montoya at his *estancia* near Puerto Natales, several hundred of his 18 000-strong flock are being rounded up for the annual sheep shearing. The giant central barn is a hive of activity. Sheep are corralled in pens. Periodically a sliding gate is raised and the shearer grabs one of the sheep by its back legs. The sheep is tackled and pinned efficiently to the ground while the shearer starts removing its thick woolly coat. There are eight shearers. They can each shear 200 sheep per day.

The power-driven shearing tools they use are ancient and 'Made in England' is still visible on the metal casing in solid 1950s lettering. Other members of the itinerant shearing team collect the wool fleeces and compress the wool from 70 sheep into compact 270 kg bales using hand-operated presses. The bales are covered with plastic sheeting and tied with metal bands. They are now ready for export. There is still an export market and in 1997 wool exports from the Magallanes region of Chile totalled 6410 tonnes, mainly going to Italy (32%), Uruguay (19%) and China (14%).[10]

Throughout the early and mid-twentieth century, high wool prices meant that the sheep industry in Patagonia focused on wool rather than on meat production. Times have changed. Eduardo explains that he now receives US$1/kg of wool; each sheep produces about 4 kg of wool per year. In the 1960s he used to receive US$3/kg. The price of wool is so low that sales just about cover the running costs of his *estancia*: any profits come entirely from the sale of meat. Lamb sells at US$1.30/kg and each sheep weighs approximately 15 kg. Producing meat is far more profitable than wool, and this is the direction in which Eduardo would like to move. He is partly able to do so because southern Chile also has conditions that favour the rearing of the Romney Marsh breed, the only serious rival to the predominance of Corriedale, and a breed that produces high-quality meat.

The seasick sheep that we saw on the *Puerto Edén* travelling south from Puerto Montt to Puerto Natales were destined for Eduardo's *estancia*. He explains that the new Romney Marsh breeding stock are currently in quarantine but as soon as they arrive he will start a breeding programme in order to produce stock that is geared primarily to meat rather than wool production. And Eduardo has an important advantage over many other sheep farmers in making this switch from wool to meat production. He has close links with an abattoir and freezing plant in Punta Arenas and market connections in Europe. As we were later to see in Argentina, this is not a facility on which all farmers can rely.

Eduardo is confident that there is a future for lamb exports. Figures from 1997 show that lamb exports from the Magallanes region totalled 3636 tonnes, chiefly to Spain (18%), Mexico (16%) and the United Kingdom (14%).[10] According to Eduardo, the health scare in Europe over mad cow disease in beef (bovine spongiform encephalitis) has improved the market for lamb. Eduardo believes that by focusing on quality and adopting aggressive marketing tactics, Chile can increase lamb exports to Europe. The government of Chile is facilitating this by helping to improve conditions at abattoirs to ensure rigorous quality control. Furthermore, recognizing consumer demand for healthier foods, researchers in Chile are investigating ways of reducing cholesterol levels in lamb through the management of pasture and the age at which animals are slaughtered.[11]

It seems that, for some, there may be a way out of the wool crisis, but it may well be the case that only large landowners in Patagonia are able to change their operations from a focus on wool to one on meat production. Like many changes in the production process, capital is needed both for the inputs (in this case new sheep stock) and to enable the farmer to bridge the gap before reaping the benefits of higher prices from sheep reared for good-quality meat rather than wool.

As is the case with coffee, wine and forestry (see Chapters 3, 7 and 9), many farmers do not have sufficient capital to make the necessary changes that would enable them to compete more effectively in national and international markets. It is this lack of capital that partly explains why the future of some of the sheep co-operatives and smaller *estancias* is bleak. Perhaps for them the answer is to focus on the national market and supply the lower-quality meat that comes from the ubiquitous Corriedale sheep.

Who's going to eat it?

Don Chicho runs a restaurant in the southern Patagonian town of Puerto Natales. From November to March he caters predominantly for tourists and the rest of the time for locals. He has 250 sheep and rents land for grazing. They are raised for meat which is served at his restaurant. It is the only option on the menu and is accompanied by potatoes, salad and carafe after carafe of wine.

Eat, drink and be merry is our abiding memory of *Don Chicho's*, and yet the popularity of his restaurant hides a salutary fact. As Chile's economy has grown, meat consumption has increased. Between 1986 and 1996 annual meat consumption per capita grew from 28.5 kg to 60.7 kg. However, within this total, the annual consumption of lamb has dropped from 1.0 to 0.5 kg per person.[4] The problem, according to Rodrigo Alvarez at the Ministry of Agriculture in Punta Arenas, is that the market for lamb is very local. Only in the south of Chile is lamb a regular feature of the diet. As a result, the government in Chile is trying to encourage its citizens throughout the country to eat more lamb. Lamb consumption has also fallen in Argentina from an average of 5.9 kg per person in the 1960s to 2.5 kg in the early 1990s.[12]

Without a boost to national demand it is unlikely that a switch to more lamb production will be a successful option for sheep farmers in either Argentina or Chile. Perhaps, then, the only option left is to recognize that there is little future in sheep and to seek alternative income-generating activities.

El Galpón: diversify to survive

Faced with problems of overstocking, land degradation and falling demand, the Argentine and Chilean governments have both encouraged diversification of land use. While sheep farming remains the most important rural activity in Patagonia, provincial and federal agencies offer farmers incentives to move away from sheep farming and diversify into tourism, forestry and alternative agricultural activities such as growing garlic. For many, tourism is seen as the way forward.

El Galpón, 21 km from the town of El Calafate in southern Argentina, is located on the shores of Lago Argentino. El Galpón is a 'working' *estancia* in the sense that it has 3000 hectares of land and 5000 sheep. Pasture is plentiful because there is no shortage of water from the many springs dotted around the *estancia*. The *estancia* still sells wool to the town of Comodoro, several hundred kilometres away on the Atlantic coast. Meanwhile, live animals are transported to the meat-packing plant in the coastal city of Rio Gallegos. However, it is tourism that provides the life blood of El Galpón.

165

El Galpón formerly belonged to the owners of Estancia Anita, scene of the last stand of the anarchist uprising in 1921, which was sparked by a wool price slump. El Galpón was purchased from its original owners and turned into a hotel and restaurant. It is an idyllic location, and the old *estancia* buildings have been beautifully restored. Bales of wool are stacked at the entrance to the restaurant. The dining room overlooks the turquoise waters of the lake on one side. On the other, a huge glass window reveals the shearing shed so that, as they tuck into their barbecued lamb, the diners can watch a traditional sheep shearing demonstration. Horse-riding and bird watching are also on offer to the well-heeled visitors.

In 1999, El Galpón received approximately 8000 visitors. In 2000, numbers were reduced, partly because the road to El Calafate was being repaired. The *estancia* survives but it does not provide large employment opportunities for local people. In addition, the current economic and political crisis in Argentina may well lead to a further reduction in visitor numbers. Tourists visit the *estancia* during the relatively short summer season from November to May. During this period, El Galpón employs ten people, most of whom come from Corrientes in the north of Argentina. A handful of tourism students from Buenos Aires help out as part of their work experience. Throughout the rest of the year, El Galpón employs one person full time.

El Galpón is perfectly located to attract tourists. The nearby town of El Calafate is a booming tourist centre. It is the staging post for visits to the spectacular Los Glaciares National Park and particularly the nearby Ventisquero Perito Moreno: an advancing glacier five kilometres wide, in front of which viewing platforms allow visitors to watch vast high columns of ice crash into the glacial waters below. Few places have such a steady supply of wealthy tourists. However, one place that does is Ushuaia on the south coast of Argentine Tierra del Fuego.

Harberton and Viamonte: location, location, location

Looking around at the open pasture beneath a chill leaden sky, it is no surprise that Harberton has been compared to an estate in the Scottish Highlands.[7] Only the penguins out in the Beagle Channel give it away. Harberton is 50 km from Ushuaia, the most southerly city in the world. The farmhouse is tucked away in a sheltered inlet, protected from the choppy waters of the Beagle Channel, the stretch of sea named after Darwin's famous ship. Thomas Bridges, missionary and linguist, established Harberton in the 1880s. It has been in his family ever since.

We meet Tommy Goodall, whose wife Natalie is one of Bridges' descendants and the current owner of Harberton, in the cafeteria next to the house. Among the delicate china tea cups and plates of delicious cake, Tommy does not mince his words as he spells out the problems he and his family face. Harberton is relatively large, with 20 000 hectares of land. In its heyday it had 8000–10 000 sheep and 2000 head of cattle. About 20 men were employed here. But during the *Terremoto Blanco*, the 1995 blizzards, approximately 80 per cent of Harberton's stock were lost and it has never fully recovered. Sheep are simply not economical and cattle face stiff competition from elsewhere. Faced with this, Harberton now has only 400 sheep and employs four men to manage the farm.

Instead, tourism has become the *estancia*'s mainstay. A few visitors come by road, but the majority arrive by boat from Ushuaia, which is itself an important centre for tourism. Most of the cruise ships that tour the Antarctic set off from Ushuaia; the nearby Tierra del Fuego National Park also attracts many visitors. Between 7000 and 8000 people visit Harberton each year. It is one of the stops on a trip into the Beagle Channel, where visitors can see penguins, sea lions, albatrosses, cormorants and grebes. Tourism contributes about US$50 000 per year to Harberton's coffers. Tommy explains that it is better than nothing but still not much with which to pay six guides and keep the farm running.

However, there are no real alternatives to tourism. With respect to sheep ranching, Harberton faces three major problems: low wool prices, losses of sheep to theft and feral dogs, and a declining local market for lamb in Tierra del Fuego. Tommy laments the fact that in 1960 wool sold for US$3.80/kg. Now it sells for just US$0.90/kg. If you take inflation into account, he points out, the modern equivalent of the price in the 1960s would be about US$10/kg. Before the road to Harberton was built, Tommy used to pay the Argentine Navy to transport his wool to Ushuaia. The transport costs significantly reduced his profit margins. The road has reduced the cost of getting the wool to market but improved access has increased the problems of theft and dog attacks.

Changing regulations, markets and tastes for meat in Tierra del Fuego have also altered the rules of the game. For many years, imports of beef on the bone to Tierra del Fuego were prohibited, according to Tommy, as a measure against foot and mouth disease. More recently the policy has been reversed, and traders are offered a 30 per cent subsidy to bring meat into the region from the north. Outsiders who have moved to Tierra del Fuego in large numbers over the past decade bring with them a taste for sweeter, northern beef. Lamb sales locally are in decline, while local producers of beef also find it hard to compete in the local market.

With its location on the shores of the Beagle Channel, tourism is likely to continue to play a major role in the future of Harberton. In that respect Tommy is lucky: his brother faces a more serious problem. Adrian Goodall owns Estancia Viamonte, a large *estancia* of 40 000 hectares, some 100 km to the north of Harberton, just off the main road running through Tierra del Fuego. Adrian is not sanguine about the future. In contrast to Eduardo Montoya in southern Chile, who has access to a modern meat freezing and packing plant, the refrigerated meat-packing plant in the nearby city of Río Grande has recently closed down. Built in the 1950s, it was no longer economical to keep it open in the face of continued improvements in hygiene demanded by the European market.

In Australia, New Zealand or even Chile, says Adrian, newer packing plants can cope with increased quality requirements. In other countries, plants are built with an expected lifespan of ten years: the one in Río Grande had been going for fifty. The increasing quality demands, particularly in the EU, are viewed by many sheep farmers as hidden barriers to free trade, or non-tariff trade barriers.

When we met, Adrian had little idea where he was going to sell the lambs. Located inland and far from a centre of tourism, he faces the same problems as his brother Tommy in terms of low wool and meat prices but without the possibility that tourism will contribute substantially to the *estancia*'s running costs. His *estancia* offers some possibilities for camping, mountain-biking and horseriding but this part of Patagonia is not everyone's cup of tea. Being in the southern hemisphere, the tourist season lasts from October to March, coinciding with ferocious winds that sweep across the open *pampas*. We stop at a campsite on the edge of Adrian's *estancia*. Set amongst a glade of trees, it offers some respite from the wind. However, camping is unlikely to offer much respite from the economic abyss facing Adrian and other ranch owners in Patagonia.

As we leave Viamonte, Adrian pulls a wry grin and points out that at least things are not so bad in Tierra del Fuego as in the Falkland Islands where, lacking any market, the islanders throw their excess sheep into the sea. Nonetheless, there is growing evidence that Falkland Islanders are actually adapting rather successfully to the decline in the wool and meat markets and are successfully pursuing other options.

Turning the tide in the Falkland Islands

There are some circumstances where the switch from sheep to tourism, and principally eco-tourism, has worked. The irony is that one very successful venture is in the Falkland Islands from where the first sheep in Patagonia were dispatched. In the eighteenth and nineteenth centuries, visitors to the Falklands decimated local populations of whales, seals, seal lions, albatrosses and penguins. Following the occupation of the Islands by the British in 1833, keeping sheep became the main economic activity.[13]

The sheep industry in the Falklands went into decline in the 1960s but few in the outside world took much notice of this until the Argentine invasion in 1982. Since then, there have been concerted efforts to protect wildlife – the king penguin, which had been wiped out by 1870, has now returned – and eco-tourism has become an increasingly important part of the Islands' economy. The number of tourists staying on the Islands has risen to 3000 per year (almost equalling the Islands' population). In addition, some 40 000 tourists sail through Stanley harbour on their way to the Antarctic and South Georgia. Many of these visitors briefly visit the Falklands Islands' albatross, penguin and seal colonies and some farmers earn more from admission charges than they do from wool sales.

The Islanders have not, however, given up on their traditional sheep industry. Taking advantage of the recent prosperity from exploiting local squid populations, the Islands' government has just built a new abattoir which, it hopes, will meet the strict hygiene conditions demanded by the EU. The aim is to secure a niche in the growing European market for organic lamb.[14]

No easy answers

In this chapter we have looked at some of the issues that face large and small-scale farms in Patagonia, and find that there are similarities with small farms elsewhere in South America. Although a small sheep farm in Patagonia might be orders of magnitude larger than a small farm in Peru, Bolivia, or Ecuador, they face some of the same challenges: the need to specialize to improve quality of produce; poor access to processing facilities and markets, lack of credit and inability to invest. In Patagonia, these issues are exacerbated by an industry in crisis, driven by environmental stress and falling productivity, declining markets for wool, and a shrinking local market for meat coupled with an international market that demands quality beyond the ability of many farmers and processors to provide.

The harsh reality is that there are no short-term or easy solutions to resolving the sheep crisis in Patagonia. Although there is a need for government support in terms of financial incentives for those farmers who adopt more sustainable land-use practices, the Argentine and Chilean governments recognize that only large-scale enterprises that achieve economies of scale and implement sustainable land-use practices, are going to be able to compete in the wool and meat markets.[5]

Although alternative income-generating activities are clearly needed, and have been offered in some places, there are critics of the way that these have been promoted. Farmers are seldom seen as equals in the conservation and development process, and alternative development initiatives have been designed and implemented largely from the top down. In some cases, government subsidies for forestation programmes are paid 18 months after tree planting. No provision is made for farmers to have access to credit in order to buy seedlings and hire labour. In particular, farmers without formal title to their land are unable to secure the credit from banks that is needed to invest in alternatives. Farmers are understandably reluctant to embark on alternative production systems when they are unsure of the market potential they offer.

Traditional top-down models of policy design have not encouraged large-scale buy-in from farmers. Measures based on participatory and community approaches to natural resource management may have more success.[2] The need for a 'farmer-first' approach to better land management is as relevant to Patagonia as it is to smallholder farming conditions in Peru, Bolivia and Ecuador. But as the Argentine economy implodes, it is far from clear whether the government in that country will accord Patagonian sheep farmers the assistance that they need. As Tommy Goodall pointed out while we drank tea at Harberton, there are few votes in sparsely populated Patagonia. The government is much more concerned with appeasing the anger of the pot-banging urban dwellers in cities like Buenos Aires than a few remote sheep farmers.

Perhaps sheep farming has simply outlived its time. The reality is that there is a reduced demand worldwide for wool products, and the consumption of lamb is unlikely to compensate for this change It is certainly a conclusion that many British upland sheep farmers have come to in recent years. Changes in Patagonia seem to support this conclusion. Agriculture, once the mainstay of the region's economy, is losing ground to other activities. In Chilean Patagonia, hydrocarbons in one form or another now provide 44 per cent of the gross domestic product of Magallanes region; a new coal mine and a petrochemical works recently opened. In this context, the future for sheep farming in Patagonia remains very uncertain.

CHAPTER 9

Forestry and livelihoods: making trees pay

Introduction

WE SIT ON a rough wooden bench and watch as the man in the army hat and faded tattoos folds strips of palm leaf in an intricate pattern and a basket appears before our eyes. Around us the tropical forest presses in on the little clearing where the guest house stands, alone and separate from the villagers' houses. Once the basket is complete, the man and his companion show us how to make fish traps from palm stalks, and string from the long leaves of a spiky aloe plant. The bushes around us are armed with hunting traps made of branches and palm leaves; later we try the blowpipe armed with wooden darts. The visit is a celebration of the richness of the forest, and the ingenuity of indigenous communities to put that richness to use. This is Salazar Aitaca, one of the ten communities in an eco-tourism scheme near Tena in the Amazonian part of Ecuador, which is run by the Red Indígena de Comunidades del Alto Napo para la Convivencia Intercultural y Ecoturismo (RICANCIE). Together, RICANCIE and the communities are working out a way of making a living from the forest without destroying it.

The preceding chapters have demonstrated some of the opportunities that the global and national markets present for farmers and the problems they face in taking advantage of those opportunities. Intensification, diversification, specialization: each brings its economic, environmental and social costs and benefits to farmers. In coffee, banana and coca-growing areas, agricultural expansion has often gone hand-in-hand with forest destruction. As farmers grapple with fickle markets for their agricultural produce, can forestry be an alternative?

Forests and trees offer a huge range of products and environmental services. Existing natural forests may provide timber, non-timber forest products (NTFPs) such as medicinal plants, seeds and fruits; or the forest may provide environmental services like protection of watersheds, fisheries, or conservation of bio-diversity. New trees may be established in plantations or combined with crops in agroforestry systems to provide products, like timber, firewood and fodder, and services like soil conservation, shade and windbreaks. Products from trees and forests may be sold in the market, or there may be non-market benefits, on which it is difficult to place a monetary value. In many societies, forests have an important cultural role to play.

171

Forests usually provide a range of these products and services simultaneously, often to different people, so forest management needs to balance a
number of potentially conflicting needs and values.

Throughout Latin America, people are looking for ways to make forests
and trees attractive options, by harnessing these products and services to
provide a decent livelihood for smallholder farmers. In a world that increasingly emphasizes monetary values and market integration, can forests which
provide long-term and often intangible services survive? How can trees,
which take so many years to grow, provide benefits in the short term for
farmers who cannot afford to wait? Is it possible to make trees pay? This
chapter seeks answers to these questions by looking at a range of forestry
activities from Argentina to Ecuador.

Sustainable forestry: have your cake and eat it

Logging or sustainable forestry?

The word 'logging' normally invokes images of deforestation, wildlife hunted
to extinction and general Armageddon. And in many parts of the world,
there is justification for that image: estimates continue to show the world is
losing almost 16 million hectares of natural forest in the tropics every year.[1]

But does it need to be that way? For many years, sustained-yield forestry
was the aim for professional foresters throughout the world.[2] This approach
aimed to harvest trees for timber in the forest only as fast as they grow. If
we know how long it will take a tree to reach a commercial size, and how
many of those trees there are in the forest, we can calculate how many trees
we can cut down every year. It would work fine if the only thing forests
produced were timber.

Over the past few decades, however, the concept of sustainable forest
management has broadened, to recognize the fact that forests provide many
other products and services. Sustainable forest management moves away
from the focus on timber as the primary product, and aims to fulfil multiple
environmental, social and economic objectives.[3] While forests can provide a
range of products and services, there are usually trade-offs between them.
Maximizing timber yields is not generally a compatible objective with
maximizing wildlife values, for instance. Faced with the huge diversity of a
tropical rainforest producing many different products and services,
sustainable forest management can become very complicated indeed.

From coca to conservation: forestry in the Chapare region, Bolivia

The Chapare region of Bolivia used to be famous as one of the main
sources in Latin America of the coca leaf. Much of the coca from the

Chapare was processed into cocaine and was smuggled to the USA and Europe. Now, with a considerable amount of military and economic assistance from the USA, EU and the UN, coca has largely been eradicated. Without the coca, everyone is looking for alternatives. The focus has been on alternative and licit crops (see Chapter 6, Coca eradication and alternative development) but sustainable forest management is also seen as a viable alternative to growing coca.

Near the village of Israel B in the Chapare, the noise of a chainsaw shatters the quiet of the forest. Wilson, one of the extension agents from the UN-funded Jatun Sach'a Project (the 'Big Tree' Project in Quechua), leads the way through the trees. Further down the shady path a thin man in army fatigues is waving a large chainsaw. Antonio Arce works with the Israel B community logging and sawmilling company, set up with help from Jatun Sach'a. The aim of the company is to enable the community to harvest trees from the natural forest on their land on a sustainable basis, add value to it by saw-milling, and market the timber in Cochabamba, the nearest city.

We stop to talk to the farmers. As soon as we do so we are surrounded by a cloud of mosquitoes. Antonio and Wilson seem unaffected by the swarm as they explain that the project started to work with the Israel B community in 1999. The forest here is divided into small blocks which are individually owned by the villagers. Twenty-four farmers, including many of those working today, put their blocks of forests, about six to eight hectares each, into the plan, making a total of 180 hectares. Other farmers, who also own land within the same forest block, decided not to participate. During 1999, Antonio told us, they had started cutting lines to demarcate the boundaries between the forest inside and outside the plan area. Now they were clearing some access tracks for logging, along lines planned with the project.

With the assistance of Jatun Sach'a, a formal company was set up to carry out the felling and extraction. Seventeen of the 25 shares in the company have been sold for US$100 each to members of the community. The idea is for the forest owners to sell their trees, standing, to the company. The company cuts the trees, extracts them to the edge of the forest, saws them up and sells the sawn timber. Although the price an owner receives for the trees is not high, at US$30–40 per tree, the aim is to add value through sawmilling. Sawmill equipment is provided at a subsidized rent by Jatun Sach'a: the company pays only for fuel and maintenance costs. Jatun Sach'a has also helped to carry out an inventory of the trees in the forest, training the community as they go. A management plan – a legal requirement for forest management in Bolivia – has been put together by the project. At a cost of US$3000 to prepare, this represents a significant contribution to the local farmers' forestry company. To get the company going, Jatun Sach'a is providing training in tree measurement, saw milling, forest conservation, chainsaw use and business administration.

If work goes according to plan, the company should make US$30 000 from sales of timber in its first year. From this, they will need to pay themselves, pay for equipment hire and fuel, invest in equipment, pay marketing costs and perhaps even have a profit for shareholders. The benefit of creating a company in the community is that the participating farmers get paid three times over for their trees: once when they sell the tree, once for their work for the company, and once through dividends if they own shares.

There are, however, a number of pitfalls that need to be overcome. Sustainable forestry is something of a gamble: for many trees it is simply not known how fast they will regrow and what effect the logging damage will have on the composition of the forest that grows back. Perhaps the extra light getting to the forest floor will encourage different species to grow. Perhaps it will encourage more timber trees to grow. Nobody really knows for sure. As part of the management plan, Jatun Sach'a has planned for the regrowing forest to be monitored, to check the speed of growth and types of trees that come back. Before starting, the inventory also checked the seedling trees on the forest floor, to verify what types of trees would be available to grow into the spaces left by harvesting.

With traditional methods of forest exploitation, loggers tend to exploit an area of forest first for the valuable trees like mahogany and cedar. They then return again and again to extract steadily less valuable species. This way of logging never gives the forest a chance to recover. Gradually the forest is degraded until only the very fast-growing, uncommercial tree species are left. When the forest has no value left, it is more likely to be cleared for agriculture. In order to try to avoid this, forest law in Bolivia stipulates that any area of forest that is opened up for logging must be closed off again after two years and left to regenerate for a further 20 years.

For a small forest area, like that surrounding Israel B, this law brings its own problems. Each forest block is open for only two years. During this time, all the trees identified for cutting must be felled and removed. That might amount to perhaps four or five trees in each hectare. In Israel B, the inventory identified about 20 species of trees that have commercial uses. The result of this diversity is that there is never very much of any one type of wood per unit area.

If the 180-hectare total area of Israel B was divided up over the 20-year logging cycle, about nine hectares could be harvested each year. This might provide 45 trees, with perhaps only a couple of each sort. For a small forest, this is a marketing nightmare. Where buyers want supplies in quantity of the same species, the small forest offers them small amounts and variety. Further, the high cost of machinery for extraction and processing is unfeasibly large in comparison to the small volume of timber produced each year.

For Israel B and other similar Jatun Sach'a forestry projects, the answer has been to do the logging over a shorter period of time. At Israel B, the forest area has been divided into six annual felling blocks. When the last of these is logged, the area will be closed off completely for 14 years to allow the forest to regenerate. The company, and the community it supports, will need to find alternative sources of income for the intervening fallow period. The project hopes that by then they will have adequate resources and skills to work for other villages in the Chapare region, felling, extracting and sawing their timber. While a good opportunity for the Israel B company, this would not offer the same benefits to other small forest owners, who would not receive all the benefits of 'value added' by sawmilling.

The participating farmers in Israel B are optimistic about the future. They show us the portable sawmill already in place on the edge of the forest. Jatun Sach'a has also promised three sets of carpentry equipment for use with off-cuts from the sawn logs. In Cochabamba, a possible buyer has been identified for two of the 20 species likely to be harvested from Israel B. Work is going ahead with demarcating boundaries and cutting access tracks for the tractor. For now, the important thing is to get to work and start implementing the management plan.

Forestry: a technical or administrative challenge?

There are, however, some concerns about the long-term future of sustainable forest management initiatives like the one at Israel B. Once chainsaws are widespread and contacts with buyers in Cochabamba established, will the community and the forestry authorities in the Chapare be able to enforce a 14-year fallow period? When funding from Jatun Sach'a ends, will the farmers in Israel B be ready to take on the enterprise? These are problems that have been faced by other forestry professionals working in Bolivia and worldwide.

The lowlands of eastern Bolivia have many years of experience of community-led forestry enterprises. For several years, Freddy Peña Flores has assessed sustainable forestry in indigenous communities in the lowland Santa Cruz region. We meet Freddy at his offices in the vibrant city of Santa Cruz. In his experience, the problems are not technical so much as organizational and administrative. Sustainable forestry needs good organizational skills, planning, marketing and long-term business management.

According to Freddy, the problem is that far too often well-meaning organizations inadvertently undermine the long-term future of their development work. Organizations that seek to help communities to manage their forests tend to do so in a paternalistic way. The communities rely on outside help and never develop their own capacity for management. Short project funding cycles mean that communities do not have enough time to develop their own skills. When the external assistance is withdrawn, the project may collapse. Freddy suggests that in Bolivia much development aid to date, and not just that directed at the forestry sector, has had a negative impact by breeding dependency.

Communities also have bigger organizational problems than private companies. Where the forest is a common resource, it belongs to everyone and no one. People swap between jobs so it is difficult to develop skills for good-quality workmanship and marketing. These points were emphasized by Omar Quiroga and Gerardo Rasens. They work with a small development NGO in Santa Cruz called Centro de Investigación y Promoción del Campesino (CIPCA). The timber business, they suggest, is so complex and specialized, that it needs a full-time professional to get a sawmill off the ground. Aid agencies, which often work on three to five-year project cycles, do not have the expertise or the determination born of necessity to make this work. In their view, communities need to work with a commercial partner, and an NGO's role is best confined to helping draw up forest management plans for designated areas of forest.

Omar and Gerardo add that if the sawmill is owned or run by the community itself, there is a potential conflict of interest between forest owners and the sawmill. Forest owners feel that the sawmill should pay a 'fair' price rather than a 'market' price. If the sawmill pays a higher than market price for the raw logs, it is effectively subsidizing the forest owners. The sawmill itself may then become uncompetitive. Sometimes the same people may own both the forest and the sawmill, but not always. Without clear objectives, the danger is that conflicts will develop within the community.

The lessons from the Santa Cruz area are very relevant to the situation in the Israel B community in the Chapare. Jatun Sach'a is working hard to establish a new NGO to take over the responsibilities of maintaining and renting out the sawmilling equipment, and providing technical and organizational assistance. By providing training in business management skills to the Israel B community they hope to increase its sustainability. Ensuring adequate skills and long-term funding will be essential.

Israel B is one of many communities in the Chapare with the potential to get involved in sustainable forest management. Until recently other communities interested in forest management found themselves in a Catch-22 position. Until the end of 2000, external funding via projects such as Jatun Sach'a, was conditional on farmers eradicating all their coca. As with alternative agricultural crops (see Chapter 6, Coca eradication and alternative development) many farmers were, understandably, reluctant to do so because in some cases the viability of the alternatives is unproven and, where there are benefits, they often materialize months or years after the coca has been eradicated. A USA-based forest economist commented that many more communities in the Chapare would get involved in forest management if the 'coca eradication before outside assistance' conditionality was removed. Now that this has happened, it remains to be seen whether there will indeed be a positive impact on sustainable forest management in the region.

A cruel irony in Bolivia is the impact of coca eradication on the general economy. Prior to eradication, coca was an important component of the Bolivian economy. Eradication has removed one of the biggest sources of wealth in Bolivia. This has been manifested in the precipitous decline in house building in Cochabamba. Few would deny that some of the investment in housebuilding during the coca boom came from the sale of cocaine. For Israel B and other communities involved in forest management as an alternative to growing coca, the current housing slump means that the demand for their timber has also dropped.

The challenge posed by forest certification

Bolivian forests produce wood products for markets worldwide, including Europe and the USA. Many people in these regions have a very negative image of forestry and logging. We are constantly assailed by facts and pictures, illustrating the destruction of the world's forests. Reassurance from forestry companies and spurious claims of sound environmental practices made repeatedly during the 1980s and early 1990s proved worthless. In 1991, a survey of the UK wood retail market found that, of over 600 claims of sustainability, only three could actually substantiate their claim.[4] Many people, led by organizations such as the World Wide Fund for Nature (WWF), Friends of the Earth and Greenpeace, felt it was time for independent checks to be made on claims of good forest management.

In 1993, a new organization, the Forest Stewardship Council (FSC), was set up, bringing together environment, social and industry groups concerned with forest management. The FSC developed a 'standard' which sets out what is meant by good forest management, including environmental, socio-cultural and economic aspects. Independent auditors visit the forest to check whether the standard is adhered to. Forests that pass the test are awarded a certificate, the proof that they are doing it right. Finally consumers have a way of identifying which products come from a well-managed forest. By May 2002, almost 29 million hectares of forest in 56 countries had been certified under the FSC system.[5]

Bolivia has been in the forefront of forest certification. One of the first community forests in the world to be certified was Lomario near Santa Cruz. Jatun Sach'a in the Chapare is considering the benefits of applying for certification. In theory, having an FSC certificate can open doors to markets. Certainly, not having a certificate can close doors, particularly to markets in Europe and the USA.

For small forest owners and community forests, however, certification brings its own problems.[6] Fulfilling the requirements of the standard demands good organizational capacity, as well as the technical ability to harvest a forest without damaging it. For forest management to be certifiable a level of management ability is needed that many communities do not have, and cannot develop in the short term. Additionally, the markets where certification is valued tend to be export, niche markets for high-value products. For some communities, these markets may be too demanding, requiring access to skills and equipment that they do not have.

For owners of small forests, certification can also work out disproportionately expensive. So far, it has often failed to provide the access to markets that was expected automatically to follow certification. Without external help to pay for the audit and make the changes required to meet the standard, many small and community-run forests cannot achieve certification. But donor help has tended to encourage dependence, which itself prejudices their long-term management.

Certification aims to encourage good forest management by opening markets to products from such forests. It recognizes good forest management where it already exists. In the short term, though, certification cannot provide all the answers to the deeper problems of small forests and community forests.

Given the long-term uncertainty associated with sustainable forestry, and the large capital investment needed to extract and process timber, many forest owners and development workers in Bolivia and other regions of Latin America are looking for lower-impact ways to make a living from their forests. Rather than felling and extracting the trees and taking them to the market, eco-tourism offers the chance to bring the money to the forest.

Eco-tourism: bringing the money to the forest

The riches of the Amazon

The taxi drops us at the end of the road some 30 km from Tena in the Amazon region of Ecuador. We walk in slowly to the Salazar Aitaca Community guest house. We pass through steaming pasture land, then through a mixed plot of banana, cassava, naranjilla fruit and maize, before plunging down the hill into secondary and finally tall, primary forest. It is wonderfully cool in the forest, as we slip and slide on the thick carpet of leaves. We spend two delightful days at Salazar Aitaca, staying in a basic but comfortable palm-thatched hut, and eating simple but very good food, cooked by one of the women from the village.

Carlos, our guide, introduces us to a vast array of sights in the surrounding forest. In a cave, we dodge missile-like oilbirds, which were formerly hunted but are now protected by the community as a tourist attraction. Within the forest, countless trees, plants and vines are sources of medicines to cure everything from haemorrhages to problem flatulence. Carlos tells the story of an American woman crippled by arthritis. She was carried to one of the indigenous communities and was treated there for 21 days. By the end of her stay she could walk again – a miraculous cure – using medicines from the forest and the knowledge of the indigenous people.

On a huge rock in a sacred spot, Carlos points out petroglyphs and tells us the stories behind them. There are carvings of spacemen similar to petroglyphs that we had seen in Chile and eerily similar to one of the huge figures etched in the desert sands in Nazca, Peru. We try target practice with a blow-pipe, paddle the river in a dug-out canoe, and walk the single-file paths through the forest.

In the evening we are invited to Doña Blanca's house to see how *chicha*, a mildly alcoholic drink, is made. We sit on a low wooden bench next to the fire while Doña Blanca expertly peels, boils, mashes and kneads cassava into a pliant dough, which she leaves to ferment overnight. The house is cramped: three small rooms built of flattened bamboo and thatched with palm leaves. Thirteen people live in these three rooms, Doña Blanca tells us, unrolling whatever bedding they have on the floor. Eco-tourism has the potential to bring much needed income to some of the poorest communities.

Deep within the forest are small agricultural plots. Local people traditionally clear small areas of forest and grow food crops such as yucca, plantain, papaya and pineapple. After a few years the plots are abandoned and the forest slowly regenerates. Within a few years it will be difficult to tell which area had until recently been cleared of forest by the farmers. While forest regenerates in one plot, the family clears another one. This type of agriculture is perfectly sustainable as long as the population is small and the forest has long enough to recover between cycles.

This trip was organized and run by RICANCIE. The organization was formally founded in 1993 with the aim of improving life for 200 native Quechua families in the area of Tena, some six hours from the capital, Quito. The main objectives have been to provide economic alternatives to logging and unsustainable agricultural practices which destroy the forest, and the mining and oil exploration that encroach on the Quechua lands.

Economic alternatives are needed. Oil is the mainstay of the Ecuadorian economy but oil exploration in the Amazon region is highly destructive. At 2-km intervals within an oil concession, 3-m wide trails are cut through the forest and dynamite is detonated every 300 m along the clearing. The seismic waves are recorded and analysed to determine the geological profile under the forest floor and the probability that oil is there. Within a typical concession, approximately 1300 km of trail are cut, 1500 helicopter pads are made and all in all about 900 hectares of forest are destroyed. All this just for the seismic testing!

Reacting to the growing demand in the developed world for 'environmentally-sound' tourism, Tena has become a centre for eco-tourism in Ecuador. Numerous tour companies run eco-tourism trips from here. Many have built their own cabins in Quechua communities around Tena. The vast majority of these tour companies, says Emilio Grefa, RICANCIE's co-ordinator, are run by people from outside the area, often foreigners or businessmen from Quito. Outsiders have many advantages when dealing with tourists: they have contacts and access to all the communication channels, they understand how to cater for tourists, and they have money to invest.

Eco-tourism is not necessarily benign. Internal divisions have appeared in many communities when some families become involved in tourism without consulting the rest of the village. Traditional forms of community organization are weakened, and traditional culture is eroded. The people themselves are converted to a tourist attraction and in many cases there is little emphasis on cultural understanding. Often, little of the money spent by visitors is left in the host communities. The communities feel they are being exploited.

RICANCIE has sought to provide an alternative. The organization started in a single community. Since then it has grown to encompass another nine communities in the Upper Napo River basin. While they have received some external help with training and infrastructure, RICANCIE is fiercely proud of its self-determination and independence. The cabins in each village are built and maintained by the communities; guides are drawn from the villages; the co-ordinating office in Tena is run by people from the communities. All important decisions are taken by a Council, whose members are drawn from the participating villages.

Training is an important part of RICANCIE's work and participating villagers are trained in administration and guiding foreign tourists. The organization is acutely aware of the danger of bringing tourists into indigenous communities. It is a fine balance between bringing tourists in and losing the culture they aim to protect. Tourists bring with them a different culture and a level of wealth beyond the dreams of most villagers. Without careful management, tourists can unwittingly act as a catalyst for social division, breakdown in community institutions and out-migration.

To help minimize the negative aspects of eco-tourism, RICANCIE has established rules for tourists, guides and communities. The cabins for tourists are located on the edges of the villages to minimize impacts on community life. A limited number of trips is permitted to each community every month to prevent overload, and tourists are not allowed to stay on in communities after their tour has finished. Donations, swaps and sales of clothes to the community are not permitted, and intimate contact with guides and the community is strictly forbidden.

RICANCIE deals with about 1000 tourists per annum. Approximately 75 per cent of the revenue from tourists stays in the communities, in comparison to 5–10 per cent with externally owned eco-tourism operations. After paying costs and wages for members of the community who work with the tourists, any profit is passed to the members of RICANCIE in the community. Profits have been used for health and education facilities, schoolteachers and as credit. The remaining 25 per cent of the revenue is used to support the office in Tena, although the office staff are also required to bring in their own funds through donor-aided projects and consultancy fees.

While we left Salazar Aitaca feeling refreshed and filled with respect for the people to whom this is home, it was clear that it has not all been plain sailing for RICANCIE. Under Ecuadorian law, 'community companies' like RICANCIE have no legal status. Having refused to convert to private company status, the organization was closed down several times. At the same time, RICANCIE was recognized as being among the top 100 responsible tourism projects worldwide, and was invited to participate in the Expo 2000 exhibition in Germany. Embarrassed by the international recognition afforded to RICANCIE, the Ecuadorian government is now reviewing the legislation to allow them to operate.

Furthermore, when RICANCIE started up, there were initially 30 communities who wanted to participate in the project. With insufficient visitors to provide an income for all the communities, two-thirds of the villages left the organization. Many of these were the more distant communities, with difficult access for tourists and which require a longer stay to make a visit worthwhile. Location and access are key issues for developing eco-tourism, as exemplified by another forestry project in southern Ecuador.

The pros and cons of isolation

In the Province of Loja, in southern Ecuador, we visit a project assisted by the Food and Agriculture Organization of the United Nations (FAO). The Desarrollo Forestal Comunitario (DFC) project is working with small farmers in the village of El Tundo. During the bumpy five-hour ride by four-wheel drive to the community, Jeanneth Ordóñez, who runs the project, explains what they are trying to do. Near the village are some 70 hectares of walnut forest, a relatively rare asset in Loja. When the previous owner threatened to fell the forest, it was bought by an association of villagers called the Asociación de Productores Agroforestales del Tundo (ASOPAFT). They were concerned by the environmental impacts of felling the forest and applied for assistance from several northern European countries and the FAO project to buy it. Arcesio Tandez, a member of ASOPAFT says, 'It's important to protect the forest because it's protecting the springs and we need the water downhill'.

Sixteen local families make up ASOPAFT. The idea is to link up with a local NGO called Fundación Arco Iris, which manages 150 hectares of forest nearby for conservation and eco-tourism purposes. According to a survey of birds carried out by Arco Iris, of the 80 species recorded, seven were found only in this area. This is a very high level of endemism, which may provide the subject for more scientific study. The members of ASOPAFT hope that, together with Arco Iris, they can develop the possibilities of 'scientific tourism' in the area. To this end, they have built a cabin in the 70-hectare forest to accommodate up to seven visitors at any one time.

Don Flavio, the vice-president of ASOPAFT, offers us fresh lemonade on the shady patio of his house. He tells us that while he and others in the community have always recognized the importance of conserving the forest, they still needed outside assistance to encourage villagers to work together and, more importantly, to draw up a realistic management plan for the 70-hectare forest. Villagers are limited to cutting trees only for domestic use – Don Flavio explains he is thinking of taking two or three trees this year to repair his house. On the whole, however, the forest is to be managed for eco-tourism and non-timber forest products (NTFPs). But a major problem for developing an eco-tourism project in this area is the lack of transport.

El Tundo has no public transport from the nearby town of Sozoranga, which itself is in a pretty isolated part of Ecuador. During the rainy season, the road may be cut off for months at a time, so that the only access is on foot. El Tundo is faced with the same problem as the more remote communities involved in RICANCIE's scheme: although eco-tourists may like to feel they are in the wilds, they generally do not like to walk very far to get there. For those trying to conserve the walnut forest, the problem is accentuated by the fact that far fewer tourists visit southern Ecuador than flock to the Amazon around Tena.

Another problem, and one shared by many rural areas throughout the Andes, is labour shortages. The DFC project has provided training to the 16 families in ASOPAFT but the enterprise is jeopardized by out-migration among participating farmers. Continuity and skills are lost, an inexorable brain-drain. Seeking their economic fortunes elsewhere, approximately half a million people left Ecuador between 1999 and 2001, from a population of only 14 million.[7] Three of Don Flavio's sons work in Spain, and while the migrants often send back considerable sums of money to their families, it presents a challenge for development among those who stay behind. Ecuador's economy may be picking up but the migration phenomenon continues.

The project in El Tundo is not relying solely on eco-tourism to provide value from the forest. As in several other locations, they are attempting to reap market benefits from some of the non-timber forest products and services which the forest offers. This, together with eco-tourism, may provide local villagers with a sustainable income from the forest, helping them to protect and conserve it.

Scientific tourism

A variation of the eco-tourism theme is scientific tourism. Scientists, aspiring scientists, and others who are just interested in learning more about tropical forests, can and do contribute to local forest communities' livelihoods. They do so by paying to work for a period of time on different aspects of forest management.

Jatun Sacha is an Ecuadorian NGO (not to be confused with the Jatun Sach'a project in the Chapare, Bolivia). Jatun Sacha's principal objectives are to promote biological investigation, environmental education, conservation of tropical forests, and the management of biological reserves. The NGO manages five biological reserves where forest management is combined with development programmes in neighbouring settlements. These programmes include agroforestry, health and education.

The biological reserves have rustic accommodation, and each year around 300 volunteers from Ecuador, the USA and Europe spend anything from a few weeks to several months working at the reserves. The overseas visitors pay to work at the reserves and carry out useful scientific research. The money raised is used to subsidize some of the Ecuadorian students and also to pay for Jatun Sacha's development programmes in the local communities. Farmers in the area benefit from the programmes and recognize that the forest is a valuable resource that is worth conserving. In some communities, women's groups have started to make money from the sale of handicrafts, such as woven baskets, made from material that comes from the forest. The sustainable use of non-timber products like these can offer opportunities for benefiting from forests without cutting down the trees.

Non-timber forest products and services: looking beyond the trees

Under-appreciated walnuts

We tend to forget that forests produce much more than just trees. NTFPs are all the other things a forest produces apart from the wood in the trees: nuts, flowers, berries, mushrooms, vines, and so on. NTFPs offer a way of harvesting products from the forest without destroying it. In some parts of the world, low-income farmers may earn 10 to 25 per cent of household income from NTFPs.[8] In El Tundo, Ecuador, the DFC project is not working only in eco-tourism. It is also investigating walnut as a possible NTFP, another way of generating income from the forest.

Apart from its excellent timber, walnut produces nuts, which can be used for making sweets, or simply sold as seed for walnut reforestation projects. A syrup can be made from the leaves, which is used as a herbal remedy for anaemia. At Don Flavio's house, we meet Miriam Lapo, a local promoter for the project in El Tundo. She tells us that walnut syrup was known locally and made for domestic use before the arrival of the project here. Now the community makes syrup and sells it at local markets as well as through fairs in Quito and Loja.

So far, income from the syrup has not been high, Miriam admits, but expanding sales through shops is difficult. The syrup can be kept for only a month without it starting to ferment. Shops often keep stock for longer than a month, leading to quality problems. The project contracted a university specialist to look at means of stabilizing the syrup as well as at possibilities for marketing, recommended doses, and so on. Once the study is complete, the community will need to apply for their product's health certificate, aquired after a chemical analysis, which is required for all foodstuff distributed through the supermarkets in Ecuador. In recent times the study had stopped because the leaves on the evergreen walnuts had turned brown – nobody was quite sure why.

Sweets can also be made from the walnut seeds but the high labour costs involved in extracting the seeds from the shells render it unprofitable – labour costs that are exacerbated by the shortage of labour due to migration to Spain. So far, income from the walnut and syrup has not been high, Miriam says. They are trying to organize a micro-business, to learn more skills; they need an accountant, someone to oversee quality control and more ability to seek out market opportunities. In short, they need similar business skills to any other agricultural enterprise we have seen.

The fungal connection

In several parts of Ecuador, the collection, drying and selling of mushrooms from pine plantations is a commonplace activity.[9] In the mid-1970s forestry plantations of the non-native trees *Pinus radiata, Pinus patula* and *Cupressus macrocarpa* were established for timber production in the community of Salinas in Bolívar province. Following plantation establishment, wild edible mushrooms *(Boletus luteus)* began to grow. Local people recognized the commercial value of the mushrooms and a small-scale industry was born. Interest in the commercial value of the mushrooms has generated interest in establishing more pine plantations: in fact the mushrooms are valued more highly than the timber. One women's group earned income of US$17 863 in 1996, from the collection and sale of these mushrooms.[10] This is a substantial sum of money in Ecuador.

Meanwhile, in Pichincha in northern Ecuador, another project started by the DFC has advanced with their NTFPs. Here, the DFC is working though the local federation of popular organizations known as the Federación de Organizaciones Populares de Ayora-Cayambe (UNOPAC). The Federation buys produce from local farmers and helps to market it, both through the UNOPAC shop and wider afield. We visit a small community where a women's group collects mushrooms from the government-owned pine plantations nearby. With driers designed and built with assistance from the project, they clean and dry the mushrooms, which have medicinal uses. With help from UNOPAC, the women have applied for and received their 'health certificate'. This allows them to sell their dried mushrooms to the big supermarkets in the capital, Quito and throughout the country.

As the pine trees approach the age when they would normally be felled, the women have asked for 40 hectares to be given to the community to manage. However, the ownership of the pine plantations is currently in dispute between the Ministries of Agriculture and Environment. The community needs to ensure that they have some control of the plantation and that the trees are not felled for their primary purpose: timber. If the trees are felled, the women's source of mushrooms is gone. It is a common problem with NTFPs: people who use the NTFPs may not have rights to manage the forest. Their destiny is in the hands of others, who may have other objectives. Uncertainties about forest tenure and restricted forest access are the biggest constraints worldwide to the development of local forest-based businesses.[8] A similar issue arises with environmental services like watershed protection, which are provided by forests.

Environmental services: let the beneficiaries pay

We stand in damping rain that drips from the leaves of the cloud forest overhead. All around, glinting from behind the trunks of trees, are bright yellow orchid flowers. This 500-hectare area of forest is on the edge of a buffer zone surrounding a reserve in Imbabura province, northern

Ecuador. It has no legal protection even though the watershed it covers provides water to 1200 people in the town of Pirmapiro further down the valley. The forest provides a service to the people of the town, protecting the fragile soils of the watershed and ensuring a regular, albeit limited, supply of water to the town.

The people who own the 500 hectares of forest, 21 families in the community of Nueva America, do not benefit from providing this essential environmental service to their neighbours downstream. The DFC project has been working in this area for about five years, with local bodies such as the Municipality and a number of NGOs. They aim to find a way of making the forest an economic asset to the people of Nueva America, without felling the trees. To do so, they need to see beyond the trees and look at other forest products and services provided by the forest.

Initially the DFC's efforts focused on developing markets for NTFPs. Medicinal plants from the forest are known from this area of Ecuador and are used by local people. This offered a potential product for sale in the market. Some trial exports to the USA were successful, but the resulting orders demanded container-loads of herbs, quantities that could not be supplied from this forest.

Another possibility was the cultivation of orchids. About 30 different species are found in this forest: bright, intricate flowers that surely must be saleable. NTFPs can be over-exploited just as timber trees, and to ensure the wild population is not depleted the orchids must be cultivated. Orchids, however, are difficult to propagate from seed. They need to be produced vegetatively from the stolon, the root-like bulb that holds the orchid to the tree on which it grows. With some species, the stolon can be divided and grown to produce flowers relatively rapidly.

In Nueva America, the community established an open-air orchid house and tried to propagate the numerous species. They found that only two of the thirty species could be produced in this way. The problem, explained Mario Añazco of the DFC project, is that these flowers are really popular in Ecuador only on Mother's Day – a limited season, you might say. Orchid sales alone are not going to save this forest.

With medicinal herbs and orchids proving too difficult to market, the DFC project is going back to basics. If the main service that the forest provides to the town below is water, perhaps a system can be found to pay for the service. Pirmapiro currently receives only about one hour of water per day; inhabitants are unwilling to pay their water rates for such a limited service. However, the Municipality is constructing a tunnel so that water from another river can be diverted into the river that supplies Pirmapiro. The Municipality plans to increase water provision up to ten hours a day. Nueva America's watershed will need to provide half of the expected water demand.

The FAO proposes to establish a fund to pay the Nueva America forest owners US$1/ha per month to protect their forest for the next ten years. In the meantime, the increased water supply in Pirmapiro could justify the Municipality raising the water rates of the existing 1200 users in the town, a figure that is likely to grow once the supply of water improves. Over the ten years, the Municipality could save money from the higher water rates charged to those living in Pirmapiro. Hence, when funding from the DFC comes to an end, the Municipality will be in a position to pay the Nueva America forest owners for the watershed protection service their forest provides. The system would have become self-sustaining.

When we visited Nueva America, the plan had not yet been put into action. It remains to be seen how well it works. Will the people pay their water bills? Will the Municipality prove stable enough to save funds over a ten-year period? Will the forest owners feel the funds are sufficient payment for preserving the forest? It is still too early to judge whether the project will be a success, but 18 months after our visit the omens are good. The scheme is now up and running and the residents of Pirmapiro are seemingly prepared to pay for a more regular supply of water.[11]

In the light of concerns about global warming, a worldwide market is also developing fast for the carbon storage capacity of forests and trees. Essentially this allows producers of large amounts of carbon dioxide, such as electricity companies in developed countries, to pay other people to plant trees or manage forests, thus locking up some of the carbon in the atmosphere. Carbon off-set certification is already available. In Ecuador, one organization called Programa Face de Forestación (PROFAFOR), is working with indigenous communities in the Andean region to plant trees, taking advantage of carbon off-set opportunities. PROFAFOR is one of only two organizations to have achieved certification in Ecuador under the FSC; it has also been certified for its carbon sequestration, allowing it to receive funding from a Dutch electricity company. As the market becomes clearer and the rules better defined, carbon off-set may offer a huge opportunity for other small landowners and communities to sell this environmental service of their trees and forests.

And so to market . . .

There is little doubt that direct payments for environmental services, or a clear market for NTFPs, can offer small forest owners direct short-term benefits from the protection and management of their forests or plantations. As the women collecting mushrooms have shown, the benefits from NTFPs can far exceed the timber value of the trees.

El Tundo and Pichincha's experiences point to a number of obstacles for projects attempting to develop markets for NTFPs. The products themselves may not be well known, so that the project needs to develop production methods, such as the propagation of orchids, or the stabilization of walnut syrup. Once developed, there may be bureaucratic or administrative barriers to the market. In Ecuador, all products sold in shops need a health certificate (see page 184). This costs about US$200 for each product, which is prohibitive for many small community companies in the absence of outside help. A legal company registration costs another US$100 and takes time to acquire. Only once these barriers have been overcome can the work of marketing and selling the product, in adequate quantities and consistent quality, begin.

NTFPs may provide a means of creating wealth from an existing forest without destroying it, but it is not always a simple route. Similarly, developing markets for a forest's environmental services, for which people have not previously paid, is often difficult. For farmers who do not own pre-existing forest, making trees pay can be even more difficult. Trees take a long time to grow, even in the tropics, tying up space, invested time and money. Can trees provide an alternative and decent livelihood for smallholder farmers?

Agroforestry: bringing the trees to the farmers

Agriculture + Forestry = Agroforestry

Most of us think of forestry and agriculture as separate, and potentially conflicting activities. Agroforestry describes a wide range of land-use systems where trees and shrubs are grown together with crops and pasture.[12] This might be at the same time, or one after the other.

Agroforestry as a discipline became widely recognized in the 1980s. Long prior to this, however, farmers had been incorporating trees into their farms and recognizing benefits. Since the 1980s, many rural development projects have encouraged farmers to plant trees for a variety of reasons, including environmental benefits such as soil conservation, increasing diversity, and production of timber or firewood. In addition, trees can provide inputs to the farm system, such as shade and fodder for animals, or green manure for crops. It sounds great, but the reality is not always so simple.

Who decides what?

Near the town of Aguaray in northern Argentina, we visit Don Alejandro on his small patch of land. He has received help from a state-funded forestry project to improve his land by planting trees. He was supposed to have finished planting an area with trees but admitted he had fallen behind on the task. Although he had planted a number of timber trees in his plot as part of the project, it was evident that his heart was not in them. On the other hand, the fruit trees that the project had helped him plant were much more to his liking. He could imagine them producing something useful during his lifetime. It was clear that Don Alejandro had not been actively involved in planning for the trees. As we walked through his recently planted field, he admitted that he planted some of the timber trees because the extension agent told him to.

Another farmer who has received assistance from the project is Don Felipe. His farm is tucked against the foot of a small hill, with mandarin trees shedding delicious fruit, and small patches of maize, potato and cassava for home consumption. He is interested in the leguminous cover crop the project can help supply in order to reduce soil erosion between his fruit trees. He also planted some timber trees as part of the project he says, but he much prefers fruit trees. His family makes jam from the fruit and sells this in a local farmers' market that has been set up by the project. The small plantation of cedar trees in the corner of one field is being attacked by an insect pest. With few trials of the growth of this species in the region it is not clear to Don Felipe when they will be ready to fell and what use they will be.

The extension agents are well aware of local farmers' preferences and try to meet them wherever possible. They point out that their hands are tied by government officials in Buenos Aires, the capital of Argentina, who insist that timber trees be promoted as part of the agroforestry activities. This is a problem that is not confined to this particular project in northern Argentina. Too often development projects are designed by outsiders without the active participation of the 'beneficiaries' (in this case the local farmers in Aguaray). Furthermore, when it comes to forestry projects, many forestry professionals shun fruit trees. As far as they are concerned forestry means timber trees or multi-purpose trees and shrubs. Fruit trees are part of horticulture and not forestry. Unfortunately farmers seldom make such a clear distinction and, as is the case with the project in Aguaray, they may well prefer fruit to timber species.

Fruit or timber, you still need a market

It would be easy to conclude that when it comes to agroforestry, fruit trees are the way forward, but it is not always the case. Down the road from Israel B in the Chapare region of Bolivia, the Jatun Sach'a project has been working for several years on developing agroforestry systems. In the village of Tres Rios, Doña Marina shows us the agroforestry system she established with the project in 1995. We stand in the dappled shade of the 10-m tall

Cerebo (*Schizolobium amazonicum*), extraordinarily fast-growing trees, native to Bolivia. Beneath the rows of Cerebo are scattered citrus trees, producing bright orange fruit in such profusion that they fall to the ground uncollected (see Chapter 6, Coca eradication and alternative development).

Everything here has its expected life span: the Cerebo can start to be harvested after about 10 years. A variety of slower-growing trees mixed with the Cerebo will extend the harvest period for timber. The citrus trees will produce for 15 years. However, not everything has gone quite according to plan for Doña Marina. The oranges rot on the ground because the price is so low. At less than US$0.30 per hundred fruits, she does not bother to pick them. The Cerebo market in Santa Cruz is currently good, but markets are unpredictable, especially in Bolivia. By the time the Cerebo is ready to harvest, who knows what the price will be?

In another village in the Chapare region, extension agents from Jatun Sach'a offer local farmers' leaders assistance with the establishment of plantations of agroforestry systems, including fruit trees. Politely, the farmers reject the offer. They do not have enough land to plant the trees. Instead, the farmers have decided to focus all their effort on growing bananas. Planting trees is not a high priority for some farmers.

Listening to farmers

Even though trees take a relatively long time to grow, research on experimental stations in the past has demonstrated the benefits of trees. Many agroforestry development projects have subsequently promoted tree-planting, but uptake among farmers is patchy. If farmers do not participate in tree-planting initiatives, they are often seen as being uncooperative. An alternative approach is to question whether farmers' unwillingness to follow technical advice stems more from the fact that forestry initiatives devised by outsiders do not, in general, fit in with farmers' resources, needs and priorities.

Farmer decision-making takes place within a framework of constraints and opportunities which forces the farmer to make compromises on the optimum technical management of most of the farming system. While tree planting may lead to the protection of a farmer's water supply or reduced soil degradation, farmers have not paid for these services previously. Hence, the cost of planting the trees, and maintaining them until they can be harvested, are often seen by farmers as extra costs. For many farmers, who have little extra time or money to invest in long-term projects, planting trees does not always seem like a good option. The farmer may decide not to plant trees because it is too labour, or land-intensive.

Often what farmers are looking for are activities that give tangible short-term benefits, regardless of how important the environmental benefits of alternatives may be in the long term. In the Santa Cruz area in Bolivia, farmers were encouraged by one local NGO to plant windbreaks using a species called *Grevillea robusta,* a large timber tree. Local farmers insisted that they add another species, tamarind (*Tamarindus indica*), which is less effective as a windbreak but more useful to the farmer because the fruits can be eaten.

In development organizations' agroforestry programmes, the costs in labour and money are frequently not fully calculated. In order to overcome farmers' lack of interest in planting the trees that development practitioners feel that they ought to plant, incentives such as money and material goods have been offered to participating farmers. Another incentive, as exemplified by the project in Aguaray, is to piggy-back planting timber species on more popular activities such as growing fruit trees.

Agroforestry does have a role to play in rural development and can contribute to farmers' livelihoods. In some areas, such as Yapacani near Santa Cruz in Bolivia, farmers are spontaneously adopting agroforestry systems promoted for several years by development projects in the area.[13] For them, the benefits outweigh the costs of establishment and maintenance. More could be achieved if projects were to listen to farmers and find out more about their needs.[10] In Potosí, Bolivia, this is exactly what they have done. Pierre-Henri Dimanche works with the FAO-funded Desarrollo Agroforestal Comunal project and he explained how the project has evolved.

Initially, the forestry project promoted tree planting by local communities. Timber trees were produced in nurseries. To avoid distortions created by subsidizing planting, local people were expected to buy the trees and plant them as an investment for the long term. The project works in the harsh highlands of Bolivia at an altitude of 3500–4000 metres. At this height the trees grow very slowly. The farmers involved in the project were unimpressed by results and were reluctant to spend time and money protecting their trees from grazing. Project results were poor in terms of the area planted with trees and people's level of enthusiasm. After five years, project personnel realized that there was a need for a major rethink and turned to the farmers themselves for some suggestions.[14]

As a result, the revised project changed its focus away from timber trees, some of which had been promoted as small-scale plantations. Fruit trees within agricultural and grazing plots became a focus. The project also realized there was a need to help farmers with the early investment needed: even if they wanted the trees, farmers could not afford to buy the seedlings. Returns from the trees and other components need to come more quickly than originally expected.

The project also started to establish marketing links for the fruit products between the participating farmers and a number of Bolivian towns. The project looked more widely than the trees. Assistance was provided to recuperate river beds using stone walls, called gabions, to stabilize the river. Once the river bed was stable, willow could be planted, which could also be used for basket making. Fencing around fields provides shelter from frost and wind; cactus fences also provide fruit and protection for forage crops and waterholes. The project also began to work with farmers in establishing irrigation systems.

Now, says Pierre-Henri, the project is seeing renewed interest from local people. In some areas where the project works, there is even a reduction in the number of people migrating each year to find work elsewhere, an indication perhaps that the project is helping to improve small farmers' livelihoods. The project is also realistic about who is likely to participate. The reality is that farmers without land are very unlikely to be interested in growing trees or investing considerable amounts of labour in activities that they will not benefit from.

Farmers' decision-making with respect to tree planting is influenced by a number of factors, some of which may not have been considered in the past. Often forestry projects are designed on the basis that tree planting can make a positive contribution to farmers' livelihoods. While in theory this is often the case, the complexity of a farmer's reality means that farmers seldom view 'trees' as a well-defined component. A successful agricultural development programme cannot be built on a single component such as tree-planting. All other relevant components of a farming system have to be considered. The Potosí project is unusual in the depth of the rethink and the significant move away from focusing on tree-planting as the primary activity.

Weighing up the evidence

Trees can pay

Smallholder farmers work with trees and forests in a very diverse range of situations, from tropical rainforests to the high Andean mountains, and from existing forests to newly planted trees. Trees have the potential to contribute to small farmers' livelihoods in many different ways, including sustainable timber production, eco-tourism, collection of NTFPs, fruit trees, or through developing markets for environmental services and other indirect benefits. However, approaches are needed that take into account the agro-ecological, social and economic constraints that prevent farmers from attaining their production goals and targets.

Although trees have the potential to contribute to farmers' livelihoods in some situations, they are not a panacea or an easy solution. Those trying to sell timber and NTFPs face similar challenges to farmers marketing any other product: they need quality, quantity and consistency of supply. Whether it is the quality and consistency of eco-tourism ventures, or the ability to market adequate quantities of good-quality sawn timber, small farmers need training and capacity-building to enable them to take advantage of the market.

As some of the examples described show, forests can be made to pay. RICANCIE increased the number of visitors to its communities during 2001, promising a brighter future. Community forestry initiatives in Bolivia have received new powers from the government and the rights to manage large areas of forests which were formerly granted to private companies. Meanwhile, initiatives such as the FAO project in Ecuador are searching for innovative mechanisms to ensure that people who own forests are paid for the environmental services they provide.

The forest sector is diverse and complex, and farmers can benefit from it in myriad ways. However, in order to ensure that farmers benefit from their forest resources, the professional foresters who advise them need adequate training.

Improving the training of professional foresters

Forestry has moved on from the sustained timber yield focus of the 1960s and 1970s to become a complex, multidisciplinary profession, incorporating aspects of environmental, biological and social sciences, as well as a dose of economics. The complexity of forestry is such that the management and use of forest resources involve a wide range of people and interests: the government, indigenous communities, private companies and NGOs. Forestry professionals need new skills and knowledge to manage and guide this sometimes volatile mix of players.

Unfortunately, forestry training in Latin America, and in many other parts of the world, has yet to catch up with this new focus. Graduates emerging from universities may have a theoretical understanding of how to grow and harvest trees for timber, but rarely have adequate training in the wider aspects of the field. A greater focus on the way that forestry can contribute to farmers' livelihoods means that foresters need to have much more training in the social science disciplines such as rural sociology and anthropology. This signifies a major departure from the way that forestry has traditionally been taught in Latin America. Ecuador illustrates how some of these changes can be brought about.

In Ecuador, the five universities that offer a forestry degree are funded by the state. The teaching staff at the universities recognize that the forestry curricula need updating but they point out that low salaries mean that many of them work part time and they do not therefore have the time or resources to improve teaching material. In the present economic climate, the publicly funded universities are unlikely to receive additional government funds.

A wholesale reform of the curricula is a long-term process which will require substantial financial assistance, but much can be achieved in the short term and relatively cheaply. Private forestry companies, NGOs and indigenous groups in the country all have a vested interest in seeing that the forestry sector flourishes. These organizations represent a rich source of knowledge and experience on a number of topical issues, such as sustainable forest management and forest certification, watershed management, carbon sequestration and payment for other environmental services, and eco-tourism. Many of these organizations have expressed their willingness to present seminars and modules on their work and to offer internships to undergraduates. By doing so, students will be able to get first-hand practical experience of the forestry sector as opposed to the theoretical teaching that characterizes the forestry curricula.

The reform process at the forestry universities in Ecuador is at an early stage, but it offers a pointer towards what can be done when there is a will to bring about positive change. If smallholder farmers and forest owners are to benefit more from forestry, they need technical skills to manage the forest, but perhaps more importantly for long-term sustainability, they need business and institutional management skills to help them compete in the market. While the technical challenges may be different, in this respect forestry does not differ from any other land-use sector that we have looked at in earlier chapters. A new cadre of forestry professionals, sufficiently trained in the cross-disciplinarity of the forestry sector, is needed to work with communities, smallholder farmers and forest owners, to ensure that forestry initiatives work more effectively to contribute to farmers' livelihoods.

CHAPTER 10
Conclusions: the need for trade and aid

Welcome to the globalized world

WE LIVE IN a globalized world. Decisions taken in one part of the world can have a major impact on smallholder farmers in another part. In this book, we have looked at a number of different land uses and told the farmers' side of the story as they seek to benefit from the opportunities offered by growing local, national and global markets. In South America, farmers are intricately connected to markets. Farmers cannot escape these connections, and a retreat into isolation would deprive the poor of the opportunities offered by trade. The farmers we met expressed no desire to escape from markets – they recognize that markets can bring them benefits, and without trade they would have much reduced access to the education, health services and consumer goods that they want to buy.

Global markets and attempts to control them are also not new phenomena. In the late eighteenth century Chile, still a part of the Spanish empire, was so successful at producing and exporting wines that Spanish exports to its colonies were threatened. A Royal Order was issued prohibiting the sale and shipment of Chilean wines to protect Spain's markets. For millennia people have travelled and carried goods with them to trade, sell or barter. As long as this has happened, some people have been winners, and others losers. The change in recent years has been the rapidity with which goods and money can be transferred, and the dismantling of many of the structures that aimed to protect farmers from competition. Local markets have become linked to national markets, which in turn are linked to international markets.

When we embarked on our research we were unsure what farmers would talk about. With backgrounds in agriculture and forestry, we expected that farmers would mention some of the problems associated with the bio-physical processes of growing, harvesting and processing, sometimes referred to as transformation costs. The clear message from Patagonia to Ecuador is that farmers are, and want to continue being, active participants in the market economy. Furthermore, some of the greatest problems they face surround their participation in markets, the so-called transaction costs.

Our research illustrates the way that farmers' participation in inter-national and national markets involves a complex system of agricultural inputs, technical extension, packing, processing and marketing activities.

These demands are being placed on farmers at precisely the same time that structural adjustment and cuts in fiscal deficits have led to a dismemberment of classical agricultural extension and research services, to the extent that these services are unable to serve the needs of farmers living in complex, diverse and risk-prone environments. Our research demonstrates some of the overlapping and often contradictory problems faced by smallholder farmers, and offers insights into some of the changes that are needed.

In this chapter we discuss, first, the main barriers faced by the smallholder farmers we met as they seek access to local, national and global markets. Second, we outline some of the practical assistance, based on our case studies, that would help farmers to grasp new opportunities and to overcome barriers to market participation. Third, we argue that this assistance needs to take place in the context of an enabling national and international policy environment: more support for small farmers in the developing world and reduced protectionism in rich countries are discussed in the context of international trade policies. Finally, we suggest that recognition of farmers' desire to participate in the market, and the changes that are needed to facilitate this process, may provide the basis for a more productive debate than has been the case to date about how globalization can act to reduce poverty.

Barriers to market participation

Quality, quantity and continuity of production

Time and again during visits and meetings, farmers and development workers brought up the issues of market demands for good-quality produce, adequate quantities to interest buyers, and consistent supply of both quality and quantity. In Spanish these translate as *calidad, cantidad*, and *continuidad*. One development worker in the Chapare in Bolivia referred to them as the 'three Cs'. Meeting the demands of the three Cs should not be underestimated.

Faced with competition from elsewhere, and operating in increasingly open markets, farmers are being asked to supply higher-quality goods. Witness, for example, the wine market in Argentina, where consumption of poor-quality table wine has dropped dramatically during the 1990s, while demand increased for fine wines. Both to maintain their national market niche and to enter international markets, farmers and processors must be aware of this demand and must supply good-quality products.

Meeting the demand for quality is linked to a number of other barriers faced by smallholders. For farmers to offer good-quality products they may need to specialize in the production of one crop or one variety. Farmers may be excluded from new or quality-demanding markets by intermediaries who have no interest in quality management; entry into niche and certified markets requires farmers to implement and to demonstrate the quality of production processes and products. For example, in the coffee market, the race is on to secure a niche in the more lucrative fair trade, organic and gourmet markets. Discerning customers are highly unlikely to pay more for a product if it is of poor quality. However, as we demonstrate in Chapter 3, farmers' ability to produce high-quality coffee is hampered by, among other things, the role of intermediaries and lack of access to credit.

Increasing competition and the relentless drive to reduce cost, also means that buyers continually seek to reduce transaction costs: those costs related to the trading of products. Transport, processing and transaction costs are all disproportionately high for products sold in small quantities. These economies of scale, particularly at the international level, mean that buyers seek to purchase large quantities of produce. For example, the CIRNMA in Peru, when investigating export markets for quinoa in Canada, received orders for 20 tonnes per month. While the organization might have met this order size once, it is unlikely that they could have done so consistently over time, with good-quality produce. CIRNMA did not pursue this market opportunity.

Quantity requirements are particularly challenging to smallholder farmers, who by definition produce on a small scale. Farmers face particular risks in entering a new market, yet without sufficient participants, the new market cannot be supplied. Only by working together with other farmers, can smallholder farmers accumulate enough supply-power to fulfil the market demands for quantity and continuity of production.

Farmers we met often complained during interviews that 'there is no market for our produce'. Perhaps a more accurate view is that there is no market for the quality and quantity of produce smallholders can typically offer. This is certainly the view of some of the development practitioners working in the Chapare in Bolivia. The alternative development project in the Chapare, known as Consolidation of Alternative Development Efforts in the Chapare (CONCADE) is convinced, for example, that one of the reasons that pineapple producers in the area were unable to develop a market for their produce was poor quality rather than lack of demand.

Price fluctuations

As countries in South America have liberalized their economies, farmers have become more exposed to the price fluctuations of traded commodities. Market liberalization in producer countries means that national governments are less able to control or predict crop availability, in terms of volume and timing. Where states previously provided protection for their own farmers from foreign competitors, or offered price support to farmers for their crops, many of these safety valves no longer exist and price fluctuations are passed on direct to the farmers. Simultaneously international commodity agreements, which could help restrict some of the excess production and price fluctuations, have largely fallen by the wayside.

Coffee is a good example. World oversupply of coffee, and the high volatility of international coffee prices, have led to low and fluctuating prices being paid to smallholder coffee producers in South America. Coffee producers throughout the Andean region are faced with prices that have plummeted since the mid-1990s, and those selling in the conventional coffee market can hardly cover their production costs.

In small towns in Bolivia, Peru and Ecuador, farmers' leaders and development workers linked to various NGOs log on to the Internet and track the price of coffee on world markets. They are well aware that the world price of coffee is low, but they also feel that the price they are getting from the intermediaries is too low. Meanwhile, the coffee exporters complain that farmers have little idea of processing costs, and that if they understood these costs they would realize that the prices paid to them are fair.

Meanwhile in the Chapare region of Bolivia, farmers who have been persuaded to eradicate their coca and grow alternative and licit crops, such as bananas and palm heart, are also faced with low and fluctuating prices for their crops, caused by changing production levels or more aggressive marketing by producers in other parts of the world. In the Chapare, organizations such as CIAPROT are working to ensure that the system linking palm heart producers with the processing plants is transparent.

CIAPROT aims to ensure that farmers are kept informed as to why the prices fluctuate and why the processors have to vary the price they offer. Farmers still suffer when prices are low but have greater faith that the palm heart processors are paying them a fair price. They are also aware that by improving quality, and meeting contractual obligations with respect to timing of delivery, they may be able to capture a larger share of the world market.

Price fluctuations are part of the reality of the market economy but farmers in South America and the rest of the developing world bear the brunt of these price fluctuations, while many farmers in Europe, Japan and the USA are protected by a complex array of subsidies and price supports. These are discussed in more detail below. Low and fluctuating prices leave farmers extremely vulnerable to risks and unable to invest in farm improvements. Dealing with low and fluctuating prices will be one of the greatest challenges for international policy makers in their quest to ensure that globalization leads to a reduction in poverty.

Intermediaries

Although they are often portrayed as villains, intermediaries play a vital role in many farmers' livelihoods, providing a number of services including transport and credit. Intermediaries are also often responsible for gathering together adequate quantities of product to fulfil market demands and reduce transaction costs of further sales. They assume a high degree of risk, and often make significant investments in vehicles and credit to farmers. Without them, many isolated farmers would not be able to participate in markets at all.

Intermediaries may also form a significant barrier to farmers trying to meet market demands. Produce from many different farmers is mixed together by the intermediaries, leaving farmers with little incentive to try to meet market requirements for specific types or quality of produce. In the coffee sector in Bolivia, for example, intermediaries do not separate out good from poor-quality coffee, leaving farmers unable to meet existing quality requirements. Some intermediaries are also known to deliberately moisten the coffee to increase its weight and thereby its apparent value. This in turn decreases its quality and makes it more difficult for farmers and exporters to reduce the price differential of Bolivian coffee with respect to the international price.

In long and complex market chains, a large part of the final price may be made up of intermediaries' costs. In the national market for quinoa in Peru, transport costs and intermediaries' margins may make up 70–80 per cent of the final price in the market. The complex chain thus adds cost while simultaneously reducing quality.

In some situations, however, intermediaries may be adding value to the product by separating out different qualities, for sale in different markets. In the potato market in Escoma near Lake Titicaca in Bolivia, local farmers sell a mixture of potato types to intermediaries who separate them and sell the segregated classes in La Paz for a higher price. In theory, farmers could carry out this quality management themselves and realize the added benefit; it remains to be seen whether the intermediaries will offer them a higher price for ready-sorted tubers.

Intermediaries can also have the effect of locking farmers into a poor-quality market chain. Farmers who need credit before the harvest often turn to intermediaries as sources of finance; in return, the farmer promises to sell some or all of their crop to the intermediary. In this case, even if the farmer would like to explore different market channels, such as improved quality, organic or fair trade markets, they are unable to make the switch because their crop is promised to the intermediary.

Many development projects and NGOs are trying to establish alternative market channels, which offer better terms to farmers and effectively compete with intermediaries. In some situations, however, it may be practical and more sustainable to work with intermediaries, rather than trying to bypass them. The problems noted may be due to a lack of interest in, or knowledge of, changing market demands, or possibly due to a lack of facilities and skills to manage different product quality classes. It should not be forgotten that intermediaries often have a knowledge of farmers and markets, business and negotiating skills, and investments in transport facilities, all of which are necessary for farmers to have access to markets.

Specialization and risk

International and national markets demand good quality and quantity of produce from farmers. Smallholder farmers can often meet these demands only by focusing their time and investment on fewer products, and working together with other farmers. The demands for quality and quantity almost inevitably push farmers towards specialization. Sheep farmers who keep 'dual purpose sheep' to supply both wool and meat markets find they need to restock with breeds appropriate to one market only to meet demands for meat quality. Similarly, smallholder potato farmers supplying processors in Ecuador often need to specialize in one potato variety and work together with other farmers to meet quality and quantity demands of the processor.

Specialization brings new risks for farmers. The reduction in diversity implied by growing a reduced number of crop varieties leaves farmers more vulnerable to pests and diseases, environmental fluctuations, and longer-term risks of biodiversity loss. In marginal agricultural areas particularly, diversity may provide an important safety net against total crop failure.

Farmers may find themselves locked into production of a crop, with no flexibility to switch to alternatives in the face of severe price fluctuations or poor terms offered by intermediaries. This is especially the case if the crop is perennial such as coffee, and if the farmer has made considerable investments in farm infrastructure. In both the coffee and banana sectors, farmers are selling at below the cost of production, because they have few alternatives.

Specialization on small farms also raises the issue of economically versus environmentally sustainable units. While economists and marketing specialists promote the development of economically sustainable units, such as larger banana plantations in the Chapare, Bolivia, other development workers encourage farmers to aim for diversity and environmental sustainability. Participation in markets tends to push farmers along the path of consolidating landholdings. In the long term, however, and particularly in fragile environments susceptible to soil degradation and loss, this may not be environmentally sustainable.

Transport

A perennial problem faced by many farmers is the lack of transport facilities. Transport is an issue for farmers at many levels; it can increase farmers' costs considerably, and may leave them vulnerable to the power of the intermediaries who carry their goods. Neither can they develop services, such as the type of forest-based eco-tourism discussed in Chapter 9, without adequate transport facilities to bring people to the area.

The importance of transport was recognized by the CONCADE project in the Chapare in Bolivia. As part of the alternative development programme, the road infrastructure in the region was improved, creating one of the most extensive road networks in the country. There are still problems though. The absence of a good road between the Chapare and the large potential market for bananas in Argentina means that road hauliers are unwilling to invest in refrigerated trucks to carry the fruit. Expansion of the market for farmers is stymied.

Similarly, coffee producers in Quillabamaba in Peru complain that road transport to the Pacific coast takes a week and transport costs are twice those of shipping the coffee from the Pacific port to Europe. Although both the Bolivian and Peruvian governments are committed to improving road infrastructure in their countries, pleas from their farmers coincide with governments that are cutting spending in order to reduce budget deficits.

The issue of transport has long been recognized as critical to development. While globalization may eventually lead to greater convergence between the developing and developed worlds, the stark reality is that many developing countries will be left behind. They will be disabled by geography and the fact that sea-based trade is less expensive than overland, despite the advent of railways, cars and air travel. In South America, land-locked countries such as Bolivia are at a grave disadvantage compared to countries such as Chile, with its extensive coastline.

Securing a niche market

Farmers' participation in markets is more likely to contribute to their livelihoods if they can secure a niche in more lucrative fair trade, organic and, in the case of coffee, gourmet markets. Coffee producers working with organizations such as COCLA in Peru and Fundatierra in Ecuador were unequivocal about the extent to which their livelihoods rested on their having access to these niche markets. Meanwhile, banana producers see the niche markets as a way to circumvent the power and influence of the banana exporting companies that pay them low prices. Timber from well-managed forests may also find a niche in environmentally conscious markets, and organizations like Jatun Sach'a in Bolivia are exploring the opportunities offered by niche export markets for sustainably produced timber.

These niche markets, while often providing better returns to smallholders, have additional requirements that must be met. Gourmet coffee markets require extra-quality coffee; organic markets demand that farmers' production processes do not include agrochemicals; sustainable timber markets demand that forest management is environmentally and socially beneficial. These create higher entry barriers to niche markets than for the general market. It is unlikely that small farmers can meet the additional requirements and take advantage of niche market opportunities without external assistance.

A word of caution is also needed: while increasing numbers of farmers are trying to tap into niche markets, it is also clear that these markets are not large enough to accommodate all aspiring participants. At present, this applies particularly to coffee producers. It is not possible for all smallholder coffee producers to participate in organic and gourmet niche markets, even if they meet the requirements, without depressing their price too. If the world price for coffee remains depressed (and there is every sign that it will) many farmers will be unable to make a living from coffee and will have to seek alternative livelihoods.

The fair trade market offers the best hope of decent prices for farmers because the price does not drop with increasing supply. Without wholesale changes to international markets, however, it will remain a tiny niche and most farmers will be excluded. The answer may lie in making fair trade mainstream; taking fair trade out of its niche and ensuring that some of the principles behind the movement are adopted more widely.

Consumers of niche products often live a long way from producers: the main niche markets for developing countries' coffee, bananas and timber are among the rich consumers in the developed world. Given this geographical separation, consumers are unable to see for themselves the environmental and social benefits their purchases are designed to bring. They therefore want independent assurances about the environmental and social standards associated with the products they buy. This is particularly manifested in the different types of certification explored in earlier chapters. These include fair trade and organic schemes for food, and the Forest Stewardship Council (FSC) certification of forest management.

The growing demand for organic produce in the developed world does offer a more rewarding market for coffee, banana and quinoa producers in the Andean region. Smallholder farming can be very suitable for organic production because the farmer is often able to manage soils and crops more carefully than on large farms.[1] In theory, at least, smallholders should also be able to meet the social requirements of FSC certification with relative ease, compared to large plantations or natural forest concessions.

The issue of certification can, however, be a major obstacle to farmers in accessing these markets. The certification processes can be complex and involve an initial certification assessment and annual reinspections. At times the procedures are so daunting that some of the coffee and banana farmers we met voiced their suspicions that the certification process is essentially a non-tariff barrier imposed by the EU and USA.

Smallholders often find certification demands particularly difficult to meet. For example, some European-based organic certification bodies insist on forms being filled out in English, German or French. The high cost of certification, the complexity of the process and the choice of certifying body for particular export markets are all issues for smallholders. Certification schemes generally require documented and formalized planning and record-keeping; while very simple systems can be adequate, farmers often need assistance to understand requirements and develop systems which they can apply.

Producers are also confronted with a variety of different certification schemes and may not know which programme to choose in order to improve their access to markets. For organic foods, many of these schemes comply with the basic standards set by the International Federation of Organic Agriculture Movements (IFOAM), but certification bodies working in different consuming countries are more acceptable to national consumers. For example, certification by the USA-based Organic Crop Improvement Association (OCIA) sees little demand in the United Kingdom, while Soil Association certification may be relatively unknown in the USA; and yet they offer the same assurances. As outlined in Chapter 2, farmers like the Cañartes in Ecuador opt for multiple certification for their organic banana production, but this is expensive and time-consuming.

The need for new skills

Globalization places a premium on flexibility and adaptability, and those least able to respond to change are also likely to be those adversely affected by globalization.[2] In order to have more control over their lives and to benefit from global markets, be they conventional or niche markets, farmers need to be aware of market requirements and to sell their produce accordingly. Aside from the challenge of meeting strict quality criteria and ensuring consistent supply, farmers need leadership qualities: contacts need to be forged, negotiations need to be carried out and capital is needed to improve farm infrastructure, purchase agricultural inputs and, in some cases, pay for certification. Farmers also need to be adept at financial planning and control, and forecasting. In other words, they must become more businesslike.

Where do farmers learn these skills? While local or indigenous knowledge is a powerful tool when it comes to meeting the demands of growing a crop, it is highly questionable whether it is sufficient to meet the quality requirements and transaction costs associated with market opportunities. Programmes of assistance that try to expand rapidly, bringing new skills and opportunities to many farmers, tend to do so prescriptively. Technical assistance is offered as a defined package; farmers are told what to do in order to produce for a perceived market opportunity. While this may work to help farmers rapidly expand their production of a particular crop, it is less likely to provide them with a deeper understanding of how to adapt to changing world markets. It is not really empowerment, and once the external assistance is withdrawn there is a danger that the development initiatives will peter out.

Practical assistance

Market opportunities are not enough

The preceding chapters and the outline above clearly demonstrate that just because there is a market opportunity it does not necessarily mean that smallholder farmers are able to benefit. For example, under the Lomé Convention, the EU gave preferential market access to the African, Caribbean and Pacific (ACP) countries, and yet exports from these countries to the EU fell from US$23 billion in 1985 to US$20 billion in 1994.[3]

The case studies that we have presented demonstrate that improved market access is only one of the requirements for strengthening the links between trade and poverty reduction. Around the world, thousands of development practitioners see similar stories daily.[4] Our research shows that if globalization is going to fulfil a role as the cure for poverty then more, much more, is needed. This sets a number of challenges for governments and international organizations that are working to improve smallholders' access to markets.

Smallholder farmers in South America and worldwide need both market access and access to affordable credit, along with technical and marketing assistance in order to take advantage of market opportunities. If the developed world really is prepared to offer this assistance, how should it be directed?

The steps that can be taken to improve market opportunities and reduce the barriers to accessing these markets come at two levels. First, at the practical level, there are ways in which current aid programmes can be directed to make these programmes more relevant to the needs of smallholders. Second, there is a desperate need for reform at the national and international policy level in order to bring about an enabling policy environment.

From our own experience, we can offer some insights into the factors that have helped small farmers in their quest for market access. These are of relevance to policy, research and extension agendas. In this section we describe some of the types of practical assistance that could enable small-holders to grasp new opportunities and to overcome barriers to market participation. They include the need to facilitate farmers' access to credit; develop farmers' associations as viable business units; assist farmers in meeting social and environmental criteria for certification schemes; improve basic infrastructure such as roads, packing sheds and processing machinery; and encourage sustainable agriculture.

Providing access to credit

In our travels we came across numerous examples of smallholder farmers who had succeeded in benefiting more from markets. There were also countless examples of those whose efforts have been frustrated. In almost every case, access to credit emerged as an issue for farmers, processors and exporters.

Government-supported agricultural development banks, state-supported co-operatives and state marketing boards all previously offered some mechanisms for providing credit on favourable terms at various levels. Corruption and mismanagement of many institutions, combined with structural adjustment programmes to reduce government spending, have often closed down these sources of credit for farmers and agro-industry. Often, state banking services have been replaced by private banks that charge high rates of interest, demand evidence of secure tenure not available to many farmers, and threaten to confiscate farmers' land should they default on their loans.

According to The Fairtrade Foundation, the lack of access to credit has become one of the key factors undermining the position of smallholder farmers.[5] Farmers need to be able to meet the rapidly changing demands of the market, as seen, for example, in the wine sector: in order to invest and meet new quality demands, farmers need access to credit to replant their vineyards with new grape varieties. Processors need credit to be able to pay on delivery for produce from smallholder farmers who cannot afford to wait a lengthy period between delivery and payment. Processors and exporters need credit too, in order to purchase sufficient stocks to ensure continuity of supply to the market.

This was illustrated particularly in the coffee sector. COCLA in Peru has focused on developing honest relationships with farmers, and ensuring that their creditworthiness with banks has been built up by timely repayment of loans. COCLA's access to credit means that it can pay its farmers most of the final sale price when the farmers deliver their coffee to the main warehouse in Quillabamaba. New or expanding organizations like Fundatierra in Ecuador are limited by the amount of credit they can raise. Although Fundatierra has identified a market demand for organic coffee, and has enough farmers participating to produce the quality and quantity of coffee required, it has insufficient capital to pay the farmers in advance for their coffee. Desperate for cash payment, many of these farmers are forced to sell their coffee to intermediaries before or at harvest time.

Provision of low-cost credit to smallholders would assist them to overcome a number of difficulties. Farmers could invest in new equipment or production techniques, allowing them to meet new market demands for quality or product type. Credit availability to NGOs, processors, and exporters allows them to pay farmers promptly on delivery, reducing their reliance on intermediaries for credit.

A corollary of the provision of low-cost credit is the need to assign to smallholder farmers a clear title to the land that they cultivate. This would make the land a more productive asset and one that could, if farmers chose, be used as collateral for credit, in addition to being bought and sold more easily. The issue of land titling is, however, often caught up in the more controversial ones of land distribution and large landowners' ability to block meaningful land reform. Furthermore, even a relatively simple process such as land titling can get bogged down in controversy. In the Chapare region in Bolivia, according to a local NGO, an EU-funded land titling project was viewed with great suspicion by the intended beneficiaries, because smallholder farmers believed that the measurement and recording of their plots were the first steps to their being confiscated by the government.

Working together: developing new management skills

Many of the barriers described in the previous section lead directly to the need for new management skills. Production of consistent quality and quantity also means that farmers need to acquire new knowledge, facilities and skills.

To meet quality requirements, farmers need to understand what is needed, have facilities and technical ability to meet them, and the management skills to maintain quality and adapt to changing demands. Similarly, farmers need to work together in order to be able to specialize in the production of particular crops, and to offer adequate quantities to buyers. Working together successfully requires that farmers have management skills, institutions that allow them to make decisions and to delegate responsibility for negotiation, quality control and decision-making. Farmers must agree to establish and comply with rules.

In the Chapare area of Bolivia, a handful of farmer associations have secured a niche in the export market for bananas to neighbouring Argentina, with assistance from USAID. Farmers have consolidated their individual farms into larger units to facilitate aerial spraying and the central installation of infrastructure, such as roads, packing sheds, wells and cable lines. The associations export bananas as a group. They have established quality control and pricing systems to help them run as a business. The establishment of these systems has relied on assistance provided by CONCADE.

Strengthening the link between agriculture and industry

Support for agriculture needs to be embedded in the wider context of rural development and to move away from an exclusive reliance on agricultural development as the only means of improving farmers' livelihoods. Traditionally, agricultural extension services have worked predominantly on improving and increasing production at the farm level. A new focus is needed in agricultural extension, development projects and NGOs on the integrated chain of production from farmer to the consumer. Working with, or around, existing networks of intermediaries may be as important as working with farmers and processors.

Modern agriculture requires co-operation with agro-industry in order to meet successfully the demanding quality standards of national and international markets. For example, the development of an understanding between small potato farmers and the processor, as part of the CESA/INIAP programme described in Chapter 4, illustrates how co-operation between farmers and industry can bring benefits to small farmers. Similarly, the development of long-term contracts with small grape producers, aiming to ensure the quality of their production, represents a new focus on quality from the farm to the finished product. The growing link between agriculture and agro-industry will entail additional public and private promotion of rural non-agricultural employment in industry and services.[6]

Developing marketing skills

If smallholder farmers are to take advantage of the market, they need to be able to seek out and develop opportunities. In particular, for them to benefit from the niche markets such as organic, fair trade, gourmet and FSC certified markets, they need marketing skills.

Successful organizations such as Fundatierra and COCLA and the Asociación Nacional de Productores de Quinua (ANAPQUI) employ specialists whose sole remit is to identify market opportunities. To what extent can a new farmer association emulate these organizations without the services of marketing specialists? Similarly, were it not for the efforts of Radiofónica in Ecuador it is almost inconceivable that the farmers in the village of Guantug, described in Chapter 5, would be able to export their quinoa. This might seem rather self-evident, but in development circles there are still those who focus on the existence of a market per se and do not question whether farmers have the technical skills and knowledge to take advantage of these market opportunities.

Some projects are specifically seeking to identify market opportunities where small farmers have a competitive advantage. The Papa Andina project, based at the Centro Internacional de la Papa (CIP), Lima, recognizes that developing new markets for products that will ultimately be more easily supplied by large farms, will not benefit smallholders or alleviate poverty. The project aims to identify specific markets where small farmers have a competitive advantage over larger farms. For example, some market niches require small potatoes that imply high planting density and manual harvest. This is difficult for large-scale mechanized farms to achieve. Again, the question arises as to how a group of farmers acquires the necessary business skills to identify and build on these niches. Small farmers are unlikely to develop sophisticated marketing skills overnight. This type of development needs careful inputs from outsiders, whether from government organizations, NGOs or private companies.

Participatory extension and research

Experience in Latin America with a range of participatory extension and research models, such as Farmer Field Schools (FFS) and Local Agricultural Research Committees (CIALs), demonstrates that these may be effective in empowering farmers and by doing so provide them with some of the marketing skills needed to compete more effectively in the global market.[7] FFS is a training approach that was developed for helping farmers to understand integrated pest management and to reduce farmers' use of chemicals. The format is now being extended to help farmers learn about market demand and product requirements as well as how to negotiate in new markets. CIALs develop farmers' research and learning capacities; they aim to encourage farmers to learn by doing, to criticize their own and others' work, and to adapt their processes to changing conditions.

These participatory methods can stimulate local innovation, because the emphasis is on principles and processes rather than recipes or technology packages. In some cases, farmers who participate in CIALs are learning how to manage funds, plan time, launch micro-credit schemes, prepare proposals to access external resources, and deal with outside agronomists and professionals on a more equal basis.[8] A number of CIALs have launched small businesses involving the production and marketing of seed, and selling fresh or processed food products.[9]

Suitably empowered, farmers are better able to influence formal research and extension systems to their own benefit and to gain access to potentially useful skills, information and research. The FFS and CIAL approaches to extension seem to offer encouraging results. However, it is important to acknowledge that these approaches take time and resources. Cost has been a major argument against wider promotion of FFS and CIAL approaches.

Improving access to certification

The importance of niche markets to smallholder farmers has been clearly demonstrated, as have the difficulties of meeting the administrative and management demands of certification along with the costs. Certification schemes are aware of these issues and are working to reduce the barriers for small farmers. Organic schemes operate mutual recognition schemes, although the initial cost of assessing each others' standards and procedures remains a barrier. The FSC is working specifically to address barriers to the certification of small and community-managed forests in terms of certification costs and the requirements of the standard. Nonetheless, certification remains a significant transaction cost, which may at times exceed the benefits it brings.

To reduce some of the certification costs, farmers can, in theory, form a group and establish an internal control system so that the certification body inspects the system and a sample of farms, rather than each individual farm. Both organic and FSC certification offer such schemes. A very successful example is COCLA, which maintains the group certification for its coffee producers. However, once again the issue arises as to how farmer associations acquire the management skills to establish and maintain internal controls.

Partial solutions include more direct marketing channels between producers and consumers, so that farmers can more readily generate the resources needed to obtain certification. Fair trade certification reduces the cost barrier for farmers by charging the importers and retailers a royalty fee for use of the fair trade label; farmers do not have to pay for certification. If farmers are able to sell their produce through fair trade channels, they may be able to raise the necessary funds to pay for organic certification.

Farmers can also seek external help from a private company or NGO. For example, in Ecuador Inagrofa shared the costs of organic certification with some of its quinoa suppliers, and the banana producers in Cumandá are being helped to meet organic certification requirements and costs by a Dutch solidarity organization. An increase in the number of accredited local certification bodies that are accepted as operating equivalent standards and procedures would also increase accessibility of certification. It is far cheaper to be assessed by local certification bodies than it is to pay for people to visit from Europe or the USA; local bodies are also likely to understand better local conditions, language and culture.

Do not forget the land

Agricultural development efforts have often been directed at increasing production, with less attention focused on whether there is a market for the produce. Our research demonstrates that for many farmers, access to markets is their main concern. It is important, however, not to go to the opposite extreme and emphasize the importance of markets while ignoring the production side of the equation. It is also important to recognize that, irrespective of farmers' ability to access the market, there remain major technical challenges to production. These include low and variable yields, inappropriate farming systems, and land degradation. There is little point in farmers growing surpluses if there are no markets for their produce. Conversely, efforts to improve farmers' access to markets will be wasted if the natural resource base becomes so degraded that they are unable to farm.

In some parts of Latin America and other parts of the developing world, land degradation is so advanced that it is undermining farmers' livelihoods. For a variety of reasons, some of which are perfectly rational, farmers have not always adopted the improved agricultural practices and technologies promoted by development projects. Often farmers' unwillingness to follow recommendations stems from the fact that the technologies and practices devised by researchers and extension agents do not accord with farmers' resources, needs and priorities. Sheep farmers in Patagonia, who continue to overstock in the face of land degradation, may not have the resources available to invest in other approaches such as forestry.

The complexity of working with farmers to improve land management has been well documented and in recent years there has been much success in promoting a more sustainable agriculture.[10] In this context development specialists, be they agriculturalists, soil scientists, marketing experts or foresters need to work together. They need to think beyond conventional sectoral or disciplinary boundaries and to identify interventions that meet the needs of smallholder farmers' livelihoods.

The policy context

An enabling policy environment

The preceding section describes some of the practical measures that need to be taken if farmers are to benefit more from market opportunities.

Fundamental changes, however, are also needed at the policy level. Without these changes, it is very unlikely that the potential benefits that come from accessing markets will be realized with or without the types of assistance detailed above.

Globalization has led to increased inequality: changes in the system are needed. Joseph Stiglitz, the former chief economist at the World Bank, is quoted as saying that received wisdom took 'privatisation and trade liberalisation as ends in themselves, rather than means to a more sustainable, equitable and democratic growth'.[11] What is needed is a system of global governance capable of managing a process of globalization with equity. The challenge is to make trade contribute to poverty reduction by changing the institutions, rules and policies that marginalize the poor. Or as Amartya Sen wrote in his foreword to Oxfam's trade report in 2002, there is a need 'to combine the great benefits of trade ... with the overarching need for fairness and equity which motivates a major part of the anti-globalization protests'.[12]

The example of coffee producers in the Andean region has shown how vulnerable primary commodity producers are to global price fluctuations. Primary commodities still account for over 40 per cent of the export earnings of developing countries. In 2000/2001, developing country coffee exporters sold nearly 20 per cent more coffee on world markets than in 1997/98, for which they received 45 per cent less foreign exchange. Had they received the same price in 2000/2001 as they did during 1997/98 they would have been US$8 billion better off.[12]

For traders in international markets, changes in commodity prices register as blips on a computer screen and opportunities to generate profit. But for the people who produce the commodities, changes in international markets have a major impact on their livelihoods. In response, organizations such as Oxfam have called for the creation of a new international commodities institution to promote diversification and end over-supply in order to raise prices to levels consistent with a reasonable standard of living for producers, and for changing corporate practices so that companies have to pay fair prices.

What is needed is essentially the institutionalization of the principles and practice of fair trade, with a deliberate focus on facilitating smallholder farmers' access to markets without unfairly supporting or subsidizing them. The idea that developing country smallholder agriculture should be given special and differential treatment is being pursued by development NGOs, particularly with respect to the World Trade Organization (WTO) Agreement on Agriculture. The proposed 'Development Box' would contain a package of measures for developing countries to enable them to take account of their development needs by implementing policies to strengthen their domestic production, promote food security and maintain and improve rural livelihoods. The Doha Ministerial Declaration, following the launch of new trade talks in November 2001, agreed that future negotiations should recognize the need for this special and differential treatment for developing countries.

Specific measures may include exempting government subsidies for low-income producers from reduction commitments. Other measures could include the use of incentives to encourage exporters to buy produce from certain farmer groups. The CONCADE project in Bolivia, for example, already pays local exporters an incentive to buy bananas from farmer associations that have been established by the project. Additional measures also include the active use of locally produced products such as quinoa as part of government-funded food programmes.

Care is needed, however, because a fine balance needs to be achieved between subsidizing smallholder farmers to produce goods that people do not want, like cheap wine in Argentina in the 1970s, and facilitating them to meet market demands. The type of protectionism used in the past to protect Argentine wine makers is no more a panacea for poverty than rapid import liberalization. It remains to be seen whether trade negotiations granting developing countries special and differential treatment bear fruit. Much of the success of any endeavour rests on the developed world opening up its own markets to exports from the developing world.

Protectionism in the developed world

Some of the policy changes that are needed pose a major challenge for the developed world. Trade can indeed contribute substantially to poverty reduction, but while developing countries are pressured into liberalizing their economies they are excluded from opportunities in international markets, particularly in the agriculture and textile sectors, by protectionism in the developed world.

This protectionism includes an array of direct payments, intervention prices, storage facilities for surplus production and export subsidies. Developed countries' farm support amounts to over US$360 billion a year, which is US$30 billion more than Africa's entire gross domestic product,[13] and six times as much as rich countries' total foreign aid budgets.[14] Meanwhile, the USA's programme of 'emergency' farm payments exceeds the whole of the UN's humanitarian aid budget.[12]

The 'rules of the game' for international trade in agricultural produce, set by the EU and USA, remain largely inimical to the interests of the developing countries. In Europe, over 46 per cent of the EU's budget, manifested in the Common Agricultural Policy (CAP), goes on farm subsidies to the tune of an average of US$17 000 per full-time farmer per annum.[15] In 2001 alone, the EU spent approximately US$40 billion supporting EU agriculture and fisheries and about US$6 billion on development aid.[16] This imbalance, along with the host of tariff and non-tariff barriers, does few favours for developing countries.

Oxfam, in its trade report launched in April 2002, points out that when developing countries export to rich-country markets they face tariff barriers that are substantially higher than those encountered by rich countries. Those barriers cost developing countries US$100 billion a year, which is twice as much as these countries receive in aid.[12] Meanwhile, subsidies to farmers in the developed world generate overproduction. The resulting surpluses are dumped on world markets with the help of yet more subsidies. The USA and EU, for example, account for around half of all wheat exports, but their export prices are 46 per cent and 34 per cent respectively below the costs of production. In the Andean region, nutritious grains such as quinoa could play a large role in ameliorating malnutrition, but cheap and subsidized wheat imports to Peru from the developed world encourage the switch from quinoa to less nutritious wheat-based foods. The result is that local farmers' livelihoods are undermined.

The dismantling of protectionism in the developed world would indeed lead to greater market access for developing countries. It has been calculated that if developing countries increased their share of world exports by just 5 per cent, this would generate US$350 billion – seven times as much as they receive in aid.[12] But what hope is there that developing countries' access to markets in the developed world will be enhanced?

Progress in opening up developed world markets has been desperately slow. The Agreement on Agriculture, negotiated during the Uruguay round of trade talks that ended in 1994, mandated the continuation of negotiations in agriculture. The subsequent agreement at Doha in 2001 set the agenda for a new round of trade negotiations aimed at improving market access for agricultural products, substantially cutting export subsidies on agricultural goods with a view to phasing them out, and substantially reducing domestic agricultural support mechanisms that distort trade.

The CAP has been partially reformed in recent years: there have been some moves away from price and production-based subsidies to less trade-distorting measures such as direct payments to farmers, but much remains to be done. In the case of sugar, for example, the EU supports its own sugar-beet farmers to the tune of US$1.6 billion a year. As a result, the price of sugar in Europe is three times the world market price. Cheap sugar imports are still kept out because the EU imposes 140 per cent tariffs on many imports from Africa. The array of tariffs and quotas means that developing countries, such as Mozambique, are denied access to EU markets. Furthermore, the EU dumps surplus sugar on world markets to such an extent that the EU is the world's biggest exporter of white sugar.[17]

The issue for many developing countries is that there remains a huge gulf between developed countries' rhetoric and concrete action. The Doha round of trade talks are scheduled to end by 1 January 2005 but there are few signs that political leaders in the developed world have the courage or political will to open their markets further to farm products from Latin America, Africa and Asia. At the United Nations' World Summit on Sustainable Development in Johannesburg in September 2002, talks on market access and farm subsidies merely reconfirmed promises on freeing trade which had been made at Doha.

In the USA, new legislation has actually signalled a move towards greater rather than less protection. The USA Farm Bill signed by George W. Bush in May 2002 runs counter to what was agreed at Doha. The Bill extends and, in some cases, reintroduces subsidies on a host of farm products from honey to chickpeas. It raises the level of federal subsidies to farmers by over 89 per cent, although most of the money will go to the biggest and richest 10 per cent of farmers. In the case of the USA's biggest crops such as soyabeans, corn and wheat, the Farm Bill invents new payments that are related to prices and production – precisely the sort of trade-distorting measures that Doha was designed to get rid of.[18]

Meanwhile, farming in Europe, even with its current levels of support and protection, is in crisis. While the British and German governments tout vague plans for further reform of the CAP, the French government, the largest beneficiary of CAP spending, is implacably opposed to any meaningful reductions in the generous subsidies offered to some European farmers. There is a danger that the USA Farm Bill may give the EU, faced with a politically powerful farming lobby, an excuse to delay real reform of the CAP.

Faced with the blatant hypocrisy displayed by the developed world with respect to free trade, is it any wonder that farmers in developing countries direct their ire at the World Trade Organization, which allows rich countries to subsidize their farmers while insisting that the developing world dismantle protection measures for its own farmers?

There is also the suspicion that, even in the event that current protectionism were dismantled, trading blocks in the developed world, particularly the EU, would use unjustifiably high environmental and social standards as new forms of protectionism. For example, if the EU is obliged to lower agricultural trade barriers it may simply keep out food products by finding some 'green' objection to them. Many forest owners in South America already suspect that moves by some EU governments to require evidence that imported timber comes from legal and sustainable sources, are in fact non-tariff barriers to trade.

Who pays and why?

Ensuring that smallholder farmers benefit more from global markets will cost money. The big question is who pays and, if funds are not made available, does it matter? Substantial and well-targeted aid is needed. That in itself is a tall order. The US foreign aid stands at 0.1 per cent of gross national product and, with the exception of the Scandinavian countries and the Netherlands, Europe's record is not much better. The UK, for example contributes just 0.35 per cent of gross national product to aid. The aid budgets of most of the developed world, therefore, fall well short of the UN's target to increase development aid to 0.7 per cent of gross national product.

The amount of aid is one issue; another critical factor is the proportion of this aid that is directed at the agricultural sector. Over the past 15 years, this has also declined so that it represents under 10 per cent of total Overseas Development Assistance (ODA). This has occurred at a time when, despite rapid urbanization, an estimated 70 to 75 per cent of the world's poorest people live in rural areas where their livelihoods are largely dependent on agriculture.[16]

Agriculture has a major role to play in the development of many countries' economies and, as described in Chapter 1, there are grounds for treating smallholder farmers differently from other sectors of the rural economy. Smallholder agriculture is fundamental to the livelihoods of many of the world's poorest people and it is also an important store of cultural and social knowledge and a country's identity. Furthermore, farmers can play an important role in providing environmental services such as the conservation of soil and water.

Aside from the humanitarian argument in favour of more development assistance, and for more of this assistance to be directed at the agricultural sector, state instability caused by poverty continues to undermine Western interests through terrorism, drug-trafficking, money-laundering and mass refugee flows.

Action is needed sooner rather than later. It is indeed correct when the World Bank states that to develop markets, and the institutions that support them, takes time.[19] The key questions, though, are how much time is needed and, perhaps more importantly, how much time is available? Approximately half a million people left Ecuador between 1999 and 2001, from a population of only 14 million. Often it is the most dynamic who leave and, while the remittances that they send back can contribute much to the country's economy, it can be argued that their skills are precisely those that could best be harnessed to bring about development at home. Without an adequate standard of living at home, this kind of migration will surely continue.

There is also evidence that Latin Americans are wavering in their support for democracy, and that the main cause is disillusionment with the way that their economies are performing. The optimism that accompanied the rebirth of democracy in the region two decades ago now seems to have evaporated. Eighteen months before Argentina's economy collapsed at the end of 2001, the people we met from Tierra del Fuego to the northern border with Bolivia had nothing but contempt for what they considered second-rate, corrupt and venal political leaders.

The anger of ordinary Argentines was palpable. The argument that it is not the fault of the economic model but rather the quality of political leadership did not hold much water with them. They saw little distinction between the two, and argued that corrupt and unscrupulous politicians flourished in the political and economic environment ushered in by liberalization and deregulation. As the economic crisis in Argentina deepens, the risks grow that, when given the opportunity, the Argentine people will elect a populist leader who will be unwilling to bring about the painful economic reforms that some argue are necessary for the country to achieve some degree of economic stability.[20]

Making markets work better for farmers

Many smallholders are currently disadvantaged by globalization and are unable to benefit from markets. Our research has demonstrated that markets can be made to work more effectively for the rural poor. To do so, research and extension agendas funded by public and private institutions are needed, which focus less on technologies and more on the real transaction problems faced by farmers. An enabling policy environment is needed in which the principles and practices of fair trade are institutionalized. External support is essential to assist farmers to develop market networks, often through the development of agro-enterprises, and to gain access to credit and infrastructure. Farmers also need to be empowered to solve their own problems through extension methods that emphasize active participation and innovation.

As we neared the end of writing this book, the Overseas Development Institute in London sponsored an e-mail discussion on globalization and pro-poor agricultural development. There were 166 subscribers from more than 30 countries and contributions were made by participants from Asia, Africa and Latin America. The summary of the discussion mirrors the experiences described in our book in terms of the problems farmers face in accessing markets and how markets can be made to work better for the rural poor.[21] This is both depressing and heartening. It is depressing because it confirms that the farmers' stories that we portray in this book could be repeated countless times using examples from other parts of the world. But it is also heartening because it demonstrates that a new direction and consensus may be emerging about the changes that are needed to make markets work better for smallholder farmers in South America, Africa and Asia.

These changes may provide a basis for a more rational debate about globalization. If the anti-globalization protesters could accept some of the pro-market messages emanating from farming communities in South America and elsewhere, a more productive protest manifesto would emerge. The proponents of globalization, in turn, need to recognize its shortcomings and to seek actively to rectify these deficiencies. We hope that this book will contribute to a more positive and productive debate about globalization and subsequently to the changes in policy, research and extension agendas which are needed to ensure that national and international markets work better for farmers worldwide.

Notes

Chapter 1 Introduction

1 Oxfam (2002) 'Rigged rules and double standards: trade, globalisation, and the fight against poverty'. Oxford, Oxfam. Available at www.maketradefair.com
2 Ellis, F. and Seeley, J. (2001) 'Globalisation and Sustainable Livelihoods: An initial note'. Background briefing. London, Department for International Development.
3 Oxfam (2000) 'Globalisation: Submission to the Government's White Paper on Globalisation'. Oxford, Oxfam.
4 The Economist (2002) 'Globalisation: Is it at risk?' *The Economist*, 24 February 2002.
5 Wade, R. (2001) 'Global inequality: winners and losers'. *The Economist*, 28 April 2001.
6 The Economist (2001) 'Development in poor countries: not by their bootstraps alone'. *The Economist*, 12 May 2001.
7 Department for International Development (2002) 'Making trade work for poor people'. Development Policy Forums 2002. Issues paper 2. London. Department for International Development.
8 The Economist (2001) 'Bush the anti-globaliser'. *The Economist*, 11 May 2002.
9 The World Bank (2001) 'World Development Report 2000/2001: Attacking Poverty'. Washington DC, The World Bank.
10 The Economist (2001) 'Globalisation and its critics: A survey of globalisation'. *The Economist*, 29 September 2001.
11 The Economist (2002) 'Latin America: Losing its way?' *The Economist*, 2 March 2002.
12 The Economist (2001) 'Central America: Small, vulnerable – and disunited'. *The Economist*, 11 August 2001.
13 Inter-American Development Bank (1999) 'Strategy for Agricultural Development in Latin America and the Caribbean'. Washington DC, Inter-American Development Bank.
14 Kydd, J. (2002) 'Agriculture and rural livelihoods: is globalisation opening or blocking paths out of rural poverty?' Agricultural Research & Extension Network Paper No.121. London, Overseas Development Institute. Available at www.odi.org.uk/agren/
15 Tripp, R. (2001) *Seed provision and agricultural development: the institutions of rural change*. London, Overseas Development Institute.
16 Department for International Development (2002) 'Better livelihoods for poor people: the role of agriculture'. London, Department for International Development.
17 Maxwell, S., Urey, I. and Ashley, C. (2001) 'Emerging issues in rural development'. London, Overseas Development Institute.

Chapter 2 Green gold: Ecuador's banana producers

1 The Fairtrade Foundation (2000) 'Unpeeling the Banana Trade'. Available at www.fairtrade.org.uk/unpeeling.htm
2 van de Kasteele, A. (1998) 'The Banana Chain: The macro economics of the Banana Trade'. Available at www.bananalink.org.uk/trade/btrade.htm

3   Chambron, A-C. (1999) 'Bananas: The TNC's Green Gold', in: *Hungry for power: The impact of transnational corporations on food security*. UK Food Group, pp.46–65.

4   José Riofrio, University of Guayaquil, Ecuador, personal communication.

5   Wunder, S. (2001) 'Ecuador goes bananas: Incremental technological change and forest loss', in: *Agricultural technologies and tropical deforestation*. Angelsen, A. and Kaimowitz, D. (eds.) Wallingford, CAB International, pp.167–95.

6   The Economist (2002) 'Ecuador's economy: Banana skins'. *The Economist*, 27 April 2002.

7   Chambron, A-C. (2000) 'Straightening the bent world of the banana'. Available at www.bananalink.org.uk/trade/btrade.htm

8   Hellin, J. and Higman, S. (2001) 'The impact of the multinational companies on the banana sector in Ecuador'. Oxford, Oxfam.

9   Oxfam (2001) 'The Coffee Market – A Background Study'. Oxford, Oxfam.

10 Glover, D. (1983) 'Contract farming and the transnationals'. PhD dissertation, University of Toronto, p.3.

11 Gibbon, P. (2001) 'Agro-commodity chains: an introduction'. London, Overseas Development Institute, Available at www.odi.org.uk/speeches/gibbon.pdf

12 Logli, P. (2001) 'What future for fair trade?' *ACP-EU Courier,* Issue 181, pp.63–66.

13 Tallontire, A. (2000) 'Partnerships in fair trade: reflections from a case study of Café-direct'. *Development in Practice*, Vol.10, No.2, pp.166–177.

14 FAO (1999) 'The impact of banana supply and demand changes on income, employment and food security'. 'Intergovernmental group on bananas and on tropical fruits'. Available at www.fao.org/docrep/meeting/X1390E.htm

15 Banana Trade News Bulletin (2002) 'Fair trade sales up 30%'. *Banana Trade News Bulletin*, March 2002, p.3.

16 Hellin, J. and Higman, S. (2002) 'Smallholders and niche markets: Lessons from the Andes'. *Agriculture Research & Extension Network Paper*, No.118. London, Overseas Development Institute, Available at www.odi.org.uk/agren

17 Anne-Claire Chambron, European Banana Action Network, personal communication.

18 Tallontire, A. (2002) 'Challenges facing fair trade: which way now?'. *Small Enterprise Development*, Vol.13, No.3, pp.12–24.

Chapter 3 Niche markets: a solution to the coffee crisis?

1   The Fairtrade Foundation (1997) 'Spilling the Beans'. London. The Fairtrade Foundation. Available at www.fairtrade.org.uk/spilling1.htm

2   Oxfam (2001) 'The Coffee Market – A Background Study'. Oxford, Oxfam.

3   World Bank (2002) 'Global economic prospects and the developing countries'. Washington DC, The World Bank.

4   The Economist (2001) 'Commodity Price Index'. *The Economist*, 27 January 2001.

5   The Economist (2001) 'Coffee: Trouble brewing'. *The Economist*, 10 March 2001.

6   Bentley, J.W. and Baker, P.S. (2000) 'The Colombian Coffee Growers' Federation: Organised, Successful Smallholder Farmers for 70 Years'. *Agricultural Research & Extension Network Paper* No.100. London, Overseas Development Institute. Available at www.odi.org.uk/agren/

7   Oxfam (2002) 'Rigged rules and double standards: trade, globalisation, and the fight against poverty'. Oxford, Oxfam. Available at www.maketradefair.com

8   Moriset, J. (1997) 'Unfair trade? Empirical evidence in world commodity markets over the past 25 years'. Washington DC, The World Bank.

[9] Oxfam (2000) 'Preliminary draft report of field research in coffee farming communities, Kilimanjaro, Tanzania'. Oxford, Oxfam.

[10] Southgate, D. (1994) 'The rationality of land degradation in Latin America: some lessons from the Ecuadorian Andes' in: *Adopting conservation on the farm: An international perspective on the socioeconomics of soil and water conservation*. Napier, T.L., Camboni, S.M. and El-Swaify, S.A. (eds.) Ankeny, Iowa, Soil and Water Conservation Society, pp.331–340.

[11] Katrin Linzer, Tierra Viva, Santa Cruz, Bolivia, personal communication.

[12] Robert Simmons, LMC International Ltd, Oxford, personal communication.

[13] The Economist (2001) 'Drowning in cheap coffee'. *The Economist*, 29 September 2001.

[14] Blake, J. (2000) 'A good deal better for the producers'. *The Times*, 2 September 2000.

[15] Madeley, J. (2001) 'Holding back the beans to perk up the price of coffee'. *The Observer*, 18 February 2001.

[16] Céline Charvériat, Oxfam International, personal communication.

[17] LMC International Ltd. (2002) 'Coffee: LMC Commodity Bulletin'. February 2002.

[18] Oxfam (2002) 'Mugged: poverty in your coffee cup'. Oxford, Oxfam.

[19] The Economist (2001) 'Changing the Plan'. *The Economist*, 8 September 2001.

Chapter 4 Potatoes and Andean tubers: losing diversity?

[1] Dandler, J. and Sage, C. (1985) 'What is Happening to Andean Potatoes? a view from the Grass-roots'. *Development Dialogue* 1, pp.125–138.

[2] National Research Council (1989) 'Lost Crops of the Incas: Little known plants of the Andes with promise for worldwide cultivation'. Washington DC National Academy Press, p.103.

[3] Tapia, M. (1993) 'Visión general y características del agroecosistema Andino'. In: *El Agroecosistema Andino: problemas, limitaciones, perspectivas. Anales del taller internacional sobre el ecosistema andino*. CIP, Lima, pp.51–61.

[4] Brush, S.B. (1991) 'Farmer Conservation of New World Crops; the case of Andean Potatoes'. *Diversity* 7 (1&2), pp.75–79.

[5] Thiele G. and Devaux, A. (2002) 'Adding value to local knowledge and bio-diversity of Andean potato farmers: The Papa Andina project'. CIP, Lima.

[6] Gonzales, T.A. (2000) 'The Cultures of the Seed in the Peruvian Andes'. In: *Genes in the field: on-farm conservation of crop diversity*. Brush, S.B. (ed.), Rome, Italy, International Plan Genetic Resources Institute, pp.193–216.

[7] Iriarte, V., Terrazas, F. and Aguirre, G. (1998) 'Memoria: Primer encuentro taller sobre el mantenimiento de la diversidad de tubérculos Andinos en sus zonas de origen'. Cochabamba, PROINPA.

[8] Frolick, L.M., Sherwood, S., Hemphill, A. and Guevara, E. (2000) 'Eco-papas: through potato conservation towards agroecology'. *Newsletter of the Centre for Research and Information on Low External Input and Sustainable Agriculture (ILEA)*, December 2000, pp.44–45.

[9] Thiele, G. (1999) 'Informal potato seed systems in the Andes: why are they important and what should we do with them?' *World Development* 27(1), pp.83–99.

[10] Graham Thiele, CIP, Quito. Personal communication.

[11] Centro Internacional de la Papa (CIP) (1998) 'La Papa en Cifras'. CIP, Lima.

[12] Crissman, C., Espinosa, P., Durcot, C. and Carpio, F. (1998) 'The Case Study Site: Physical, health and potato farming systems in Carchi Province'. in: *Economic, Environmental and health trade offs in Agriculture: Pesticides and the sustainability of Andean potato production*. Crissman, C., Antle, J.M. and Capalbo, S.M. (eds.) Dordrecht/Boston/London, Kluwer Academic Publications, pp.85–120.

13 Oscar Ortiz, CIP, Lima. Personal communication.

14 PROINPA (2000) 'Caso por caso y paso por paso: Por qué vale la pena investigar con plantas transgénicas?' *Los Tiempos*, 16 July 2000, Cochabamba, Bolivia.

15 Andrade, H., Cuesta, X. and Oyarzun, P.J. (1999) 'Breeding in Ecuador: facing increasing late blight severity' in: *Late blight: A threat to global security. Volume 1. Proceedings of the Global Initiative on Late Blight Conference, 1999*. Crissman, C. and Lizárraga, C. (eds.), Quito, CIP, pp.38–40.

16 Ortiz, O., Fano, H., Winters, P., Thiele, G., Guaman, S., Torres, R., Barrera, G., Unda, V.J. and Hakiza, J. (1999) 'Understanding farmers' response to late blight (LB): Evidence from a base-line study in Peru, Bolivia, Ecuador and Uganda'. In: *Late blight: A threat to global security. Volume 1. Proceedings of the Global Initiative on Late Blight Conference, 1999*. Crissman, C. and Lizárraga, C. (eds.), Quito, CIP, p.34.

17 Ortiz, O., Winters, P. and Fano, H. (1999) 'La Percepción de los agricultores sobre el problema del tizón tardío o rancha (*Phytophthora infestans*) y su manejo: Estudio de casos en Cajamarca, Peru'. *Revista Latinoamericana de la Papa* 11, pp.97–120.

18 SWISSAID (1999) 'Un ejemplo en la conservación de suelos: la granja de Don Mariano y Doña Mercedes'. In: *Granjas Biologicas Campesinas*. Quito, SWISSAID, pp.31–54.

19 Brush, S.B. (2000) 'The issues of *in-situ* conservation of crop genetic resources'. In: *Genes in the field: on-farm conservation of crop diversity*. Brush, S.B. (ed.), Rome, Italy, International Plan Genetic Resources Institute, pp.3–26.

Chapter 5 Quinoa and food security

1 Jacobsen, S-E. (2001) 'El potencial de la quinua para Europa' in: *Memorias Primer Taller Internacional en Quinua: Recursos Genéticos y Sistemas de Producción*. Jacobsen, S-E., Mujica, A., and Portillo, Z. (eds.) Proyecto Quinua CIP-DANIDA.

2 National Research Council (1989) *Lost Crops of the Incas: little known plants of the Andes with promise for worldwide cultivation*. Washington DC, National Academy Press.

3 Aroni, G. (2001) 'Producción de Quinua en Bolivia'. In: *Memorias Primer Taller Internacional en Quinua: Recursos Genéticos y Sistemas de Producción*. Jacobsen, S-E., Mujica, A., and Portillo, Z. (Eds.), Proyecto Quinua CIP-DANIDA.

4 Risi C. (2001) 'Producción de quinua en el Altiplano sur de Bolivia'. In: *Memorias Primer Taller Internacional en Quinua: Recursos Genéticos y Sistemas de Producción*. Jacobsen, S-E., Mujica, A., and Portillo, Z. (Eds.), Proyecto Quinua CIP-DANIDA.

5 Alejandro Bonifacio, PROINPA, Bolivia, personal communication.

6 Jacobsen, S.E. (2002) 'Quinoa: research and development at the International Potato Center (CIP)'. CIP-DANIDA.

7 Repo-Carrasco, R., Espinoza, C. and, Jacobsen S-E. (2001) 'Valor Nutricional y usos de la Quinua y de la Kañiwa' in: *Memorias Primer Taller Internacional en Quinua: Recursos Genéticos y Sistemas de Producción*. Jacobsen, S-E., Mujica, A., and Portillo, Z. (Eds.), Proyecto Quinua CIP-DANIDA.

8 Ayala, G. (2001) 'Uso de la quinua en poblaciones marginales'. In: *Memorias Primer Taller Internacional en Quinua: Recursos Genéticos y Sistemas de Producción*. Jacobsen, S-E., Mujica, A., and Portillo, Z. (Eds.), Proyecto Quinua CIP-DANIDA.

9 Macdonald, B. (1999) 'Socio-economic correlates of rural women's nutrition: the special case of re-introducing quinoa in Ecuador'. PhD thesis, McGill University, Montreal, Canada.

10 Berti, P.R., Leonard, W.R. and Berti, W.J. (1997) 'Malnutrition in rural highland Ecuador: the importance of intra-household food distribution, diet composition and nutrient requirements'. *Food Nutrition Bulletin* 18(4), pp.352–262.

[11] Tripp, R. (1982) 'Including dietary concerns in on-farm research: An example from Imbabura, Ecuador'. Working paper 82/2. International Maize and Wheat Improvement Center, Mexico.

[12] Equaquinua: National Quinoa Programme for Ecuador, Profile, Jan 24, 2002. Citing Carolin Reed, Issue no. 5, Quantum Magazine.

[13] Nieto, C. (2001) 'Cultivo, producción y conservación de la quinua en Ecuador' in: *Memorias Primer Taller Internacional en Quinua: Recursos Genéticos y Sistemas de Producción.* Jacobsen, S-E., Mujica, A., and Portillo, Z. (Eds.), Proyecto Quinua CIP-DANIDA.

[14] Salas, S. (2001) 'La quinua poscosecha y comercializacion'. In: *Memorias Primer Taller Internacional en Quinua: Recursos Genéticos y Sistemas de Producción.* Jacobsen, S-E., Mujica, A., and Portillo, Z. (Eds.), Proyecto Quinua CIP-DANIDA.

[15] Ordinola, M. (2001) 'Nuevos esquemas para la comercialización de la quinua' in: *Memorias Primer Taller Internacional en Quinua: Recursos Genéticos y Sistemas de Producción.* Jacobsen, S-E., Mujica, A., and Portillo, Z. (Eds.), Proyecto Quinua CIP-DANIDA.

[16] FAO Statistical databases FAOSTAT. Available at www.fao.org

[17] Colila, J., Quispe P. and Mujica, A. (2001) 'Aspectos económicos de la producción de quinua'. In: *Quinua* (Chenopodium quinoa *Willd.*), *Ancestral Cultivo Andino, Alimento del Presente y Futuro.* Mujica A., Jacobsen, S-E., Izquierdo, J and Marathee, J. (eds.) Santiago, Chile. FAO, UNA-Puno, CIP.

[18] Roberto Valdivia, CIRNMA, Puno, Peru, personal communication.

[19] Laguna, P.F. (2000) 'The impact of quinoa export on peasants' livelihoods of Bolivian highlands'. Paper presented at Xth World Congress of the International Rural Sociology Association, Rio de Janeiro, Brazil, August. 2000.

[20] Rivera, R. (1999) 'Los cultivos nativos: situación y estratégias para su desarrollo' in: *Memorias: Reunión Técnica y Taller de Formulación de Proyecto Regional Sobre Producción y Nutrición Humana en Base a Cultivos Andinos.* Mujica, A., Izquierdo, J., Marathee, J.P., Morón, C. and Jacobsen, S-E. (eds.) FAO, UNA-Puno, CIP.

[21] Mujica, A., Marca S. and Jacobsen, S-E. (2001) 'Producción actual de la quinua en el Peru'. In: *Memorias Primer Taller Internacional en Quinua: Recursos Genéticos y Sistemas de Producción.* Jacobsen, S-E., Mujica, A., and Portillo, Z. (Eds.), Proyecto Quinua CIP-DANIDA.

[22] Bolivian Times (2001) 18 January 2001.

[23] Bonifacio, A. (1999) 'Aspectos agrícolas y de mejoramiento de la quinua en Bolivia' in: *Memorias: Reunión Técnica y Taller de Formulación de Proyecto Regional Sobre Producción y Nutrición Humana en Base a Cultivos Andinos.* Mujica, A., Izquierdo, J., Marathee, J.P., Morón, C. and Jacobsen, S-E. (eds.) FAO, UNA-Puno, CIP.

[24] Juan López and Alejandro Bonefacio, PROINPA, La Paz, Bolivia, personal communication.

[25] Aroni, G. (2001) 'Producción de quinua en Bolivia'. In: *Memorias Primer Taller Internacional en Quinua: Recursos Genéticos y Sistemas de Producción.* Jacobsen, S-E., Mujica, A., and Portillo, Z. (eds.) Proyecto Quinua CIP-DANIDA.

[26] Garí, J.A. (1999). Bio-diversity conservation and use: local and global considerations. Technology and Development Discussion Paper No.7, Centre for International Development and Belfer Center for Science and International Affairs, Harvard University, USA.

[27] Scott, G.J. and Maldonado, L. (2001) 'Quinua y comercialización: métodos de análisis y evaluación de mercados'. In: *Memorias Primer Taller Internacional en Quinua: Recursos Genéticos y Sistemas de Producción.* Jacobsen, S-E., Mujica, A., and Portillo, Z. (eds.) Proyecto Quinua CIP-DANIDA.

28 Sven-Eric Jacobsen, CIP, Peru, personal communication.

29 Jacobsen, S-E. (2001) 'El potencial de la quinua para Europa'. In: *Memorias Primer Taller Internacional en Quinua: Recursos Genéticos y Sistemas de Producción*. Jacobsen, S-E., Mujica, A., and Portillo, Z. (Eds.), Proyecto Quinua CIP-DANIDA.

30 Dawkins, K. (1999) 'Intellectual property rights and the privatisation of life'. *Foreign Policy in Focus*. Albuquerque, New Mexico. Inter-hemispheric Resource Center and Institute for Policy Studies, 4(4).

31 Oxfam (2002). 'Rigged rules and double standards: trade globalisation, and the fight against poverty'. Oxford, Oxfam. Available at www.maketradefair.com

32 Coila, J., Quispe, P and Mujica, A. (2001) 'Aspectos economicos de la producción de quinua'. In: *Quinua* (Chenopodium quinoa *Willd.*), *Ancestral Cultivo Andino, Alimento del Presente y Futuro*. Mujica A., Jacobsen, S-E., Izquierdo, J and Marathee, J. (eds.) Santiago, Chile. FAO, UNA-Puno, CIP.

Chapter 6 Coca eradication and alternative development

1   Smith, M., Thongtham, C.N., Sadeque, N., Bravo, A., Rumrill, R. and Dávila, A. (1992) *Why people grow drugs: Narcotics and development in the Third World*. The Panos Institute, London, Panos Publications Ltd, p.12.

2   Cabieses, F. (1992) 'La coca: Dilema trágico?' Empresa Nacional de la Coca S.A.: Peru, p.13.

3   Ereira, A. (1990) *The heart of the world*. London, Jonathan Cape, p.28.

4   Higman, S. (2000) 'Town meets country, but for how much longer?' Letter from Argentina. *The Guardian Weekly*, 21 December 2000.

5   Coffin, P. and Bigwood, J. (2001) 'Coca eradication'. *Foreign Policy in Focus*, Vol.6, No.7.

6   Jones, J.C. (1990) 'The Chapare: Farmer perspectives on the economics and sociology of coca plantation.' SARSA and Institute for Development Anthropology, Binghamton, New York, p.4.

7   Tosi, J.A. (1983) 'Ecology and Land Capability Analysis of the Chapare Project Area'. Report for USAID/Bolivia, Cochabamba, Bolivia, p.37.

8   Painter, M. and Garland, E.B. (1991) 'Socioeconomic issues in Agricultural Settlement and Production in Bolivia's Chapare Region' Binghamton, New York. Institute for Development Anthropology, Clark University, p.6.

9   Painter, M. (1990) 'Institutional analysis of the Chapare Regional Development Project (CRDP)'. Binghamton, New York. Institute for Development Anthropology, p.1.

10 The Economist (2000) 'A crop that refuses to die'. *The Economist*, 4 March 2000.

11 MacDonald, N. (1992) 'The Andes, a quest for justice'. Oxford, Oxfam, pp.43–44.

12 Dirección General de Reconversión Agrícola (DIRECO) (1998) Memoria DIRECO. La Paz, Bolivia, p.20.

13 Bunch, R. (1982) *Two ears of corn: A guide to people-centred agriculture*. Oklahoma, World Neighbors, p.120.

14 Viceministerio de Desarrollo Alternativo. (2000) 'Consolidating Alternative Development Efforts'. La Paz, Bolivia, Nuevo Gran Angular, No.1, p.16.

15 The Economist (2001) 'Coca's second front'. *The Economist*, 6 January 2001.

16 Hellin, J. and Higman, S. (2000) 'Substituting alternative crops for coca: a viable alternative for farmers?' *Appropriate Technology* 27(4), pp.10–13.

17 The Economist (2000) 'Like Peru?'. *The Economist*, 30 September 2000.

18 Kathryn Ledbur, Andean Information Network, Bolivia, personal communication.

19 Arlacchi, P. (2001) 'Bolivia's coca crop'. Letter in *The Economist*, 13 January 2001.

20. United Nations Office for Drug Control and Crime Prevention (UNODCCP) (1998) 'Bolivia: Status of the country'. *Gran Angular* Magazine on development in the Cochabamba Tropics, No.34.
21. Charles Foster, CONCADE, Bolivia, personal communication.
22. Edwards, M. (1989) 'The irrelevance of development studies'. *Third World Quarterly*, Vol.11, No.1, pp.116–135.
23. Pretty, J.N. and Shah, P. (1997) 'Making soil and water conservation sustainable: From coercion and control to partnerships and participation'. *Land Degradation & Development* 8, pp.39–58.
24. Lemoine, M. (2000) 'South America's hostages and victims: Narco-trafficking and war in the Andes'. *Le Monde Diplomatique*, translated by Julie Stoker, February 2001, issued with *The Guardian Weekly* Vol.164, No.9.
25. Hellin, J. and Higman, S. (2001) 'Supplanting coca?'. Letter in *The Economist*, 3 February 2001.
26. The Economist (2001) 'Commodity Price Index'. *The Economist*, 27 January 2001.
27. Tullis, L. and Painter, J. (1994) 'Illicit drugs: Social impacts and policy responses'. Geneva, Switzerland, United Nations Research Institute for Social Development, p.11.
28. Zeese, K. (2000) 'Just say no to more money for the Colombian drug war'. *The Wall Street Journal*, 28 April 2000.
29. Krauss, C. (2001) 'Desperate Farmers Imperil Peru's Fight on Coca'. *The New York Times*, 23 February, 2001.
30. The Economist (2001) 'The drug war: Trouble for Plan Colombia'. *The Economist*, 4 August 2001.
31. The Economist (2001) 'The drug war: The struggle to exterminate a much-loved Andean Shrub'. *The Economist*, 26 May 2001.
32. The Economist (2001) 'Changing the Plan'. *The Economist*, 8 September 2001.
33. The Economist (2002) 'Drugs in the Andes: Spectres stir in Peru'. *The Economist*, 16 February 2002.
34. Tiempos del Mundo (2000) 'Debaten sobre los cultivos ilícitos'. *Tiempos del Mundo*, 6 July 2000.
35. Reuters (2001) Reuters press release, 4 September 2001.
36. The Economist (2001) 'Colombia's conflicts: into battle'. *The Economist*, 8 September 2001.
37. Pendergrast, M. (1993) *For God, Country and Coca-Cola*. London, Weidenfeld and Nicolson, p.355.
38. Spokesperson, United States Embassy in La Paz, Bolivia, personal communication. Spokesperson, Empresa Nacional de la Coca (ENACO), Peru, personal communication.

Chapter 7 Wine and Pisco: success or sour grapes?

1. Johnson, H. (1994) *The World Atlas of Wine*. London, Octopus Publishing Group.
2. Read, J. (1994) *The Wines of Chile*. London, Reed International Books Ltd.
3. Instituto Nacional de Vitivinicultura. (1999) 'Viticultural Argentinian Regions'. *Vinifera*, Revista del Instituto Nacional de Vitivinicultura, Mendoza, Argentina, November 1999, p.24.
4. Krauss, C. (2001) 'Argentine Wine Slowly Comes to Life'. *The New York Times*, 4 March 2001.
5. Allen, M., Atkin, T., Cooper, M., Neill, R., Platter, J. and St. Pierre, B. (1997) *New World of Wine*. London, Reed International Books Ltd.

6 Johnson, H. and Robinson, J. (2001) *The World Atlas of Wine*. London, Octopus Publishing Group.
7 Morris, A. (2000) 'Globalisation and Regional Differentiation: the Mendoza Wine Region'. *Journal of Wine Research* 11 (2), pp.145–153.
8 Javier Luciano Aguerre, Instituto Nacional de Vitivinicultura, Mendoza, personal communication.
9 Aguerre, J.L. (2002) 'El sector vitivinícola en la República Argentina a partir de 1990'. Internal report based on thesis submitted to the Universidad de Congreso, Mendoza. 2002.
10 Hansis, R.A. (1977). 'Land tenure, hazards, and the economy: viticulture in the Mendoza Oasis, Argentina'. *Economic Geography* 53(4), pp.368–371.
11 Instituto Nacional de Vitivinicultura (1999) 'Argentina in the viticultural world'. *Vinífera*, Revista del Instituto Nacional de Vitivinicultura, Mendoza, Argentina, November 1999, p.8.
12 Stevenson, T. (1997) *The New Sotheby's Wine Encyclopedia*. London, Dorling Kindersley, p.512.
13 Wines for the World (1998) *Asociación Vitivinícola Argentina*, Número Especial.
14 Figures provided by the Instituto Nacional de Vitivinicultura.
15 Casucci, F.P. (1999) 'En Mendoza la finca rentable no puede tener menos de 11 hectáreas'. *Diario Los Andes*, Suplemento Económico, 13 June 1999.
16 Arther Morris, University of Glasgow, personal communication.
17 Bustos, G. (1999) 'Uruguay Vitivinícola. De lo masivo a lo artisanal, del precio sostén a la competencia'. Revista de la Bolsa de Comercio de Mendoza.
18 The Economist (1999) 'Wine survey: glug, glug, glut'. *The Economist*, 16 December 1999.

Chapter 8 Sheep in Patagonia: blown by the winds of change

1 Wheeler, S. (1994) *Travels in a thin country: a journey through Chile*. London, Abacus.
2 Aagesen, D. (2000) 'Crisis and conservation at the end of the world: sheep ranching in Argentine Patagonia'. *Environmental Conservation* 27(2), pp.208–215.
3 Butland, G.J. (1957) *The human geography of southern Chile*. London, George Philip & Son, Ltd, p.56.
4 Ministerio de Agricultura, Chile (1998) 'Programa de desarrollo del cordero de Magallanes'. Ministerio de Agricultura, Chile.
5 Secretaría de Agricultura, Ganadería, Pesca y Alimentación (SAGPyA), Argentina. (1999) 'Hacia una diversificación productiva y sustentabilidad ambiental'. *SAGPyA Forestal* 11, pp.2–5.
6 Childs, H. (1936) *El Jimmy: outlaw of Patagonia*. London, J.B. Lippincott Company.
7 Chatwin, B. (1977) in Patagonia. London, Picador, p.96.
8 Rodrigo Alvarez, Ministerio de Agricultura, Punta Arenas, Chile, personal communication.
9 Allende, I. (1996) *Paula*. Flamingo, p.330.
10 Minsterio de Agricultura, Chile. (1997) 'Estadísticas Ganaderas años 1996 y 1997. Región de Magallanes y Antártica Chilena'. Minsterio de Agricultura, Chile.
11 Caro W.T. and Olivares, A.E. (1999) 'Carne de cordero con menos grasa'. *Nuestra Tierra* No.204, pp.23–25.
12 Secretaría de Agricultura, Ganadería, Pesca y Alimentación (SAGPyA), Argentina (1992) Available at www.sagpya.mecon.gov.ar/

13   The Economist (2002) 'Conservation in the Falkland Islands: virtue rewards'. *The Economist*, 19 January 2002.
14   The Economist (2002) 'The South Atlantic: a breezy, squid-free paradise'. *The Economist*, 30 March 2002.

Chapter 9   Forestry and livelihoods: making trees pay

1   Matthews, E. (2001) 'Understanding the Forest Resources Assessment 2000'. Forest Briefing No.1, Washington DC, World Resources Institute. p.5. Available at www.wri.org/wri/forests/fra2000.html
2   Westoby, J. (1989) *Introduction to World Forestry*. Oxford, UK. Blackwell, p.228.
3   Higman, S., Bass, S., Judd, N., Mayers, J. and Nussbaum, R. (1999) *The Sustainable Forestry Handbook*. London, Earthscan.
4   World Wide Fund for Nature (1994) 'Truth or trickery, timber labelling past and future'. Godalming, UK. WWF.
5   FSC website: www.fscoax.org
6   Bass, S., Thornber, K., Markopoulos, M., Roberts, S. and Grieg-Gran, M. (2001) *Certification's impacts on forests, stakeholders and supply chains*. Instruments for sustainable private sector forestry series. London, International Institute for Environment and Development, p.20.
7   The Economist (2002) 'Emigration from Latin America: Making the most of an exodus'. *The Economist*, 23 February 2002.
8   Scherr, S., White, A. and Kaimowitz, D. (2002) 'Making markets work for forest communities'. Washington, DC, Policy Brief. Forest Trends, and Bogor, Indonesia. Center for International Forestry Research, p.22. Available at www.forest-trends.org/resources/publications.htm
9   Proyecto FAO-Holanda (1995) 'Pequeñas Industrias Forestales: Metodologia y Estudies de Caso' in: *Desarrollo Forestal Participativo en los Andes*. Quito, Ecuador. Serie Validaciones Proyecto, FAO-Holanda.
10   Kenny-Jordan, C.B., Herz, C., Añazco, M. and Andrade, M. (1999) *Construyendo cambios: desarrollo forestal comunitario en los Andes*. Rome, FAO.
11   Mario Añazco, FAO, Ecuador, personal communication.
12   Young, A. (1997) *Agroforestry for soil management*. Wallingford, UK, CAB International, p.7.
13   Katrin Linzer, Tierra Viva, personal communication.
14   Ocaña, D. (ed.) (1999) *Agroforestería comunitaria: experiencias del Proyecto Desarrollo Agroforestal Comunal Potosí – Bolivia*. Potosí, Bolivia. Proyecto FAO/Holanda/Prefectura.

Chapter 10   Conclusions: the need for trade and aid

1   Barrett, H.R., Browne, A.W., Harris, P.J.C. and Cadoret, K. (2001) 'Smallholder farmers and organic certification: Accessing the EU market from the developing world'. *Biological Agriculture and Horticulture*, Vol.19, pp.183–199.
2   Ellis, F. and Seeley, J. (2001) 'Globalisation and Sustainable Livelihoods: An initial note'. Background briefing. London, Department for International Development.
3   United Kingdom Government (2000) 'Eliminating World Poverty: Making Globalisation Work for the Poor'. Department for International Development, London, p.73.
4   E-mail Discussion on Globalization organized by the Overseas Development Institute, London. Available at www.rimisp.cl/

[5] The Fairtrade Foundation (1997) 'Spilling The Beans'. London, The Fairtrade Foundation.

[6] Berdegué, J., Reardon, T., Escobar, G. and Echeverría, R. (2000) 'Policies to promote non-farm rural employment in Latin America'. *Natural Resource Perspectives*, No.55. London, Overseas Development Institute.

[7] Hellin, J. and Higman, S. (2001) 'Competing in the market: Farmers need new skills'. *Appropriate Technology*, Vol.28, No.2, pp.5–7.

[8] Sherwood, S., Nelson, R., Thiele, G. and Ortiz, O. (2000) 'Farmer Field Schools in potato: A new platform for participatory training and research in the Andes'. *Newsletter of the Center for Research and Information on Low External Input and Sustainable Agriculture* (ILEIA), Vol.16, No.4, pp.24–25.

[9] Braun, A.R., Thiele, G. and Fernández, M. (2000) 'Farmer field schools and local agricultural research committees: complementary platforms for integrated decision-making in sustainable agriculture'. *Agricultural Research and Extension Network Paper*, No.105. London, Overseas Development Institute.

[10] Hellin, J. In prep. *Better land husbandry: an international guide to effective practice*. New Hampshire, Science Publishers Inc.

[11] Oxfam (2000) 'Globalisation: Submission to the Government's White Paper on Globalisation'. Oxford, Oxfam.

[12] Oxfam (2002) 'Rigged rules and double standards: trade, globalisation, and the fight against poverty'. Oxford, Oxfam. Available at www.maketradefair.com

[13] The Economist (2001) 'Africa's elusive dawn'. *The Economist*, 24 February 2001.

[14] The Economist (2002) 'Globalisation: Is it at risk?' *The Economist*, 2 February 2002.

[15] The Economist (2001) 'From bad to worse, down on the farm'. *The Economist*, 3 March 2001.

[16] Department for International Development (2002) 'Better livelihoods for poor people: the role of agriculture'. London, Department for International Development.

[17] Oxfam (2002) 'The great EU sugar scam: how Europe's sugar regime is devastating livelihoods in the developing world'. Oxford, Oxfam.

[18] The Economist (2002) 'Dangerous activities'. *The Economist*, 11 May 2002.

[19] The World Bank (2001) 'World Development Report 2000/2001: Attacking Poverty'. Washington DC. The World Bank, p.61.

[20] The Economist (2002) Argentina's collapse: Let the voters choose their poison. *The Economist*, 1 June 2002.

[21] Overseas Development Institute. 'Summary of AgREN email discussion on globalisation and pro-poor agricultural development'. *Agricultural Research and Extension Network Newsletter*, No.46. London, Overseas Development Institute.

Select bibliography and reading list

The following is a selection of accessible texts providing further information on each of the chapters.

Bananas

Chambron, A-C. (2000) 'Straightening the bent world of the banana'. Available at www.bananalink.org.uk/trade/btrade.htm

Chambron, A-C. (1999) 'Bananas: the green gold of the TNCs'. Available at www.bananalink.org.uk/trade/btrade.htm

Clegg, P. (2002) *The Caribbean banana trade*. Palgrave Macmillan.

Human Rights Watch (2002) 'Tainted harvest: Child Labor and Obstacles to Organizing on Ecuador's Banana Plantations'. New York, Human Rights Watch. Available at www.hrw.org/reports/2002/ecuador

Josling, T. and Taylor, T. (eds.) (2003) *Banana wars*. CAB International Publishing.

The Fairtrade Foundation (2000) 'Unpeeling the banana trade'. The Fairtrade Foundation, London. Available at www.fairtrade.org.uk/unpeeling/htm

van de Kasteele, A. (1998) 'The banana chain: the macro economics of the Banana Trade'. Available at www.bananalink.org.uk/trade/btrade.htm

Wunder, S. (2001) 'Ecuador goes bananas: incremental technological change and forest loss' in: *Agricultural technologies and tropical deforestation*. Angelsen, A. and Kaimowitz, D. (eds.) CAB International, pp.167–95.

Coffee

Bates, R.H. (1998) *Open economy politics*. Princeton University Press.

Bentley, J.W. and Baker, P.S. (2000) 'The Colombian Coffee Growers' Federation: organised, successful smallholder farmers for 70 years'. *Agricultural Research & Extension Network Paper* No.100. London, Overseas Development Institute. Available at www.odi.org.uk/agren/

Coste, R. (1992) *Coffee: the plant and the product*. Macmillan.

Dicum, G. and Luttinger, N. (1999) *The coffee book: anatomy of an industry from crop to the last drop*. New Press.

Oxfam (2002) 'Mugged: poverty in your coffee cup'. Oxford, Oxfam. Available at www.maketradefair.com/assets/english/mugged.pdf

Pendergrast, M. (2001) *Uncommon grounds: the history of coffee and how it transformed the world*. Texere Publishing.

Roden, C. (1999) *Coffee*. Pavillion Books Ltd.

Roseberry, W. , Gudmundson, L. and Kutschbach, M.S. (eds.) (1995) *Coffee, society and power in Latin America*. Johns Hopkins University.

The Fairtrade Foundation. (1997) 'Spilling the beans'. London: The Fairtrade Foundation.

Potato

Brush, S.B. (ed.) (2000) *Genes in the field: on-farm conservation of crop diversity.* International Plan Genetic Resources Institute.
Crissman, C., Antle, J.M. and Capalbo, S.M. (eds.) (1998) *Economic, environmental and health trade offs in agriculture: pesticides and the sustainability of Andean potato production.* Kluwer Academic Publications.
Ochoa, C.M. (1990) *Potatoes of South America.* Cambridge University Press.
Pumisacho, M. and Sherwood, S. (eds.) (2002) *El cultivo de la papa en Ecuador.* Instituto Nacional Autónomo de Investigaciones Agropecuarias and Centro Internacional de la Papa (CIP).
Zuckerman, L. (1999) *The potato: how it changed history.* Macmillan.

Quinoa

Hermann, J. and Heller, J. (eds.) (1997) 'Andean roots and tubers: ahipa, arracacha, maca and yacon'. Promoting the conservation and use of underutilized and neglected crops. 21. International Plant Genetics Resource Institute.
Jacobsen, S-E. and Sherwood, S. (2002) *Cultivo de granos Andinos en Ecuador: informe sobre los rubros quinua, chocho y amaranto.* Food and Agriculture Organization of the United Nations (FAO)*.
National Research Council (1989) *Lost crops of the Incas: little known plants of the Andes with promise for worldwide cultivation.* Washington DC, National Academy Press.

*The FAO has produced a CD-Rom (*Cultivos Andinos: alimentos del presente y futuro*) which contains several publications in Spanish on quinoa. The CD-Rom can be ordered at www.condesan.org/principalcondesan-en.htm and includes:

Jacobsen, S-E., Mujica, A., and Portillo, Z. (eds.) (2001) *Memorias primer taller internacional en Quinua: recursos genéticos y sistemas de producción.*
Mujica A., Jacobsen, S-E., Izquierdo, J and Marathee, J. (eds.) (2001) *Quinua (Chenopodium quinoa Willd.), ancestral cultivo andino, alimento del presente y futuro.*
Mujica, A., Izquierdo, J., Marathee, J.P., Morón, C. and Jacobsen, S-E. (eds.) (1999) *Memorias: reunión técnica y taller de formulación de proyecto regional sobre producción y nutrición humana en base a cultivos andinos.*

Coca

Allen, C.J. (2002) *The hold life has: coca and cultural identity in an Andean community.* Smithsonian Institution Press.

Leons, M.B. and Sanabria, H. (eds.) (1997) *Coca, cocaine and the Bolivian reality*. State University and New York Press.

Macgregor, F.E. (ed.) (1993) *Coca and cocaine*. Greenwood Press.

Mortimer, W.G. (2000) *History of coca: the divine plant of the Incas*. University Press of the Pacific.

Painter, J. (1994) *Bolivia and coca: a study in dependency*. Lynne Rienner Publishers.

Smith, M., Thongtham, C.N., Sadeque, N., Bravo, A., Rumrill, R. and Dávila, A. (1992) *Why people grow drugs: narcotics and development in the Third World*. Panos Publications Ltd.

Wine

Young, A. (1998) *Wine routes of Argentina*. International Wine Academy.

Read, J. (1994) *The wines of Chile*. Reed International Books Ltd.

Allen, M., Atkin, T., Cooper, M., Neill, R., Platter, J. and St. Pierre, B. (1997) *New World of wine*. Reed International Books Ltd.

Johnson, H. and Robinson, J. (2001) *The world atlas of wine*. Octopus Publishing Group.

Stevenson, T. (1997) *The New Sotheby's Wine Encyclopedia*. Dorling Kindersley.

Sheep

Butland, G.J. (1957) *The human geography of southern Chile*. George Philip & Son, Ltd.

Childs, H. (1936) *El Jimmy: outlaw of Patagonia*. J.B. Lippincott Company.

Chatwin, B. (1977) *In Patagonia*. Picador.

Forestry

Higman, S., Bass, S., Judd, N., Mayers, J. and Nussbaum, R. (1999) *The Sustainable Forestry Handbook*. Earthscan.

Nasi, R., Wunder, S. and Campos, J.J. (2002) *Forest ecosystem services: can they pay our way out of deforestation?* Available at www.catie.ac.cr/news/news.htm

Powell, I., White, A. and Landell-Mills, N. (2002) *Developing markets for the ecosystem services of forests*. Forest Trends, Washington DC. Available at www.forest-trends.org/resources/pdf/powellwhite_ecoservices.pdf

Price, M.F. and Butt, N. (eds.) (2000) *Forests in sustainable mountain development: a state of knowledge report for 2000*. IUFRO Research Series No.5. CAB International Publishing.

Scherr, S., White, A. and Kaimowitz, D. (2002) 'Making markets work for forest communities'. Policy Brief. Forest Trends and Center for International Forestry Research. Available at www.forest-trends.org/resources/publications.htm

Westoby, J. (1989) *Introduction to World Forestry*. Blackwell.

Globalization and rural development

Chambers, R. (1997) *Whose reality counts? Putting the first last.* Intermediate Technology Publications.

Ellwood, W. (2001) *The no-nonsense guide to globalization.* New Internationalist Publications.

Friedman, T.L. (2000) *The lexus and the olive tree: understanding globalisation.* Anchor Books.

Loker, W.M. (ed.) (1998) *Globalization and the rural poor in Latin America.* Lynne Rienner Publishers.

Madeley, J. (2000) *Hungry for trade: how the poor pay for free trade.* Zed Books.

Oxfam (2002) 'Rigged rules and double standards: trade, globalisation, and the fight against poverty'. Oxford, Oxfam. Available at www.maketradefair.com

Stiglitz, J.E. (2002) Globalization and its discontents. W.W. Norton & Company.

The World Bank (2002) *World Development Report 2003.* Available at http://econ.worldbank.org/wdr/wdr2003/text-17926/

United Kingdom Government (2000) 'Eliminating world poverty: making globalisation work for the poor'. London, Department for International Development. Available at www.dfid.gov.uk

Wohlmeyer, H. and Quendler, T. (eds.) (2002) *The WTO, agriculture and sustainable development.* Greenleaf Publishing.

Index